D0474574

A Govan Childhood
The Nineteen Thirties

GEORGE ROUNTREE

Foreword by Elspeth King

JOHN DONALD PUBLISHERS LTD
EDINBURGH

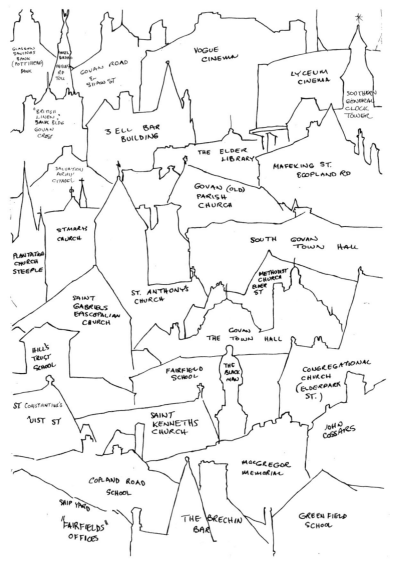

Key to buildings outlined on front cover (*Montage by Chris Fletcher* RIBA, ARIAS).

Foreword

As any Govanite will tell you, Govan is a very special part of Glasgow. When the rest of Glasgow was sporting 'Miles Better' stickers, Young Govan was wearing 'I'm Lovin' Govan' buttons, resplendent with the Govan coat of arms. Older Govanites will deny that Govan is part of Glasgow at all, for there are still painful memories of 1912, when this proud independent burgh was swallowed by the big city. At that time, many employees left municipal service, rather than work for Glasgow. Even so, every time Strathclyde Police Pipe Band (formerly the City of Glasgow, and originally the Govan Police Pipe Band) wins another trophy, there is a glow of satisfied remembrance somewhere in Govan.

Govan is a very distinctive place. An early Christian site, it has one of the biggest and finest collections of hog-backed stones in Britain, together with a splendidly carved sarcophagus, reputedly that of St Constantine. Copies can be seen in the National Museum of Scotland, but a visit to the originals in Govan Old Parish Church is infinitely more rewarding.

Like many other west coast villages in the eighteenth century, Govan depended on the weaving trade, and was chosen as the site for Scotland's first silk mill in 1824. At that time, salmon was still plentiful in the Clyde. One might have expected that all connection with the weaving trade would have been obliterated when shipbuilding and heavy engineering became the economic mainstay, and the only salmon coming up the Clyde were in John West tins bound for Princes Dock. The memory endures, for the Govan Weavers' Society is still going strong, and the Sheep's Head, the ancient symbol of Govan's wealth, is paraded through the burgh annually for the Govan Fair on the evening of the first Friday in June.

Various societies have kept the history of Govan alive — the YMCA which was given the care of Dr Barras' social history collection in the 1930s, the Old Govan Club, the Govan Fair

Association, and latterly, the Govan Reminiscence Group. George Rountree is a member of the Reminiscence Group and has now produced a substantial work of his own, honing and polishing his memory to produce both a good read and a work of reference on everyday life in Govan and Linthouse in the 1930s. While the work is firmly Govan based, the scenes and experiences described were common to many other parts of Glasgow and indeed, to other big industrial cities.

This book concentrates on the human element, and the aspects of life that other kinds of history ignore. There are practices which were so common and everyday, that when they cease, they slip entirely from our knowledge. The axe marks from the breaking of sticks on a tenement landing, which George Rountree describes with such care, are beneath the notice of the architectural historian, but could be as puzzling and as interesting to the next generation as the cup and ring marks of prehistory are to us. It is certainly the stuff of which life is made, and it is entirely appropriate that this work should have come from an individual in an area where history and tradition are cherished and fostered.

ELSPETH KING

© George Rountree 1993

John Donald Publishers Ltd, 138 St Stephen Street,
Edinburgh EH3 5AA.

ISBN 0 85976 385 4

Typeset by Newtext Composition Ltd, Glasgow
Printed in Great Britain by Bell & Bain Ltd, Glasgow

Preface

Other accounts of the thirties tell of dole queues and 'Parish' hand-outs and out-of-work loungers standing at street corners, but little of that was obvious in Govan in the years immediately before the war. No doubt it was there during the decade covered in the following pages, but almost none of these conditions were visible by the time I became aware of such things. Perhaps I was lucky in that my father, an engineer/fitter, was never out of work until he retired, but neither were any male relatives, family friends or acquaintances, or those of street pals so far as I know. For me central Govan then had a menacing and sinister aspect, so I was always grateful for the presence of an adult when away from the street where I lived. When my parents moved west to Linthouse at the end of 1936 it was like escaping from a baleful presence.

Life in Skipness Drive was more tranquil and it is this time I remember with fondness, although that impression might stem from being largely free from the health problems of previous years. These later experiences, 1937/9, are what are drawn on for most of these observations and reminiscences.

Glasgow, 1993   G.R.

Acknowledgements

While everything set down in the following pages is from my own memory, many people helped with their recollections. Someone would say – 'd'ye mind this, or that?' mentioning events, items, or things we did that were long forgotten, but had then returned, occasionally with an astonishing flash of ultra-detailed clarity, not least for myself. Most of the subjects deserve greater coverage; indeed some would occupy a chapter or even a book of their own, but restrictions had to be imposed to keep the present volume within bounds.

In addition to the individuals and organisations listed, particular mention should be made of the co-operation of members of the Govan Reminiscence Group in the project and for their generosity in allowing the use of certain photographs.

I am indebted to:

Sidney Smith — for reading an early version of the text and making useful suggestions; The Mitchell Library — for research facilities; Strathclyde Regional Archives (Head Archivist and obliging staff) — for research facilities; The Church of Jesus Christ of Latter Day Saints — for access to their International Genealogical Index (IGI); Graham McLachlan — for technical information; Margaret Thomson Davis, novelist — for encouragement and sound advice.

Special thanks are due to Chris Fletcher, RIBA, ARIAS, for extra work involved in producing drawings, particularly those which form the basis of the cover design. The plans of 7 Howat Street and 12 Skipness Drive were drawn by Colin Rountree.

A video cassette entitled *Seaward: The Great Ships* plus *Glasgow's Docklands* (Scottish Heritage Video Collection catalogue no. 53425), made by Eagle Eye Productions Ltd from Scottish Film Archive material, contains film of river, ships, shipbuilding and street activity relevant to some of the descriptions in the text. While the scenes portrayed date from post-1950 they reflect quite well the atmosphere of the 30s, especially the 'Docklands' film, except that, for example, the ratio of horse-drawn to motor vehicles seen therein would be reversed.   G.R.

Contents

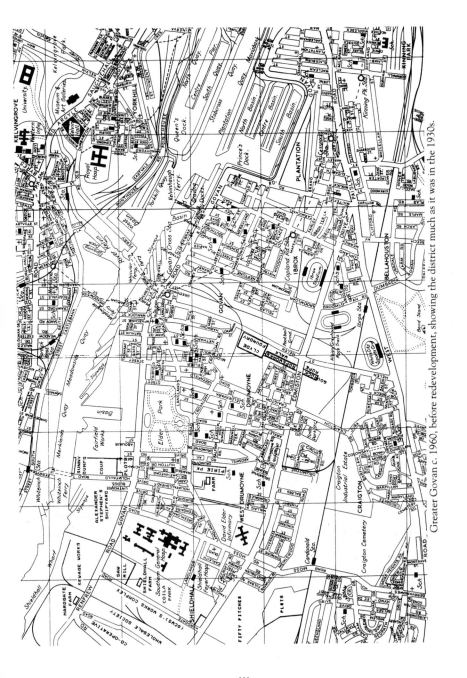

Greater Govan c. 1960, before redevelopment, showing the district much as it was in the 1930s.

CHAPTER 1

Origins

In recent years an urge to learn more of my family history, along with a desire to find out what conditions were like in the world they lived in, made me realise that some time in the future someone, descendant or stranger, might be curious about what life was like in Govan in the 1930s. In 1980 I began jotting down what memories could be dredged up, but doing so by hand proved slow and laborious. Even after a long time had passed it didn't really amount to much. Then technical assistance in the form of a word processor was acquired, and in time a couple of hundred thousand words had been produced, although a significant amount of that was devoted to family history. But much related to life in Govan in the decade before the second world war as seen through quite young eyes, and it is those experiences that have been drawn on for this book. The following pages contain much of what was felt to be interesting for entertainment's sake, as well as for serious study (although sparsely referenced) in the future by students of the period.

Both my parents had been born in Govan, my mother in Harmony Row and father in Elderpark Street. After their marriage in 1927 they lived in a sub-let room, vague details of the whereabouts of which I had heard over the years but never knew exactly where. Then a few years ago, one day I happened to look with a more perceptive eye than usual at the details in an insurance document dating from that time — and there it was, 80 Elderpark Street, with the date — 6 February 1928. They lived there for about six months before moving to the house at 7 Howat Street, where my mother lost her first baby towards the end of 1928 by a miscarriage. Then in September 1930 I arrived.

Living 'up a close'

House layout, fixtures and fittings

Number 7 is in a corner of the tenement block. It has (or had; for the last time I entered there would have been more than 50 years ago and refurbishment may have altered it), a large squarish open stairwell with the stairs winding up around the walls to the three landings. This stairwell, in common with others similarly located with no window to the outside to admit daylight, had a section of roof above it of glass for daytime illumination. Other staircases away from corners of blocks had windows on the half landings which overlooked back courts. Our house, last one of three on the first landing (one stair up), was a simple two-apartment room-and-kitchen having a short hall or lobby with two tall shallow cupboards or 'presses'. A standard feature of houses of the period was that all doors, both outer and internal, had tall narrow recessed panels in four sections bordered with a wood moulding, set two above and two below centre, which in a later age tenants took great delight in flush panelling.

Every house main door and interior apartment door had a large four-pane fanlight above it for illumination of the lobby, made necessary because originally, in the days of gas, no light was provided there. On the outside face of the door jamb, at shoulder height, on the side on which the door was hung, was a wire operated bell pull. It was a half-inch thick 3-inch by 2-inch oblong plate, of sheet brass pressed and shaped to appear solid, fixed with the long axis vertical. In the centre was a brass knob of seemingly universal shape, for every tenement house I ever saw, and many other types of houses also, had one. Pulling the knob, which was fixed on a long square rod that passed through the facing, to the other end of which a length of wire was attached, rang a bell. The wire ran round a small pulley wheel on the lobby side of the door jamb, which then passed up in the open and was attached to the free end of a piece of spring steel, or long coilspring, fixed above the fanlight, on the end of which the bell was hung. Our letterbox was in heavy brass, with a large surround, as was the nameplate with the letters deeply engraved on it. These two items stayed with us until we moved to Pollok at the end of the war where, because of the layout of the door face there, the nameplate had to be discarded for a smaller 'modern' perspex one. On entering the lobby through the main door from the landing, the kitchen was opposite with the bedroom door next to it to the left, with the two tall presses facing each other in opposing end walls.

Kitchen sink and windows

In the layout of the kitchen, the double casement windows were to the left of centre of the outside wall, opposite the door. External walls of tenement buildings are about two feet thick, and casement kitchen window recesses were something like eighteen inches deep on the inside, with a sill of six inches. Standard original fittings in all such houses were tall narrow door-like panels on either side above the sink, reaching up to the full height of the window recess, which could be used as internal shutters. From early times these doors, complete with panelling, puzzled me. Why was there a knob fixed half way up near the inner edge on each side? It really was like a small door knob and was used, it is obvious now, to free the shutters from their flush recess when closing them, although they were never used in any house I was familiar with.

Standing on one side within this recess was the sink, referred to by older people as the 'jawbox', of ordinary white glazed pottery and boxed in with wood to form a cupboard which stretched across the full width of the recess. Other older tenements had black sinks of cast iron that never looked clean. There being no such thing as chipboard or hardboard in those days (even plywood was uncommon) the sink cupboard, with a small compartment beneath and a larger one alongside, was made of half inch by two inch white pine feathered planks with bevelling, nailed upright. The top of the work surface/draining board, of inch-thick solid timber which, unlike modern drainers, had no slope, was always kept scrubbed white. A single water tap supplying cold water only, standard in nearly all houses in working-class areas, was a brass swan's neck type known as a 'crane', mounted above the sink on the side nearest the shutter. It was set in a low bulkhead built-in at the foot of the casement, which provided a small shelf to sit such items on as soap, scrubbing, nail- and tooth- brushes, pumice stone, steel wool for pots etc. The crane neck, which stood above the level of this shelf, could be turned down into the sink out of the way to allow the shutter to close, or permit another board to be placed over the sink to give extra workspace if required.

Dresser and coal bunker

To the left of the kitchen window was the wall dividing it from the bedroom, known simply as 'the room'. Against this wall, and constructed of stout planks of wood, were those standard built-in fittings of rough furniture in each house, a 'dresser' and a coal bunker. The dresser was a waist-high unit with a single compartment two-door, two-shelf cupboard below, which served as a pot press. Above the cupboard and lying side by side were two drawers. Standing next to the dresser, the bunker had a hinged lid with hinges a few inches away from the back wall so that the lid could be propped safely leaning against it. This meant there was a narrow shelf at the rear, where, if used carelessly, items might fall un-noticed through the slot left when the lid was open. The bunker front too was hinged at mid-height, so that the top half could fold down outside. Two one-hundredweight (cwt) bags of coal could be put in with the front down, and with it up and held in place by rotating catches at each top corner of the frame, it held two more. A description of a delivery of coal, telling of how much dirt, mainly in the form of coal dust, had to be coped with, will be given in the section on street hawkers in Chapter 6. Above the dresser and bunker, at a height of around six feet, were two deep shelves of heavy-gauge wood set one above the other about a foot apart. The lower shelf extended for the same length as the width of the bunker/dresser, but the upper one ran the full length of the wall, ending only to leave sufficient clearance to allow the kitchen door to swing open. On these were stored large pots, china mixing bowls and other bulky or seldom needed items.

Because it was only made use of in autumn, if the household possessed one, a jelly pan was normally kept on the higher of these two shelves until it was required for its seasonal job. The jelly pan was a large deep heavy lidless brass pan with slightly flared sides, and a single semicircular metal loop for a handle, which was used for jam making. In those days this was fairly common practice, because factory made stuff could, with a little practice, be easily bettered by any housewife. My mother had a jelly pan and used it regularly in season, the jam making process filling the house with a lovely sweet fruity smell, but with the passage of time it became too much trouble, and the jelly pan was disposed of. If it had been retained it might be worth a bit today as an antique. Cooking pots then were what could only be described as substantial. Soup, stew and potato pots were of heavy cast iron, although our frying pan was pressed steel. There's no clear recollection of any aluminium utensils but they may have been present.

Mantelpiece and range

In the right-hand inner wall and close to the outer wall of the kitchen was the mantelpiece, with its inset coal-fired cast iron range. It was a solid structure of brick, wood and plaster approximately six feet high and about five in width, which projected four to six inches from the wall. It housed the range which protruded a few inches beyond the mantelpiece line, curving in at its side edges. On top and slightly above average adult head height was the mantelshelf, broader and deeper than the rest of the structure, giving a fairly deep overhang at the front, and rather less at the sides. This shelf was a convenient place on which to keep things in regular use at the fireplace, such as tea caddy, matches and candles. As well as emergency items needed to be kept easily to hand, like a spare gas mantle or pennies for the gas, it was a convenient parking place for brassware and china ornaments like 'wally dugs'. But it invariably also became a dumping place for all kinds of odds and ends that were in occasional use. Within the mantelpiece and above the fireplace and oven that comprised the range, was a recess extending almost the full width of the range, two feet high and about eighteen inches deep.

The fireplace, set within the range, depended on the draught of the flue, or chimney, to draw smoke from the fire up and over the back, into a squared-off metal tunnel which could be positioned to increase or decrease the draught. As a further aid in varying the draught, in the back wall of the recess and above the extendable tunnel, there was a moveable tapered hood which could be pulled out to make a gap of a few inches at its widest point at the bottom. During mild weather it could be opened to create a vent, which reduced draught and combustion of the fire. Design of ranges in kitchens in different areas varied slightly, probably because they would have been supplied at different times and perhaps by different manufacturers, but the main difference was that they were 'handed'. In some ranges the fire was on the right of the oven, while in others this was reversed, a feature which might have depended on the position of the flue, where it would have lain relative to other flues passing up within the wall to the chimneyhead.

In our Howat Street house the oven was to the left of the fire and, like other tenement kitchens, had a gas stove on top. The oven was heated by gas jets supplemented by heat conducting through from the fire, but mainly because of difficulty in judging temperature, I never saw ours or any other range oven used seriously for this purpose. It was really only good for warming plates and keeping cooked food hot. There were no oven thermometers for working-class homes in those days, so skill had to be gained by experience, and most women were reluctant to experiment because of financial restrictions and fear of wasting anything. Nevertheless, stories were heard of certain women who used their oven for baking.

On either side of the range there were the flat tops of unequal width, called collectively the hob, which, being close to it, were warmed by the fire, heat which could be utilised to keep a stock pot simmering. Householders conscious of the saving always kept a big kettle full of water sitting there to warm up. A further range-fitting refinement for making the best possible use of this heat, was a thick metal plate which formed the floor of the chimney tunnel, over which smoke passed on its way into the flue. It could be slid out on guides to cover the fire when required, but normally it lay out of the way within the tunnel. Using a hooked implement provided for the purpose, pulled out over the fire it left a vent at the rear, which allowed the smoke to pass underneath into the flue. In the centre of this plate, which in the extended position would be directly over the heat, was a circular hole with a cover in three pieces in the form of two concentric rings and a plug, which sat flush like a street manhole. Using the same hooked implement, by a rod set across a depression the centre section could be lifted out, leaving a hole of a size suitable for a small pot or, with the second and third sections removed, larger holes for bigger pots or kettles.

On top of the broad section of hob over the oven sat the cooker, which was made up of thin iron strips riveted into an oblong frame. It had three burners, the largest of which lay to one side and was easily convertible for use as a grill. The two main burners were set front and rear in the frame, a layout which gave rise to the saying when referring to a project postponed but not forgotten, that it was being put on the back burner. The meaning here was that when necessary a stock pot placed on the stove over a low heat for a long time, would, in the cramped working space, be put at the back out of the way, leaving the others free for normal mealtime cooking. The stove had one end set on a pivot mounting which enabled it to be lifted up, passing over-centre away from the fire and 'parked' out of the way allowing the hob beneath it to be cleaned. Older ranges had a simple iron 'half-arrowhead' gravity operated type of hook to hold the stove frame when in the elevated position. The outer end of the frame had a pair of loose swivelling feet which swung into position as it was lowered, where its weight locked them. The burners were of course part of the frame, and the gas-pipe connection arrangement to allow this to be done was interestingly simple.

The pipe carrying gas to the stove was in the form of a 'J', lying horizontal from the point where it left the main pipe as it went up the side of the mantelpiece, and passed round the leg of the mantelpiece into the range recess. The long leg of the J was within the recess, and it was from this the three feeds to the burners emerged in a row, each with a tap directing gas into the burner pipes. Because of a need to mix air with gas to make it burn efficiently, the usual arrangement for gas burners, as in the Bunsen burner of school days, was for a rotating collar with a hole in it to be placed in a sliding fit over the burner pipe. The collar could then be turned to match up with a similar hole in the burner stem allowing, according to its setting, a variable amount of air to be drawn in. In range stoves, the pipes beyond the taps were in the form of tapering nozzles which fitted free (i.e. with plenty of room round them) into the burner pipes, these having belled ends to receive them. As with the Bunsen the amount of air allowed in was critical, so the adjustment on each of the nozzles was by a thick disc with a screw threaded hole in its centre. The disc had a knurled edge and was a little larger than the belled end, and ran on a thread behind the nozzle. When turned on the thread the disc opened or closed the gap, altering the amount of air getting in between the 'bell' and the nozzle. The advantage of this ingenious arrangement was that there was no physical connection between nozzle and burner pipe, which enabled the stove itself simply to be lifted up on its pivot without the need to uncouple piping.

Front and top of the range were cast iron, while the rest of the structure behind in contact with heat was lined with firebrick. The iron surfaces were treated with what must have been heat resistant black paint, which may have been stove enamelling, but the curled edges, projections, hinges and knobs were shiny and kept burnished with steel wool. The whole lot was given a good going over weekly with stuff known as blacklead, a graphite mixture called 'Zebo Grate Polish', which came in a tall narrow round tin with a peaked top like a Brasso tin, giving it a nice black sheen. The grate was set at knee height alongside the oven, a big disadvantage to people with cold feet, because in cold weather they had to sit with their 'plates of meat' propped up on a stool to catch any warmth. Economy style fire grate nests were curved, sitting in the fireplace on four 'feet', with the high part to the outer face of the range and the slotted body curving down to the rear. As well as holding less coal, slots on these nests were narrow and unsuitable for most pokers. This contributed to their function in restricting 'poking', and so making a loading of coal last longer, which makes me think now that perhaps they were used in summer. The normal installation had vertical bars in front, called 'ribs', with a gap between them sufficient for a poker to enter. In front was a metal door with a shiny knob, the full ten-inch width of the grate, but shallow and mounted high, which when closed concentrated the draught lower down the front through the seat of the fire.

There were two removable burnished cast steel shelves which had brackets designed to allow them to be clipped into position. One, about six inches deep and the width of the fire, was fixed conveniently in front of the bars level with the fire nest base, for resting the tea pot or other utensils that required to be kept warm. But in this position the shelf, and anything sitting on it, tended to further prevent heat from reaching floor level. Being so close to the fire it was the hottest place, but it was liable to overheat and burn pot or kettle lid knobs and handles if they were left too long, so that a pad had to be used when touching them. At the back of this shelf, level with the bottom of the firebars, was a slot opening to allow small unburnable rubbish items to be 'posted' directly into the ashpan. The other much bigger shelf, mounted to the side under the oven door, was intended for resting anything heavy on momentarily, such as a roasting tray, to get a better grip when removing it from the oven. Beneath the fire grate nest and sitting within the range at hearth level lay the ashpan, which was shaped like a deep drawer and had a shiny steel pointed knob projecting from the centre.

Along the front of the range at floor level, a flat stone or concrete projection called the hearth extended out from it about a foot and a half, which was bordered by the fender. A fender was a moveable low decorative edging of cast iron or pressed sheet brass or copper, sometimes supplemented by adornment features such as rails or, like the one we had in our next house, low corner boxes of the same metal. Assembled from sheet metal pressings, the boxes were intended for holding ready-to-use coal, paper and sticks, and fire handling tools. Those tools consisted of poker, a steel rod with handle used for stirring up the fire to get rid of ash, tongs, for lifting out stones or other unburnable material which, inadvertently or otherwise, had got into the fire, and small brush and shovel for sweeping up. Each of them usually had a loop on the end of the handle incorporated in their design, and were hung on hooks on a free standing stand, while others had a decorative shoulder on the end which fitted on a two-prong fork in place of a hook. Stand and four implements were termed 'a companion set'. The stand comprised a length of metal rod or tube set in a broad base, at the top of which was a cap surmounted by a large loop for lifting the complete unit. In the looped type, four brackets set four-square projected from the cap on which the tools were hung by their loops.

Our fender corner boxes had hinged lids with padding for use as seats, and in cold weather they were a favourite perch,for which there was much competition to gain full benefit from the warmth of the fire. They held our shoe polishing equipment and old newspapers and kindling sticks. A fender was necessary, partly to keep people from coming too close to the fire, but mainly to trap red hot cinders if they should accidentally fall out of the grate, and so help guard against setting the house on fire. A receptacle for holding ready-to-use coal found in most houses was the coal scuttle, a light brass or copper drum which stood on three feet. Ours had a narrow belt with embossed decorations in the form of entwined strings of leaves and flowers, and an elegant pagoda roof shaped lid surmounted by a broad flat round knob. It was around sixteen inches in diameter and stood about eighteen high without the lid, and had trapped, but loose, carrying loops of the same metal attached to the centre of opposite sides. There was an inner plain drum, only a little smaller than the outer one, which held the coal, with wire loop handles for carrying to the bunker for filling. Its place was at the fireplace alongside the fender. Something remaining in my memory about the coal scuttle is that when the inner drum was removed for filling, it was essential to up-end the outer on a sheet of newspaper to empty out any dust that had fallen down inside. If this wasn't done, when the inner was replaced the piston effect caused it to drive out displaced air, carrying with it any dust and grit lying inside which could get in the eyes.

Some people had nails or hooks projecting from the front and side edges of their mantelshelf for hanging things on, like kitchen cooking tools such as the ladle, grater, potato masher, toasting fork, frying pan scoop, etc. One fitment most people had was a length of flexible expanding rod, like the present day expanding curtain rail with a clip at each end, which could be fitted in tension over the outer ends of mantelshelves near the front. This 'stretch' was very handy for drying small items of washing such as handkerchiefs and socks, or dish and hand towels, for being over the fire it was the best drying place in the house. However, it was prudent to keep a close watch in case an escape of smoke occurred or the items might need washing again.

Another essential item was a taper holder, a triangular box of stiff card under a foot high and four inches at its widest, which tapered down to a point. It was usually to be found hanging from a drawing pin or nail on the outer side of the mantelpiece, holding tapers or spills. Tapers were thin strips of softwood if bought or, more commonly, of newspaper painstakingly folded or sometimes twisted into tight thin strips. There was a constant need for them to light stove and gaslight from the fire, as it saved matches, as well as cigarettes and pipes. My maternal grandfather was a pipe smoker and would spend a lot of time making his own tapers, which he kept in one of these distinctively shaped coloured-paper-covered holders, set low down within easy reach of his chair at the side of the mantelpiece. One other detail recalled of the kitchen in our house was a large oval zinc coated steel bath used for my weekly Friday night bath. For their bathing requirements my parents may have gone to the public baths about five minutes walk away in Harhill Street, or more likely, to Dad's mother's house at Shieldhall. Advantage was often taken, when visiting a friend or relation with a bath in their house, to make taking a bath part of the reason for the visit.

'Recessed' bed

Like virtually all tenement houses of the period, the Howat Street house had a bed recess in both room and kitchen, with timber battens fixed round the walls within the recess at hip height to support the bedspring frame. Bed frames were constructed of heavy timber, and if they had been made to the standard size of six feet by four feet six inches, they would fit in and be supported by the battens. Bed frame sizes from earlier years, however, could be of non-standard size, and if you had one which had been passed down through the family, maybe it had even belonged to grandparents, its dimensions might be too small to sit on the battens. Being quite expensive to replace, every effort had to be made to adapt the frame by using stout planks as supports. The surface on which the mattress lay was a dense intercoiled sprung wire mesh which, when it sagged through use, could be re-tensioned by turning a few large screws in one end with a spanner — much like a piano tuner. With a mattress laid on top, the bed was made up and curtained off from the rest of the room. As the top of the mattress was quite high, probably intentionally, to provide storage space underneath, anyone sleeping in a 'hole-in-wall' bed had to be constantly aware of the danger of falling out. People kept chairs or a settee in front, which served both as a step for climbing in and out, and a means of breaking the fall of anyone tumbling out. The space below the bed was curtained off separately and used to store seldom-required items. A cabin trunk which held linen and spare blankets, and suitcases used at holiday time, were kept in this space under the bed in my grandparent's house.

We never had a bed like this in either of the tenement houses we lived in. Being well below the critical height in stature it wouldn't have affected either of my parents, but it should be obvious that anyone six feet tall or over must have had a difficult time getting a good night's rest in a recess bed. In our house the kitchen recess was curtained off for the full height from floor to ceiling and used as a store for domestic odds and ends, so that it came to be called 'the glory hole'. On one occasion I did sleep in a recess bed for a few days in the early summer of 1942. My parents had arranged to take their summer holidays early in the season, and the school schedule was disorganised because of the war, which had caused the spring term to go on longer than usual. They went off to Ayr, and I was boarded at 13 Hutton Drive so that school attendance, which included the important qualifying exam, the 'quali', could be completed, success or failure at which would determine advancement to either Senior or Junior Secondary. At Howat Street the three of us slept in the room, Mum and Dad in a bed that was part of a bedroom suite of dark oak which was too big to fit into the recess in the usual way, so had to be placed head in, foot out. The rest of the suite consisted of wardrobe, chest of drawers, dressing table and, strangely, a pair of matching chairs.

Furnishings

In the kitchen stood a long narrow table of a type which was quite common at that time. Similar tables were encountered with remarkable regularity in other houses visited. The Govan Reminiscence Group have in their possession one just like it, and it can be glimpsed in the series of photographs of the cardboard mock-up of a single-end constructed by members of the group in 1988. Made locally at the Co-op furniture factory at Shieldhall, like ours, it has a top of unpainted frequently scrubbed wood which was always covered with a tablecloth at mealtimes. It has a full-length hinged flap along one side only, and three shallow drawers for cutlery storage along the other. Below the top the frame of ours was painted black, and a spar low down joined the turned legs at the ends. These in turn were joined by two long spars running close together near the centre line, which lay along the full length at just the right height to put your feet on — until you were spotted and received a crack on the shins for it. During a trawl among relatives and friends for surplus furniture to help fill the 14 rooms, our table was given to an aunt to help furnish a newly acquired house on Lochgoil in 1940. It was one of the few pieces to have survived an accident on the steep hill near Finnart between the Gareloch and Loch Long, involving the lorry used to transport the load, in which many other items were destroyed.

What is remembered of the rest of the contents of the Howat Street house is somewhat hazy. There were two easy chairs and a settee, each covered with shiny material that looked like leather but was, it is obvious now, a cheap substitute. It may have been fabric called Rexine, which hardened and became brittle as it aged, for it had cracked open in places and curled up along the weft of the canvas backing in areas of greatest use, leaving uncomfortable sharp edges. Heavy covers and loose cushions were added in an attempt to make them more comfortable and hide the signs of wear. At the back of the settee, on top of a row of many tiny turned wooden pillars running the full length of its seat, was a low padded rail, while at one end an extension of the seat angled sharply upward in a sloping padded section, with the top curled over, for reclining on. The floor was laid with linoleum, known then as waxcloth, on which I liked to slide in my stocking soles. Our linoleum suffered from the same fault as the chairs and settee covering, in that woven jute sacking type material was used as backing, which with wear tended to cause the lino to crack along the weft, leaving dangerous raised lips at the points of greatest wear that were liable to trip the unwary. There were also a couple of small rugs which were usually kept in position over the worn areas.

Of fittings and other furniture in the room, other than the suite the only definite detail recollected is that the bow of the three-casement oriel window, corbelled below our level, had a platform about six inches high from which I took a tumble, bumping my head quite severely in an incident talked about for many years afterwards. While the room with bay window and platform is remembered, is it not perhaps peculiar that there is no memory of the incident, which should have been impressed rather forcefully on my conscience. I would be about three at the time, but recollection is confined to hearing the story retold in later years. My cot of dark stained wood, placed at the foot of the bed, was of a design common today but made in bright coloured plastic, with barred sides that could be lowered and raised. There were coloured transfers of cartoon nursery characters on two broad slats in each side and on both ends. The reason this detail is recalled so clearly is that when I was finished with it it was kept in store, then brought out at the end of 1937 for use by an aunt, my mother's sister, for the initial members of her family, and taken back by Mum when my sister was born in 1941. The cot then went back to auntie for further use so that it would have been a familiar sight until my mid-teens.

Inside the wardrobe and in the drawers of the chest-of-drawers and dressing table of the bedroom suite, there were always a number of marble size balls with the odd appearance of looking like frosted glass, but which felt slightly greasy to the touch. They were camphor balls which gave off a strong pungent odour, regarded as essential for keeping moths at bay to stop them from laying their eggs in garments made of the natural materials of the time. Called mothballs, the effect of failing to ensure they were used became evident once or twice in later years, when articles of clothing were found to be full of holes eaten by the grubs. This protection is no longer necessary, seemingly because modern, mainly man-made materials, are not to the taste of moth grubs.

The decor of the house was typical of the period. Ceilings were whitewashed, as was the wall area above the wallpaper called the frieze, and many buildings had quite elaborate cornice mouldings. Room ceilings had in the centre a large round decorative plaster moulding called a 'rose', from the centre of which hung the gaslight and which later became the natural mounting point for electric lights. Woodwork was usually varnished or painted dark brown, and walls were papered to a height of two or three feet below ceiling level. Affordable wallpaper of the time was of poor quality, not a great deal stronger than brown paper, and was hung using a mixture of flour and water for paste. A neat finish at the junction of frieze and wallpaper was made easier for the DIYer of the period by a narrow (2 inch) embossed decorative paper strip, bought as 'border' and purchased specially for that purpose and pasted over the join to cover any unevenness. Whitewash was bought in packets in the form of a powder of about the density of flour and much like Polyfilla powder, to be mixed with water. Consistency of the mixture produced was similar to, but much less enduring than, cheap modern emulsion paint, and was brushed on with a special broad heavy whitewash brush. If used within scuffing height, dry whitewash had the serious disadvantage of coming off on hands and clothing.

The toilet cubicle on the tiny half landing of the common staircase, which was shared with the other two households on the landing, had the wooden seat and high cistern of all toilets of the period. The cast iron cistern, again like all others of the time, was mounted more than six feet up on the wall, and was flushed by pulling a hanging chain. Remoteness of the toilet from the house caused severe inconvenience if anyone was immobilised by illness, accident or old age. When that happened the chamber pot, also known as the 'chanty' had to be used. Use of the 'pot' by children was no more difficult then than it is today, except that at that time they were of white stove-enamelled iron or china, not plastic, and consequently heavier. We never had a china one, and I sometimes wondered how many serious accidents were caused if a weighty body sat on it rather too heavily, causing a breakage and leaving a sharp edge which could have had painful results on an important part of the anatomy.

Earliest memory

Another early memory, at around the age of three, is of sitting on the drainer with my feet in a basin of water being washed before going to bed in the dark of an evening. Quite clear is the recollection of looking past the side of the blind out through the window into the dim gaslit street, and seeing the many illuminated windows of houses in the building opposite. Domestic gaslight was set at a lower level than electric lighting, and at this time windows of every house had blinds of beige coloured thick paper or fabric, so that anyone working at their sink or drainer had their silhouette thrown on the blind, rendering them very visible from outside. Frequent movements were to be seen at lit up kitchen windows, of people busy at their sink with one of the never-ending household chores, like preparaing a meal, washing dishes, a man stropping an open razor and shaving with it, then washing his face, or a woman washing clothes and using a scrubbing board. In those days domestic chores took up far more time than they do today. A popular song of the period heard frequently on the radio, or 'wireless' as it was then called, was:

> Just a song at twilight
> When the lights are low
> As the flickering shadows
> Softly come and go.

Those words are indelibly imprinted in my memory. They appeared to my very young perception to have been made up specially for me, to describe this sight. It was the first of a great many occasions when a piece of music has become associated with an event or experience; indeed it is one of the three most powerful. Window blinds were wound on spring-loaded wooden rollers. When pulled down to the required level by a long cord fixed to the centre of the lower edge, winding up a spring inside the roller doing so, and held there for an instant, it caused a lock to operate in one end of the roller which retained it in that position. A quick pull freed the lock and allowed the blind to roll up. However, wear eventually caused the lock to become undependable as the brass pawl and teeth on the ratchet became worn, and people occasionally received a dreadful fright sometimes in the dead of night, when the blind unexpectedly shot up the full height, whirling round violently with a loud clatter.

Drudgery of a coal fire

Most people born after the mid-1960s with no experience of living in a house with an open fire, will have no conception of what it was like, of the amount of dirt it produced and labour involved in keeping it going. Properly looked after and fed with good quality coal, while it was wasteful source of heat it was a very efficient house warmer. But it needed constant work and vigilance to see that it didn't go out, to poke out the ash and stoke it up with fresh coal. But most important of all was to ensure that no smouldering coals fell out, bounced over the fender and burned a hole in the carpet, or at worst set the house on fire. On burning down coal reduces first to cinders then ash, a fine grey powder of the consistency but without the body of flour. The fire had to be stirred up frequently by raking it with the poker, to riddle ash through the bottom bars of the grate into the ashpan below, or it became choked and went out because of oxygen starvation. Most of the ash went down, although some of it was drawn up the chimney by the natural draught. But a certain amount always escaped into the apartment, making cleaning a frequent and never-ending job. Of course furnishings and carpets near the fireplace were worst affected.

The whole operation of keeping the fire going was dirty and unpleasant, except in cold weather when it became almost a favourite chore. From the visit by the coalman, who carried the coal in on his back in hundredweight (cwt). sacks of heavy-duty canvas through which coal dust percolated, who dumped and emptied them into the coalbunker, to the point where it finally left the house as ash to be taken to the midden, it generated a great deal of dirt.

During wet weather the bags were damp, which kept dust down, but in dry weather fine coal dust floated out as they were emptied and was liberally spread around. Coal had then to be dug out the bunker with a coal shovel, or by hand, to fill a bucket or coal scuttle and carried over to the fireplace. Often it was in large lumps which required to be broken up with a hammer, further spreading dust and fragments around and making you aware of another hazard. Unless special care was taken you might get a bit in the eye. The rest of the operation was equally disagreeable, because keeping a good fire going was a task requiring a fair amount of skill which only came with practice. If fresh coal was heaped on a fire needing stoked without first raking out the ash, it gradually settled down into a dense layer which blocked off the flow of air necessary for combustion, so that the heat generated would diminish, and it would die down and go out. This happened occasionally even to the best and most vigilant stokers, through temporary inattention or being distracted, especially if the coal was damp and of poor quality. Women gossiping with neighbours on the stairhead were particularly affected, when one might be heard saying, wide-eyed and with a gasp — 'Ah'll need tae go or ma' fire'll be oot!' It was essential to rake the embers free of ash thoroughly before putting on fresh coal, and during the coldest weather this operation required fine judgement. If it was begun too soon, unless you had a very long poker it could result in scorched knuckles. Left late so that the heat had died down past a certain point the fire, loaded up with cold coal, could take a long time to regenerate, leaving the occupants huddled round the range wrapped in coats and scarves, and holding out their hands to catch some warmth until it did so.

As bedtime approached the fire was left to die down as low as possible to reduce the chance of a cinder falling out unobserved. On winter mornings pressure was on to get it lit quickly. First, cinders remaining would be thoroughly raked to clear out all the ash. Then, after carefully checking they were cool enough, using fingers all were lifted out and placed on a sheet of newspaper which would then be made up into a rough parcel. The whole of the range, hob, cooker, all round the recess, the hearth, and, at regular intervals, up the chimney as far as the arm would reach through the sliding access hatch in the top of the range recess with a long handled flue brush, to sweep it clear of soot. All debris gathered from this operation was swept into the ashpan, and taken down to the midden in the back court and dumped there. It used to be estimated that something like 80% of all domestic rubbish consisted of ash and cinders from domestic fires, for not everyone was economy-minded enough to save cinders. Bear in mind, too, that the fire itself was an excellent way of disposing of burnable household garbage, which if it added to the output of heat so much the better.

Public health authorities advised that empty food tins should be scorched in the fire before being put in the midden, to help prevent vermin and scavenging dogs and cats. Removing them afterwards was a job for the tongs. After the cleanup, the fire was laid ready for relighting by crumpling up a couple of sheets of newspaper and placing them loosely in the bottom of the grate. Sticks were laid on top of the paper, criss-crossed to leave air passages, then the parcel of cinders was put on top along with some small pieces of coal. When applying a light it was essential to do so to the paper at the bottom, so that the sticks caught alight before the wrapping of the parcel burned away and allowed the cinders to fall down, which might smother the flame before it had got a proper hold. If that happened the operation of relaying had to be done all over again.

Firewood

Firewood could be bought ready to use in hardware stores, ironmongers and newsagents as bunches of sticks. They were often cut from old railway sleepers, which burned well having been treated with creosote. Generally six to eight inches long and split into strips, they had to be of a certain size, not too thick or they wouldn't catch alight easily, or too thin, or they would burn up too quickly to allow the cinders to catch. The bunches held about as much as could be grasped in a loop made by the hands with middle fingers and thumbs touching, and tied up with a length of twine which incorporated a carrying loop. They cost about three-halfpence, equal to the one new half pence which is no longer legal tender. I remember selling them when working in the Co-op grocers as far on as the late 1950s, but by then they cost tuppence-ha'penny. (1p). It was seldom necessary to buy sticks for our household as Dad brought home pieces of wood regularly from work, carrying them concealed in the saddlebag of his bike. Engineering works like the Govan Shafting in Helen Street where he worked, which handled heavy material, always had baulks of timber lying about as props and chocks. The smaller pieces tended to disappear after a time, for by then they would be well covered with oil and grease, when they were spirited home by workers to be used for kindling. A street trader called Drummond used to go round Govan with a light horse-and-cart. He specialised in selling cut up ordinary box and scrap wood in set quantities in small sacks. Once or twice, when the supply from the Shafting failed to materialise, a much criticised bridging quantity was bought from him.

To prepare wood for kindling it was taken out to the landing. There, kneeling on the doormat within the door and working over the doorstep on the stone floor of the landing, using a small domestic axe, the wood was split down to the required size, generally by the man of the house. This weekly job, usually done by Dad on a Friday night in our case, always fascinated me and I really couldn't wait to be old enough to get to use the axe. Landing surfaces invariably got a bit chipped by the axe, but the marks were covered up when the doormat was replaced, although people who today live on these landings, where they are original, might be curious about them. The best I could hope for then was to be allowed to gather up the sticks as they were chopped, and place them properly aligned and tidy in the box, a wooden Australian butter box scrounged from the Co-op, in which they were kept. It was most satisfying if at the start of the work the piece of timber was large enough to produce sufficient to fill the box, for it meant that all the sticks would be of the same length and lie neatly aligned. But most often they were prepared from two or three smaller pieces of different lengths, and this resulted in an irritating untidiness in packing. A childhood rhyme comes to mind at this point and is quoted here as being relevant to that description, although I know nothing of its origin —

> One two buckle my shoe,
> Three four open the door,
> Five six break up sticks,
> Seven eight lay them straight.
> Nine ten a big fat hen.

That seeming irrelevant last line was probably an expression of relief at the job, one of a never-ending series of chores, being completed.

A hazard liable to be encountered when using firewood as kindling, was that certain kinds of wood could spark when burning. This was caused by explosive bangs which shot out slivers of smouldering wood that could, and often did, land on a fireside rug and burn a hole in the pile if not spotted and dealt with in time, or on furniture or the clothes of some unwary person sitting nearby. The phenomenon was probably caused by pockets of air trapped in certain types of timber (one of the culprits may have been larch) which expansion caused to explode as the temperature rose. That type of wood had to be avoided, although we never learned to tell which was which until the first of it was burning and sparking away. Then, if it was bad enough the rest of that batch had to be disposed of into the midden. Having a lung problem like mine with air passages so sensitive to smoke, it may seem a peculiar thing to be nostalgic about, but I well remember the highly distinctive smell of burning carpet, when a tiny spark of wood or red hot cinder had fallen out un-noticed. This caused noses to twitch until it was identified, then panic set in as carpet and chairs around the fireplace were searched frantically, looking for the faint tell-tale wisp of smoke. If it wasn't spotted at once a sure way of finding the ember was to rub your hand over the surfaces. It was effective but painful.

The only aspect of the domestic coal fire and industry produced smoke absent today and missed, is that in those days of little or no weather forecasting service, it was sometimes convenient to be able to look out the window to see, by glancing at surrounding chimneys, which direction the wind was blowing from. Outdoor winter temperature is often indicated by the direction from which the weather is coming. It could be convenient to gauge what to wear before going out and a change of wind usually meant a change in weather. Also, as some industries emitted pollution in the form of soot, while these lay well to the east of Govan, it helped to be able to tell if the wind was in that airt before putting out a washing or even opening the windows. In the most unfavourable conditions soot, while invisible from inside the house, could be as palpable as gritty particles landing in the back of the throat when breathing, so it was advisable to know if the wind was coming from a direction from which it was likely to be bearing soot before hanging out a washing. The worst local constant source of pollution was the Corporation destructor, with four tall chimneys and three distinctive cooling towers, in Craigton Road.

Some people bought firelighters, which were specially prepared from highly combustible material like compressed wood shavings that had been soaked in paraffin type oil. Made in cakes that were sectioned off like toffee or chocolate bars from which the required amount could be broken off, they were sold wrapped in flimsy cellophane which tore easily, and was quite ineffective in keeping in the strong oily smell. If food was bought at the same time as firelighters, extreme care had to be taken to ensure they were not put in the shopping basket together, otherwise bread and butter and other easily tainted foodstuffs tasted of paraffin. In those days there was no material as effective in protecting food from taint as todays plastic and foil wrapping. Using firelighters, it was possible to light the fire without paper or sticks. Experience with an alternative method, a gas poker, was gained much later.

Although the gas stove incorporated a grill, in our house toast was always made at the fire. Apart from economy reasons it tasted best done that way. For this job a proper toasting fork with a long handle was essential if scorched knuckles were to be avoided. Ours was a stout instrument with a bone handle and two wide spaced vicious prongs. It was a meagre foot or so long which, if the fire was glowing bright, meant the hands were uncomfortably close. A three-pronged fork seen in another house, and coveted very much, was the same length and made of wire, but the handle could be extended to double that by an ingenious sliding arrangement. At that distance from the glowing coals, no matter how hot, there was no risk of getting burnt. Sometimes the best heat was on top of the fire, and if toasting new (soft) bread in that position, there was the chance, unless the slice was securely stitched on the prongs, of it falling off onto the coals. If that embarrassing event occurred to me and no-one else had spotted it, the slice was quickly recovered and all trace of ash and smoke removed from it. Then it was shoved on the communal pile with the fervent hope that I wouldn't get landed with it.

The flue and the chimney sweep

Another aspect of looking after a domestic fire was the state of the flue, or chimney. A local byelaw required them to be swept annually, but because it cost a couple of shillings and was an unpleasant and traumatic experience to undergo, few complied with this statute. Normally it was done only when it became absolutely necessary, usually after two to three years of normal use. By then the deposit of soot in the flue would have built up so much, it would be restricting the draught needed to keep the fire going efficiently and draw up the smoke, 'draw' being the term used to describe that efficiency. The task was performed by the chimney sweep, who was seen often in the streets with his assistant as they passed between jobs, carrying the rope and round flat stiff bristled brush with a heavy iron ball weight attached, a ladder, and a bundle of soot impregnated sacking. He became blacker as his days work progressed so that by the afternoon he began to look like a negro. If there was anyone who succeeded in appearing dirtier than the coalman, it was the sweep. That and his equipment made him instantly recognisable.

The main job of the sweep's helper was to assist in locating the correct flue to be swept. It must be obvious to anyone how disastrous it would be if the brush was put down the wrong chimney, but it seemed to have happened with surprising regularity according to the number of times it was talked about. Generally flues from all houses on adjacent sides of two closes, one from each apartment in each 'through and through' house, passed up within the dividing wall between closes to a common transverse chimney head on the roof. In our situation, with a fireplace in each apartment a chimney pot per flue gave a total for each chimneyhead of 16 pots. Single/two apartments all to the front had a different arrangement. The sweep and his helper, one on the roof and the other at the fireplace, would shout to one another via the flue in order to identify the one to be swept. When the correct chimney was found (and this is where mistakes were made, for in very dirty flues the voices would be quite muffled) after a pause to let his mate seal up the fireplace with the sacking, the sweep would drop the brush down aided by the weight. He pulled it up and lowered it down a section at a time to dislodge as much of the soot as possible. But no matter how carefully the sealing up was done some always escaped into the apartment, adding to the housewife's labours.

Chimney fires were common. Accidental fires were sometimes caused through excessive stoking, by heaping up the coal in cold weather, or by placing in the fire something highly flammable and likely to flare up, such as a handful of bacon rind or a piece of used butter wrapping paper. But to avoid paying the sweep, some people took the risk of deliberately setting fire to their chimney by shoving burning newspaper up it through the cleaning vent. However, this was recognised as being dangerous and was done in trepidation, because it meant a summons to court and a fine if you were caught. A chimney on fire was quite frightening for occupants of the house affected, as well as those in houses above where the flue passed up inside the wall on its way to the chimney head, because burning was accompanied by a loud roar and powerful draught up the 'lum'. A feeling of relief was experienced when the roar began to subside.

But if it was your chimney apprehension rose again, when on looking out the window you would become aware of people in houses round about at their windows, or in the street or back courts, looking up at the sight. The chimney pot would have been belching a thick plume of black smoke like a miniature volcano, with burning soot being scattered around to begin with, downwind, then a jet of flame would shoot up as the burning reached the chimney head, before subsiding. If washings had been hung in back courts in the path of all this muck, their owners were in for a nasty surprise when they came to take them in. Although it was seldom easy to identify whose chimney was to blame, some very lively arguments over the end result can be recalled.

Two other hazards of the coal fire were blowdowns and back smoke, both of which normally occurred in chimneys in need of being swept. In windy weather it was possible, if conditions were favourable, for a reverse draught to occur in the flue, particularly with a newly lit fire. But it could also happen just after the fire had been loaded up with fresh coal, when the flue would have cooled down and the upward draught was at a minimum. The amount of smoke from the fire at that point would be at maximum, so the effect on the household can easily be imagined when it started to pour out into the apartment. Fortunately this didn't happen often, and when it did in my experience it seldom lasted for long. In older tenement buildings, and some not so old, depending on the quality of workmanship and materials used in their construction, chimney linings sometimes began to break up. Or it could be caused, perhaps, by a sweep's too violent use of his brush in the past, with the weight hanging below it banging about and breaking up the lining, as well as weakening caused by previous chimney fires. If you lived in an upper floor where the flues were like this, as we experienced once or twice in our next house, it was possible to get back smoke from a fire in a house above or below, *even with no fire burning in your own house*.

A blowdown was caused by a strong wind dislodging lumps of soot in a chimney pot badly in need of sweeping, which, in tumbling down the flue, knocked down more soot which gathered in volume as it fell. In the worst case it could happen to a family living low down, with debris from the full height of the flue descending on them and pouring out into the kitchen, perhaps just as they had sat down to a meal. Their difficulties when trying to clean up would be compounded in having a partially smothered fire to contend with as well. At that time I used to think that soot was an unburnable product of the fire, but came later to understand that it is composed of still combustible elements escaping from coal before the fire has reached the temperature necessary to burn them, so they went up the chimney as smoke where some of it was deposited as soot.

Chimney pots generally had an extension which sat over the top, resting on three or four lugs round the outside of the pot rim. This left a narrow space all round for a draught of air to enter upwards to boost 'draw'. Some flues gave more trouble than others, which led to the cap being replaced by a metal embellishment in the form of a 'can'. Paid for by the tenant of course. Where trouble with draw persisted, fitting a can was supposed to make the flue system work better and also reduce the possibility of back smoke. Domestic chimneycans were in three forms, the most common of which was a simple tight fitting extension of galvanised metal rather taller than the pottery cap. The top rim of this type was a series of sharp points made by deep V notches cut all round, like a childs crown made from paper or card. Just how that design helped improve draw escapes me even today. Other types were more elaborate, helping draw in a more obvious way. One had a cowl on top surmounted by a fin extension, with the opening turned over through 45 degrees, which turned on a bearing to face, aided by the fin (or vane), away from the wind which then acted as an extractor. The other was a rotating dome with angled vents which turned at a rate according to windspeed. Yet another type not normally found on domestic chimneys was a plain can with a rigid T piece at the top.

Cans were invariably guyed in place with wire stays. This meant that sweeps were denied easy access, which was overcome by there being a door in the side. The corrosive effect of smoke soon penetrated the galvanising, which allowed weathering and rust to take their toll. After a couple of years the 'grannies', as the rotaring type were called, ceased to work and if they were not replaced, which was the normal state of affairs, as they rusted away, collapsed on themselves and might even block the flue. Stays too succumbed, and during every gale, apart from flying slates, falling chimneycans were a hazard to passers-by. A situation sometimes developed which, viewed from this distance in time, was comical, when as deterioration progressed a granny developed a squeak. Sometimes it became more of a penetrating variable shriek as wind strength rose and fell. Bad enough during the day, imagine what it was like for people at night within earshot trying to sleep, and the frustration this would cause because nothing could be done about it. Who would pay to call out the sweep to remove the offending can, or at least stop it turning? The owner, contemplating the looming expense of having to replace it, certainly wouldn't, so the best that could be hoped for was that collapse was imminent.

Cooking with gas — and lighting

Mains electricity had been installed in all closes by the original local electricity company. It was by this time Glasgow Corporation Electricity Department which had probably taken over the company. But only a small proportion of tenants, certainly less than half in the early 1930s, had been connected and had their houses wired. Responsibility and expense for wiring a house seemed to lie with the tenant and not the factor. Our Howat Street house had none even when my parents left in 1936/7, and the next house in Skipness Drive had none either, but my father had it installed there soon after moving in. In the past, due mainly to poverty, a technological innovation like this took much longer to filter down through the levels of society than it would today, when unless it was very expensive it would be almost instantaneous. The benefits of electricity would have been well known to Dad, for when his parents moved to the new house in Shieldhall housing scheme off Moss Road in 1925 it was all electric (but with coal fires). It may have been financial reasons that caused the delay in taking it up, so all cooking and lighting was by gas in our Howat Street home.

In the kitchen the main gas pipe came from the coin operated meter, which sat on a small shelf well above head height over one of the presses in the lobby, so that a stool or chair was needed when feeding it. The supply pipe from it reached the kitchen range at floor level, then ran up the side of the mantelpiece from where two branches were taken off it. One at a low level went to the oven, and the other, at the top of the range, to the stove. The main pipe continued up to the mantelshelf and ran along the top, at the back against the wall to the centre, where it made a ninety degree horizontal turn via an elbow bend. Reduced to the smallest gauge of pipe, it projected out over the edge a little and by another elbow ended in a high swan's neck 'up and over'. On the end of the pipe, at a height of over six feet above floor level, was a metal collar which trapped inside it, by means of three screws spaced evenly round the circumference, a round globe of usually clear, sometimes frosted, glass. In upmarket areas, as portrayed in the Buccleuch Street preserved tenement house, globes were engraved and frosted with artistic designs. The globe was about eight inches in diameter with a round opening top and bottom, the top opening having a thickened outward curling lip which located in the collar and was held in place by the screws. Inside, on the end of the pipe, which incorporated the vent necessary for the entry of air, was the device which produced the light, a mantle, a delicate affair made with asbestos type material.

When the gas was turned on to pass through the mantle and a naked light applied, it ignited with a 'plop' then gave off a continuous soft hiss. A small flow of gas was necessary to begin with until it warmed up, or else the mantle might shatter with too much heat too soon. A reasonably bright white light was produced by a single mantle which would have been roughly equivalent to a 40 watt electric bulb. Although the obvious way of improving the degree of illumination would have been to increase the number of light fittings, I expect the extra cost was the deterrent for I never saw such a thing in any working class home. Some upmarket homes did have brackets with two, or even three, mantles to illuminate large rooms.

A description of a mantle and how they might have been made, should make it easier to understand their function and appearance.

Imagine a small tea strainer, under an inch and a half across and with a very coarse mesh, made with asbestos netting and either coated with fireclay or simply produced in a mould. The circular opening of the ring had a thicker lip of the same material, with three evenly spaced lugs in the outer circumference which located and locked into a fitting within the collar on the end of the pipe. Probably because of the somewhat dim shadowy effect it produced, gaslight created a very attractive and cosy ambience that is nowhere encountered today; even dim electric lighting never succeeds, but if young people used to today's lighting standards were carried back to that time, they would probably complain about rooms being too dark. If the question is raised about how this seemingly feeble light illuminated window blinds so well, remember the effect was evened up by the same low intensity gas street lighting. In other words the streets were gloomy too. Houses with rooms in locations where sunlight never penetrated had corners which were never seen except in deep gloom, so were never cleaned properly. Apartments low down in the inside corner of that side of a block with a south-facing aspect, where the sun never reached, came into that category.

Flow of gas to the mantle was controlled by a valve with a short crossbar set in the horizontal part of the pipe, where it projected out from the mantelshelf, and fitted inverted for convenience. Other houses of the up-market type had a valve with a much longer crossbar in the vertical part of the swan's neck, from each end of which dangled a chain with a large loop on the end. This was for installations that were inconveniently high up, and pulling on one chain or the other gave complete control of the gas flow. Lighting the mantle was done with a match, or preferably using a taper, with the globe removed. If it was attempted with the globe in place, without ensuring that the taper flame was bearing directly on the mantle as the flow was turned on, gas might fill the globe which exploded when the light was applied. Some types of ornamental globes had a wider bell mouth opening at the bottom, and mantles could be safely lit with them in place.

The meter, a much bigger unit than its modern counterpart, was operated by pennies popped into a slot and registered by turning a large butterfly knob. The 'gasman' called at regular intervals to empty the catchment box, which after a month, I think it was, although it may have been quarterly, was very heavy with its load of pennies. Possibly as an inducement to their customers to be at home and alert for his visit, all meters were set to deliver less gas than was paid for, and his calls were were eagerly awaited because the excess was returned by an on-the-spot rebate. Many times, after he had taken the reading and did his calculations, I watched with impatience as he emptied out the contents of the tall narrow box onto the kitchen table, then did his bewilderingly swift count by placing fingertips on individual coins and flicking them into the palm of his hand. Three or four swift movements and he had twelve, then the shilling piles were stacked in a line and counted. The rebate was around 10% and in our case sometimes the total content was a pound's worth or more. Calculations finished, the official, in his uniform with a peaked cap, slid the pile of rebate across to where I was waiting impatiently for them. Having so many coins to play with made me feel like a millionaire. For a time anyway, until Mum carried them off and put them all back into the meter, so that for a few days anyway, there would be no need to go hunting in the increasing gloom for 'a penny for the gas' when the light began to fade.

Two good examples of kitchens of the period can currently be seen. One is the previously mentioned National Trust For Scotland's preserved tenement house at 45 Buccleuch Street, Garnethill. The other (if it is still on display) is on the upper floor of the People's Palace Museum in Glasgow Green. A third example, also mentioned previously, in the form of a very good mock-up made of heavy duty cardboard constructed by some members of the Govan Reminiscence Group, existed for a time, but the nature of its fabric meant that it did not endure for long. However, excellent photographs were taken of it, most of which were enlarged to poster print size, that really do capture some of the atmosphere of a kitchen of the 1930s.

The wireless

'Radio' was then an ultra modern term which didn't come into general use until after the war. (When called up for national service in 1949 I trained initially as a 'wireless operator'). Transmitting from established stations by the BBC was still at a fairly early stage in its development, having commenced in 1923 when the corporation was set up some ten years before the period being written about. It was necessary to have an annual licence costing ten shillings (50p) for all receivers. There are a few recollections of programmes of the period, the most noticeable aspect of which, obviously, was contained in the voices. Regional accents just did not exist as far as Lord Reith, the first Director-General, was concerned and all broadcasters spoke 'proper' English. A later age saw the same phenomenon at the beginning of television, and it is 'well seeing' that Lord Reith died about thirty years before Rab C. Nesbitt came on the scene. However, future generations might consider Rab tame compared to what they, in their more enlightened(?) age, will encounter. News bulletins carried reports of wars, in China involving the Japanese and, later in the decade, in Spain, at the end of which listeners might be rendered agog with the words 'Here is a police message'. This was a regular occurrence which featured pleas for information about mainly road accidents, or less often, crime or missing persons. They related mostly to the London area where people with helpful information were requested to telephone Whitehall 1212 or, if on the odd occasion it applied to the Glasgow area, the number was 'Glasgow Bell ****'.

There were recitals of chamber music, orchestral concerts, Scots songs, talks on intellectual subjects, and variety shows with bands, comedians and singers (crooners was the term then) with the latest popular songs, and plays. Dance music was played by a number of orchestras, Henry Hall, Ambrose, Harry Roy, Joe Loss or Billy Cotton. A variety show of enduring memory, 'Monday Night at 7 o'clock', was later changed to what would then be, as it is today, peak listening time — 'Monday Night at 8 o'clock' with the introductory song:

It's Monday night at 8 o'clock
O can't you hear the chimes
They're telling you to take an easy chair.

It contained features such as playlets, comedy spots, resident and guest orchestra playing different styles of popular music, and a quiz called Puzzle Corner, the answers to which were given later in the programme. This was conducted by a gentleman called Ronnie Waldman and featured something that began as genuine, but which generated such interest that it was made permanent — a deliberate mistake which listeners were invited to watch out for. Writing in with the correct answer held the exciting possibility of having your name mentioned the following week.

Children's Hour is remembered with fondness, with presenters Uncle Mac (Derek McCulloch), Auntie Kathleen and another with the unlikely name Auntie Cyclone, and children's story/plays such as 'Toytown' with Larry the Lamb, Mr Growser and Mr Plod the policeman etc. The Children's TV series Worzel Gummidge of recent decades, first broadcast on the wireless in the 1930s and the TV series was, initially anyway, a nostalgic exercise for me to watch. A TV programme some years ago celebrating a 50th anniversary connected with Children's Hour featured Auntie Kathleen, the late Kathleen Garscadden, being interviewed, and a thrill of nostalgia was experienced on hearing her voice again. Among many performers on variety shows one in particular remains prominent in my memory. One of the crooners, Suzette Tarry, was obviously French, speaking heavily accented English, who was introduced with a song called 'Red Sails in the Sunset'. Very little of the output was recorded because the main medium then was 78rpm discs, and playing anything of more than five minutes duration involved a pause while the record was turned over or changed, which had to be done at similar intervals thereafter. Programme timing sometimes left a gap, and one frequently used 'interval' filler between programmes was a recording of a pleasant sequential peal of bells.

The 'Paul Temple' detective series by Francis Durbridge on TV during the 1960s was first broadcast on the wireless in the 30s. Further series were continued after the war with 'Coronation Scot' as the introductory music, but programme music used for that first series was the 'Storm Music' from Sheherezade by Rimsky-Korsakov. Never, in my opinion, has a piece been employed so successfully for tension heightening effect. Whoever selected it deserved an award.

Each evening, when the weekly episode was due, Mum, Dad and I waited with mounting excitement as programme time approached. After the announcer finished his introduction, the first notes of the approaching storm always generated a spine tingling thrill of anticipation. Other excerpts from the same piece were used with equally electrifying effect during the course of each episode, which invariably ended with a cliffhanger situation leaving us on tenterhooks until the following week. Sheherezade was my introduction to orchestral music. Ever since, I never hear it without being carried back instantly to those days of seeming tranquillity.

In houses without electricity, a wireless had to be either a crystal set, or a valve operated set powered by dry batteries or an accumulator. The latter was a heavy square moulded-glass lead/acid battery rather larger than a present day motorcycle battery, with a thin metal-strap carrying frame, which had an endurance from being fully charged of a month or so, depending of course on amount of use. On running down, the accumulator was carried along to the radio shop or any establishment with charging equipment, such as certain hardware shops or a garage, to be recharged. Munley's radio shop, *The Govan Music House* in Govan Road just west of Howat Street was one place where this was done locally, and it was a common sight to see people carrying accumulators in the street to Munley's. Accumulators were quite efficient but they had one major flaw. If an evening without the wireless was to be avoided, when the accumulator ran down at teatime with no possibility of a recharge until the next day and an eagerly awaited programme was coming on, holding a fully charged-up spare was essential. The expense of that was beyond the resources of most people, who, to avoid disappointment, considered it best to save up for a mains set. Munley's shop can be glimpsed in a photograph dating from the 1950s (which also shows the Fairfield goods train), on page 19 of *Glasgow Trammerung (The Twilight of the Glasgow Tram)*, by Cedric Greenwood (1986), although by then George Munley had passed on. Early dry batteries had two disadvantages. Their endurance was poor and they tended to leak. Many a chest of drawers or sideboard was ruined by a battery coming near the end of its life, lying out of sight behind a wireless with highly corrosive fluid leaking out and ruining the polished surface. Even taking the precaution of sitting them in a metal tray was no sure protection, as metal was eaten through just as surely if more slowly.

Crystal sets were often home made. My maternal grandfather Joe Chambers had constructed one but by the time I came along he had a battery set. Their house never had electricity during their time. Mum said he had earphones for use with the crystal set, with a pair hanging on either side of the mantelpiece handy for anyone sitting there to pick up. I dimly remember seeing them, but because they had not long since bought the battery set, this equipment was redundant by the time such things came to my notice. Soon after it was all put away in a box to lie for many years with other junk, before being disposed of, much of which would have been of interest to certain museums and collectors today.

Using a crystal set had one big disadvantage that battery or mains sets didn't have. They needed an elaborate aerial in the form of long length of heavy drawn hard copper wire, and the best way to fulfil this requirement was to come to a sharing arrangement with someone living in the opposite side of the block, in the house directly opposite for preference, and have the cable strung across above the back-courts between them. However, the wire could be coiled on a wooden frame and set up inside the house, as was necessarily the case in our all-to-the-front Howat Street house, which could be inconvenient as well as less efficient. As late as the end of the 1930s and in a few instances long after this time, there were still quite a number of these aerials to be seen stretched between houses within the blocks, but by then almost all were rendered redundant by people having aquired battery or mains sets.

Aerial cables had to be insulated from contact with earth through the building, and this was done using white porcelain insulators rigged at each end. Tenants in the long sides of an oblong tenement block were ideally placed for aerial hanging, the distance involved being just about right, but what others living in the ends did to overcome the problem of arranging an outside aerial caused by the much greater distance isn't clear. A solution would be to suspend the cable at an angle between ends and sides of the block, but there is no recollection of seeing this done. Ground floor dwellers of course could not have an aerial of this type, unless they made an arrangement to share with a neighbour living higher up, allowing them to tap into their system, otherwise they and block-end dwellers were restricted to an indoor aerial. Even those living one stair up could encounter difficulty because, except near corners, the wires passed across just above the dykes and were within reach of dyke-climbers, and thus liable to be interfered with. Early valve battery/mains sets require smaller aerials that could be accommodated easily indoors. When a valve set is switched on there is a delay while they warm up, especially with the old technology large valves which were of the size and roughly the shape of a 40 watt bulb. This could take as much as a minute or so, which always produced the slighly apprehensive feeling of the 'will it/ won't it work' kind, especially if you had switched on late for something important.

Street scenes

The favourite street hawker with children of Govan was undoubtedly the candy rock man. Many Govanites of my generation and older still talk about him today with nostalgic delight. His arrival would be anticipated well in advance by the sound of his progress through nearby streets. His horse and cart was always surrounded by a milling throng of up to a hundred boisterous, noisy and excited children in a fever of anticipation. The cart was in the charge of two fellows (who ought to be labelled 'the candy rock men') most likely father and son. While one took the bridle and walked the horse slowly along the centre of the street, the other stood on the back of the cart and shouted at the surging crowd 'WHO LIKES CANDY ROCK?'. After every single voice in the crowd had yelled 'ME', he would throw a few pieces among them causing bedlam. Today this would be called a sales and marketing ploy to attract as many potential customers as possible. They would pause for a while to sell some then move on for the next performance in another street. As I was of pre-school age I never got to take part in this dangerous pushing and shoving game, and have no memory of it after we moved to Linthouse in 1937. Without a doubt an accident prevention officer today would have nightmares if he encountered anything like it, and would immediately take steps to put a stop to it.

Street lighting in those pre-war days was in transition from the low height gas lamp-posts to tall electric poles. Main streets had all been converted, assisted, no doubt, by the poles installed to carry the overhead electric power supply cables for trams, and side streets were gradually being changed over. Some Corporation housing schemes such as, in our district, Greenloan/Greengairs, Shieldhall, Drumoyne, and more distant Mosspark, all of which date from the mid 1920s (but not West Drumoyne which was built in the early 1930s), had electric street lighting from the beginning. These installations were mounted on the same type of post as the gas lights. Very distinctive low cast iron fluted poles with a crossbar and flared base, with, in the case of the electric light, a reflector that was unique in that its like was never encountered anywhere else other than in the Glasgow area. It had a naked bulb projecting out at an angle towards the pavement, from the centre of a white enamelled shallow cone shaped reflector which flared *away* from it, that is with the cone pointing *towards* the bulb. A reflector is usually designed to curve round the bulb to achieve maximum efficiency by reflecting light that might otherwise be wasted, so if the designer was aiming at the unusual he certainly succeeded here. A particular memory of these lights dates from pre-school years. It is of walking, or being carried by my father, from Rigmuir Road into Moss Road, on the way home to Howat Street after a visit to his mother's house on a dark night of heavy fine rain, and noticing these distinctive lights marching off in twin rows. They faded in a mysterious way into the mist shrouded distance down Moss Road towards Govan Road a half mile away.

Neighbours

Memories of other people who lived up the close are slight. Only one family, the Melvilles, stand out, because there were two children of around my age. They lived on the ground floor and became the first friends I had outside the family. Another acquaintance was a man who comes to mind in a rather dramatic fashion, because he had a motorcycle. Motorised transport in the area bounded by the northern section of Elder Street, Taransay Street and Howat Street, including Luath Street was infrequent because of its semi-seclusion. Those streets form a broad flat 'A' with Govan Road passing across the bottom, so only vehicles requiring access were to be seen there, mostly horsedrawn carts and handbarrows. Motor lorries, vans and cars were seldom seen. In that small area a private car in the street might belong to a doctor, but even that was rare for not all of them had a car, or was attending a wedding or a funeral.

The owner of the motorbike created an entertaining scene each time he attempted to go out on it. From recollections of its appearance it was probably even then a museum piece. It lay in the street at the close mouth propped up on its stand, the old style 'U' bracket extending under rear wheel which when not in use was held up at the back by an over centre spring. When he came to start it up he pushed it north from the close towards Taransay Street, gathering speed until he was running as fast as he could, then he leapt high in the air and came down on the kickstart, usually without success. Why he did this is puzzling unless it needed a combination of push/kick start. On reaching the north end of Howat Street he crossed over to the other side and proceeded as far as Govan Road, going through these comical and strenuous antics which included much pulling of levers and fiddling with controls. His physical attitude was like that of a predatory bird looming menacingly over the contraption, while twisting violently at controls on the handlebars. Continuing the circuit he returned to the close. This went on for a couple of circuits until either the engine started with lots of smoke and explosive backfires, or he gave up exhausted. Motorcycle enthusiasts with their noisy machines were around even then. Walking along a road when one roared past, sometimes meant being engulfed in fumes having the distinctive reek of a then popular fuel additive to boost power — ether.

Horses

The proportion of horsedrawn to motor traffic was about mid way through the long process of change, and the number of horses on the streets became steadily fewer. Nearly all had gone by the 1950s, although a few continued in use for longer because some users, usually individual business operators with one animal, obviously liked and preferred them. Studying large scale maps of urban areas dating from early decades of this century, shows that horse troughs were placed at regular intervals in localities with a lot of traffic, to provide drinking water for them. As there is no recollection of seeing any troughs, they must have been removed shortly before I reached the stage of noticing such things.

The presence of a large number of horses in the streets meant that there was always a lot of dung lying around, which made them a health hazard, particularly after a spell of dry weather. Usually rain fairly quickly flushed them clean, but an extended dry spell caused the dung to turn to dust and chopped up straw which resembled fine sawdust. A wind of sufficient strength could, and often did, whip it up and make it a danger to the eyes. Such weather conditions, which would merely be annoying today, were then rendered hazardous. Householders with gardens or plots used to send their youngsters out round the streets with a barrow or bogie and a shovel, and even a brush, to collect it for use as manure in season. More enterprising children realised there was a ready market for the stuff, and took to collecting it and selling it round houses with gardens. I can still picture the expression of glee on the face of an urchin, from his appearance not long started school, as he spotted a pile steaming in the street which a horse had just deposited while stationary. This meant that instead of having to sweep or scrape it up into a heap if it had been 'done' while the horse was on the move, he could scoop it up at one go with his coal shovel. The street sweeper, or 'scaffy', had far less litter to cope with. then but horses more than made up for it.

A simple barrow for collecting dung, which could be put to other uses, was easily made at home by acquiring from the grocers a discarded wooden box, like the one referred to before in which our sticks were kept. An Australian or New Zealand butter box was ideal, although there was strong competition for them from people looking for cheap kindling, and during the bogie building season. Butter was just one of many items bulk packed in non-returnable wooden boxes. Dried fruit, oranges, and certain canned goods were others. A single axle with a pair of wheels from an old pram could be nailed across the bottom at the centre, and a spar, or a pair of spars fixed one on either side of the box to project up at a low angle served as shafts.

Another aspect of the number of horses around was that some were nervous, easily frightened and liable to bolt off out of control with the cart. There were occasional newspaper items with the headline running something like — *Horse Bolts With Cart — Kills Man.* There were two main reasons for this. One was a sound seldom encountered today, a backfire from a motorcycle, car or lorry, a common feature of motor vehicle engines at that stage of their development. It was caused by a misfire driving fuel through the engine unburnt until it hit the hot exhaust,whereupon it would ignite and cause a bang which sounded like a gunshot. A car horn used thoughtlessly close to an animal might startle it.

Another all too common cause of a horse getting out of control was the barking of a dog. Some dogs were territorial with a natural defence mechanism that, when another animal, horse, dog or cat, appeared in what they consider to be their territory, caused them to bark and growl round the feet of any horse that appeared in the street. When that happened, and there were other causes than the ones mentioned, even apparently placid Clydesdales would snort and neigh and paw the ground and roll their eyes. It was a fearsome sight with the carter trying desperately to calm the animal as it tossed its head. Holding on tight to the bridle, he would be thrown about while trying to fend off the dog. As part of their harness all horses had to have patches, called blinkers, fitted over each eye in such a way that they could only see forward. It has been found that when motor vehicles first appeared, much trouble was caused by horses taking fright. But through the generations since then they had become used to vehicles, except in one very important situation — when being overtaken. If a vehicle passed close to a horse while travelling in the same direction, appearing suddenly in its vision it was liable to be startled, but fitting blinkers helped overcome the problem. This would be where the term 'blinkered', used to describe the attitude of a person who chooses not to see the obvious, came from.

Traffic congestion which occurred on main roads in some areas, could sometimes be severe enough to obstruct the tram lines. If a carter wished to make a delivery to a shop or other premises found he couldn't park nearby, he simply double parked. This is tolerated in some circumstances today, but in the past if it was done on a tram route it could cause a hold up if the cart fouled the line. Encountering such an obstruction, the tram driver would clang his bell furiously and bawl and shout, because he was subject to a severe regime of discipline which didn't tolerate late running. Some entertaining scenes of conflict were witnessed through this. Another even more serious cause of friction between tram and cart drivers was engendered by the fact that most carts were built to conform to a maximum standard wheel track which corresponded exactly to that of the tram lines. It will be appreciated that carters took advantage of this whenever possible by running along the rails, so as to be free from the noise and vibration of the cobbles, simply because it made life easier for themselves. A period postcard scene recently encountered showed just such a scenario, with a tram visible, running close behind a plodding horse and cart which is occupying the rails in an otherwise empty Govan Road. What was missing for me was the sound of the tram bell and the imprecations of the driver for the carter to 'Get out of the ******* road!'

The noise made by a cart rolling over cobble was so penetrating that close to it could be almost painful to sensitive ears. Carters obviously had to tolerate it while on the move, but why they did so if there was alternative employment was quite beyond me. Some seemed quite oblivious to the racket and with an empty cart, or lightly loaded one and drawing near finishing time, they 'gee'd-up' their horse to a gallop which redoubled the din. However, this was also a factor which made them choose to go by the smooth asphalt-surfaced back streets whenever possible.

CHAPTER 2

Observing Activity on the River

The ferries

Crossing the river other than by using the tunnel or bridges upstream was by ferry. Between Linthouse and King George V bridge at Oswald/Commerce Streets there were eight ferries at six crossing points. In 1938 the first vehicular ferry which also carried passengers was introduced on the Water Row to Yorkhill crossing, but they were slow and ponderous and intending passengers, except those with time to spare, preferred the passenger boats which could make the crossing in half the time. The only occasion it was quicker to use the vehicular ferry was if a passenger vessel had just left, and the vehicular boat was ready to depart. There were two locations where both types of boats operated side by side, Linthouse-Whiteinch, and Water Row (Govan)-Pointhouse (Partick), while the other four crossing points had one boat each. A vehicle/passenger boat at General Terminus-Lancefield Quay, passengers only boats at Govan Wharf-Meadowside, Highland Lane at the dry docks-Kelvinhaugh, and Springfield Quay at Kingston Dock-Anderston Quay. Curiously, they did not seem to operate to a time-table, but just went back and forward with only a short pause. On my travels with grandad, who walked a lot and took me along at every opportunity, I most likely passed over all these crossings. Clearest memories are of those at Linthouse where the terminals were at the foot of Holmfauld Road, and Water Row, because experience of using them in later decades is less distant in time.

Passenger ferry terminals, the remains of one or two of which can still be seen today, were small high wooden sided V shaped docks the wings of which projected out into the river for 20 feet or so. A flight of fairly shallow steps with metal clad edges began at ground level high up at the narrow part of the 'V', widening as they descended below low water level. A pair of upward curving metal brackets, which crossed at their high point, stretched from the top of one side wall to the other, from which hung an oil lamp for operating in darkness. Tides in these upper reaches had an average rise and fall of about ten feet, which meant that at low tide descent to the boat was about thirty steps and at high water it was as little as ten. During spring and autumn 'highs', the times of extra high and low tides, water level could be such that for a short time services had to be suspended.

Built to the same two designs, the ferry boats were quite different from the third type which operated downstream at Renfrew and Erskine, which were part funded by the two county councils in whose areas they operated. They were worked by twin chains which stretched from one cobbled ferry ramp across the river to the other. During crossings the chains were hauled in by pulleys, driven initially by steam engines but latterly by diesel, passing through engine rooms, one on either side, each with a chimney projecting above, with the slack passed out aft to lie on the river bottom clear of other traffic. The middle of the boat was a well containing three lanes for vehicles, access to which was by a kind of double-wing gate protected drawbridge, while passengers occupied enclosed spaces round the engine rooms and on open decks above. The counties operated ferries charged a fare, while those in the upper reaches provided by the Clyde Navigation Trust were free. This was a relic of the days when it was possible to ford the river in these reaches, and when work of deepening the channel began the CNT were obliged to provide ferries as a replacement at existing fords. Each of the three types of boats were bi-directional and didn't require to be turned for each crossing. CNT passenger boats were oval shaped at deck level, like a rugby ball cut in half along its length, with a heavy keel having a straight section to match the angle of the landing steps, metal reinforced to endure the stress of bumping up on them. The bulwarks of steel plating, with small openings at the ends for passenger access, had a broad flat wooden top with rounded edges.

Each passenger boat had a crew of two, and the steam engine with its coal fired boiler, water supply and bunker of coal was housed in a steel cabin with rounded corners and flat roof and a door at one end. This 'engine room' ('hut' conveys its appearance better) was set in the middle of the vessel's deck, leaving narrow passages either side for passenger movement from one end to the other. It had no windows as such but there were openings to allow the engineer to keep a lookout. Wooden slatted-type benches, which doubled as life rafts, ran most of the way along each bulwark, except in the narrow centre passages between engine room and the bulwarks. There are photographs of these boats taken in the early years of this century which show the engine and boiler with only a rudimentary cabin. But in the 30s and 40s the cabin was larger, but still just a kind of uneven-topped two level steel box with a door at one end. The section of tall thin chimney, where it emerged through the roof above the boiler, was hinged at the bottom and could be lowered on to its side to rest on a bracket at the end of the working day. In later, post-war years a small amount of shelter was provided for passengers by fitting an awning to the top of the engine house. It projected out over the side passages and curved down at an angle, to be secured on top of the bulwarks, but they would accommodate only about ten per cent of a full complement of passengers. Steering was by small conventional marine type of ship's spoked steering wheel mounted on a pillar at the entry opening, one at each end on the port side when viewed from the middle of the boat. Up to the 1940s the helmsman had no weather protection, but small cabins were added later.

The vessel was held in the terminal by hitching a mooring rope to one of the small bollards set alternately one on each step close in at the sides, by the ferryman/helmsman. With the rope looped round a bollard, here they were just steel pins about an inch thick and six inches high with a ball thickening at the top. The ferryman held it in tension so that there was as little movement of the boat as possible for passengers disembarking and boarding. Meanwhile, the engine was left running at slow to keep it pushing gently into the dock to ease tension on the rope. When ready to depart the engineer gave the engine a burst inwards which allowed the rope to be undone. Then the helmsman leapt on board and secured the coils and, as the engineer reversed direction and opened up the engine, made his way through the passengers to the opposite end, where he unlocked the wheel and began to steer as the crossing got under way. The steam engine made a quite distinctive rhythmic chuffing sound only a little bit different from a railway engine, but the exhaust smoke puffed out the chimney just the same. As the helmsman took control the engineer increased engine speed to cruise, and the vessel steamed briskly across at a speed of about 7 knots, the crew keeping a sharp lookout for other vessels passing along the main channel. Delays could be prolonged if a large ship with tugs fore and aft happened to be passing.

Other factors to be taken into consideration during a crossing were wind and tide. A combination of the two could in the severest instances result in the service being suspended, and during the worst conditions in which it was possible to operate a crossing could be lively, alarming even. A strong wind and tide flowing in the same direction often carried the boat a fair distance away from its normal path, making it slow and laborious work to return, and very tricky to steer into the dock. Nearing the end of a crossing steam was shut off at a distance of about 50 feet out. Then the engineer put the engine in reverse, the 'glunk' and slight jerk of this is well remembered, and opened it up to maximum so that it gave off a loud chuntering roar. Turning in reverse, the propeller produced a violent frothing under the 'front' of the vessel, causing it to slow down quickly as it approached the terminal steps. At this point, after ensuring the heading was correct the ferryman locked the wheel and moved to the prow and, holding onto the trail with one hand and braced against turbulence and braking effect, stood with the mooring rope in the other ready for docking. If the engineer's judgement was correct, the vessel would have just enough way left to mount a couple of steps aided by the curve of the keel. The ferryman then leapt off onto the step level with the prow and quickly put a couple of turns of rope round the mooring pin a few steps above. He stood with his back to the wall of the dock with his foot resting on the rope, while holding, and maintaining tension on, the free end, to allow passengers carried over to disembark and those for the return journey to embark.

Jumping on and off would best describe the manoeuvre, and it will be clear from the foregoing that this way of crossing the river was for the young and agile, and although I never witnessed one, accidents to people using the ferries were occasionally reported in the papers. Main hazards were falling off the open ends of the vessel during a crossing, for there was no barrier, or someone missing their footing when leaping off or on board while the vessel was moored in the dock. When departing, the time arrived when the rope was freed and the journey commenced. Men who thought they were still young and fit who arrived as the ferry was leaving, were guilty of trying, in the second or two before the gap between steps and boat became too great, of rushing down and taking a flying leap. Sometimes a lack of patience caused someone to take a dip. As indicated, the steps were set at a very shallow angle, but even so, anyone stumbling and falling was fairly certain to roll down into the water, where frantic efforts would have to be made to get them out with the long shafted boat hook. Hooks for this purpose hung on a pair of brackets, with one at each terminal and one on each side of the ferry cabin. Among other hazards encountered was the wash from passing ships, especially tugs, steaming past light (without a tow). Their tubby lines generated the worst waves, which made passenger ferries quite lively.

The story of one occurrence is a good example of what could happen. It took place during a crossing of the Govan to Partick ferry on an evening rush hour in winter. The boat was packed to capacity with shipyard workers going home, when a man who had been among the last to board, said to people in front of him that the person who had come aboard behind him, and who remained there, had disappeared. This was brought to the notice of the ferrymen who reversed the boat, and although a search was carried out for some time nothing was found. The man who raised the alarm was accused of making a mistake, but he stuck to his story, maintaining that the man was behind him when the ferry left, and could not have passed him unobserved as he was standing in the narrow part, at the point in the 'stern' between the bulwark and steering wheel. It was an evening of fog and hard frost, and in the darkness no one would have stood much of a chance of being found far less surviving for long in the water. The event became a mystery which was never solved. Newspapers took it up, and speculated on the possibility of someone being reported missing in the surrounding districts who would fit the description, but with no result I ever heard about. Another ferry accident story with a happier ending, this time on the Linthouse ferry, can be found on page 105 of the history of the shipbuilders Alexander Stephens & Sons.

Apart from being much bigger vehicular ferries were a very different kind of vessel, with an appearance that was even more interesting than the passenger boats, neither of which could be described as designed to appeal to the eye. They were of massive construction with a number of interesting technical features, and seemed ideal for the job they were meant to do. In my time the vehicular boats had a crew of three and were of two types. The older design was steam propelled and the other, introduced in 1938, was diesel/electric powered. While basically the same, both consisted of a low flat hull roughly 80 feet long by 45 feet broad, with the main deck about four feet above water level. The main difference was in the number and dimensions of the support beams, with those on the older boats appearing much heavier. In dock the deck of the hull was normally hidden by the vehicle deck, but during a crossing at low tide, when that deck would be in a raised position, the hull was exposed. The massive girders which formed the vertical supports for the vehicle deck gave the boats a very clumsy and ungainly appearance. They rose to a height of over thirty feet from around the outer edges of the hull, vertical at the sides, but leaning in slightly at the ends of the later boats, and sweeping up and curving sharply inboard at their highest point, to meet in a continuous flat sweep over the car deck.

Positioned centrally over the vehicle deck on top of the main girder and reached by a ladder and cat-walk, was perched a small cabin in which engine and steering controls were housed, and from which the 'captain' supervised the working of the boat. The overall impression conveyed by the vessels, particularly the newer one with its lighter construction of thinner beams, was of a giant spider with a heavy undercarriage, thick legs (more so the older vessel) and a tiny head. They berthed in bays that were a snug fit, set deep enough into the bank to take almost the whole boat, so that when docked they projected only a small amount out into the channel of what was after all a very busy and fairly narrow river, thus avoiding obstructing the channel. The bay itself, like those of the passenger boats, the two lay in close proximity, was of timber construction with vertical walls round the three faces, but with less of a 'V' spread than the passenger ferry docks. Standing on the level surface of the area between the bays was a stoutly built wooden hut which, because of the open aspect of the Holmfauld Road area, was very necessary, there being no other shelter for about five hundred yards. It was a square shack with a boarded over window, a pitched slated roof, and had a bench seat extending all round the walls.

To compensate for changes in water level, on the older boats the vehicle/passenger deck was raised and lowered by eight huge vertical screwed shafts, four along each side set between pairs of the massive girders required for support and stiffening. The newer vessel had a total of six shafts. These carried the weight of the deck with its load of vehicles and passengers. The hull was just a pontoon with barely a suggestion of a cutwater at each end, with hatches on top giving access to the propulsion unit, diesel engines driving a generator, and a few of the usual ship type ventilators. Engine exhaust was carried up in two tall curiously thin flattened funnels which rose to a couple of feet above the level of the control cabin at the mid point of the sides. Because of the much greater height above water level than on the passenger boats, the impression gained by passengers was of quiet stately movement, with much less engine noise even from the steam engines, than that generated by the other boats. So much so that on board you were more aware of vibration, little though it was, than noise, but that was because the engines were two decks down.

Suspended between the main girders, the vehicle deck was laid out for three lines of vehicles, while the passenger area on the newest boat was a narrow strip along one side only. In the 1930s, vehicles using the ferries were divided roughly 50/50 between horsedrawn and motor lorries and vans, plus an occasional car. The edge of the vehicle deck at each end of the boat had a metal lip projecting as an extension of the deck which, when the vessel moved up to the end of the bay when docking, engaged in a slot just below road level. The outer edge of the road had a matching lip, a metal flap hinged on the landward side, which seemed to have been levelled by two low fixed crane jib heads, in casings, with chain lifting tackle, on which the road gates were mounted. This provided a smooth transition between road and car deck, but seemed to have been operated by the aforementioned horizontal projection from the boat, as there was no other mechanism visible ashore for doing this. Lights were mounted on top of the jibs for night-time operation, the corroded remains of one of which can be seen at the riverside at Water Row more than twenty five years after it was last used. Instead of mooring ropes, the vessel was held in position by two short thick steel cables with heavy 'T' pieces on the ends. One on each side of the car deck was dropped over fairleads recessed at ground level ashore by the deck hand, then slack was taken up and the cable held under tension by a winch or hydraulic means, to hold the boat steady. It is assumed that the engine would have been kept turning over to assist in holding the boat steady.

Queues of carts and motor vehicles lined up at the gates on both sides of the road, and when the last of the arriving vehicles left, they plodded and crawled on board for the leisurely trip. That illusion persisted until the crossing ended and the two pairs of double gates were thrown open. Then, accompanied by the thunderous roar of steel shod hooves and steel rimmed cart wheels on cobbles, they all surged off three abreast, so that it sometimes developed into a dangerous race between drivers to be first at the top of ferry road. Traffic authorities of the time endeavoured to curb this practice by requiring gatemen to restrict opening initially to the centre lane only, then the others in turn. Noise made by cart wheels was lessened somewhat by laying tracks on the nearside of cobbled roads in areas with a lot of horsedrawn traffic. This was in the form of lengths of granite in long sections laid parallel at a distance apart which corresponded to the wheel track, or distance between the wheels. Certain main roads and many of the busier cobbled side streets had such strips, a few of which can still to be seen in undeveloped districts which still have that surface. These strips really helped to reduce what today would be described as a most irritating high decibel din.

Passenger accommodation was separated from the vehicle deck by a stout steel stanchion railing, the same as that round the rest of the deck perimeter. Access from the dockside was by two narrow arched drawbridges mounted on the same side of the boat, one near each end for each dock on the north and south sides of the river. When the boat had docked the landward one was lowered and raised by hand by the side rails, and in the raised position the ridged footwalk with its curved 'hump', became part of the guardrail. The ridges were anti-slip transverse wooden strips, which used to cause irritation because of their tendency to trip people up unless concentration was exercised on where they were putting their feet. Because of the many distracting sights around, for me there never was time for that so there were a few stumbles. A number of slatted liferafts similar to those on passenger boats doubled as seats.

The book of photographs entitled *Glasgow At War* by Paul Harris, published in 1986 by Archive Publications Ltd, in association with the *Evening Times* newspaper, has two illustrations of a vehicular ferry being used to carry equipment to a ship on fire. Photos numbers 69 and 70 on page 46 show one of these vessels fairly clearly although the captions are wrong. The subject of number 70 is described as a 'Special Firefighting Barge', but it is actually vehicular ferry No. 4 which had obviously been commandeered for the emergency. It would have been ideally suited to driving the fire brigade vehicles, complete with trailer pumps, straight on board and sailing to wherever it was needed anywhere in the upper reaches, then lowering the intake hoses of the pumps into the water. The other caption (60), describing the same event, states that the location was Rothesay Dock at Clydebank. But the event depicted took place at Yorkhill Basin adjacent to the Govan ferry crossing point, and was connected with a wartime incident involving the cruiser HMS *Sussex*, the story of which is already set down in preparation for a subsequent series of reminiscences. The 'ferrymaster's cabin' above the vehicle deck was normally of glass above waist height for all round vision.

But it can be clearly seen that these windows are covered over as required for wartime night-time blackout.

Two models of vehicular ferries, one of which is excellent with much detail built into it, can be seen in the Ship Room at the Transport Museum at Kelvin Hall. A good source of information on the river in general is *Clyde Navigation* — a history of the development of the River Clyde, by John R. Riddel. Another book by the same author is *The Clyde*, a much shorter edition with less text but more and more better photographs, produced in 1988 for the Garden Festival. It has a few excellent views of both types of ferries as they were in the 30s. On page 78 a passenger boat is seen, and page 81 has two very good pictures of an older vehicular vessel, showing all the detail described above including the crane jibs with lights on top.

The docks

A favourite place for walks with Granda was the docks. King George V, (opened 1931) known mainly by the abbreviation KG Five (or as Shieldhall Dock by those of anti-royalist inclination), was the most frequented as it was nearest, but Prince's Dock and the quays upriver were visited occasionally, although many of the berths there were inaccessible to the general public. He had a good eye for the unusual and exciting, and scanned newspapers for things of interest to go and look at. Sometimes we would go a long way to see a particular ship or an unusual happening. On one occasion there was a report that a tug had sunk in the river off Plantation Quay, so at the first opportunity on the following weekend, on Saturday afternoon or Sunday, off we went together to see it. Sure enough there it was, although all we could see of it was the upper half of the tall thin funnel and mast rising above the surface of the river some way out.

It had been one of a pair or tugs, the one on the stern station, in charge of a cargo ship which, as was normal practice, had her propeller turning over slowly to assist in manoeuvering, and the tug, which had been allowed to drift too close under the stern, had been struck and holed by it. It had gone down quickly but the crew had saved themselves by climbing up the mast, to quote the report in the paper as related by Granda, 'in a leisurely fashion' and hung on calmly, as they were experienced watermen and knew the depth of the river at that point, until they were rescued. (After writing the foregoing I came across an excellent book entitled *The Clyde Puffer* by Dan McDonald (ISBN 0 7153 7443 5), in which there is a photograph of the operation to recover the tug on page 37. Four puffers were used and are seen in preparation for positioning for the lift, although no part of the tug is visible. Maybe funnel and mast had been removed for the operation. The caption states that the incident occurred in April 1938.

Docks always seemed to be busy and quays a hive of activity then. With ships being unloaded and reloaded, with horsedrawn, motorised, and steam powered vehicles, and hand barrows as well, constantly coming and going, and crowds of dockers stacking the loads on vehicles as they came off the boats. But due to a fascination with railways, of greatest interest for me was the rail system. Young people today other than enthusiasts and students of the subject who study it through reading, old films, photographs and maps, would find it hard to appreciate just how extensive the network of railway lines really was, especially around docks. Some idea of what it was like can be gained from large scale maps of the period, such as the range produced by Allan Godfrey of Newcastle. They show in excellent details, to the very large scale of 15 inches to one mile, vast acres of marshalling yards with miles of sidings. Prince's Dock, General Terminus and Shieldhall Dock, with their associated access routes were a maze of lines, plus the even more extensive layouts on the north side of the river. Originals of these maps, however, can be seen free, and photocopies ordered at extremely reasonable cost, in the Glasgow Room of the Mitchell Library.

The network around loading and discharge points was constantly choked with waggons being shunted into position to be emptied or loaded, then hauled away to adjacent marshalling yards by dock shunters like the small ex-Caley class 23 0-6-0 tank engines, or the larger classes 29 and 782. Govan Cross Goods Station was also quite extensive, with plenty of facilities to serve the surrounding industrial premises, many having their own sidings. Harland and

Wolfs' Clyde Foundry on the west side of Helen Street, known as 'The Glasshouse', had a 'kick-back' siding which ran across Helen Street near Loanbank Street.

One visit to KGV Dock stands out. Sheds where cargo was stored awaiting transhipment were sometimes full, with the excess stacked on the quayside clear of the railway and travelling crane tracks while leaving sufficient room for other vehicles to pass. Sometimes there was so much that progress could be difficult even when walking, and on this occasion Granda and I were passing by an area stacked up with wooden crates from which a fruity smell emanated, when a policeman came running up from behind. Passing us he went on ahead and turned into a recess in the stacks. After a few seconds he reappeared holding by the scruff of their necks two youngsters of about ten years of age, each of them holding an armful of oranges, and heading, I was certain, for the nearest jail. Granda bent down and said, in his east coast accent, 'Dunae you ever be caught daen ae' thing like that!'

Sentinel and Trojan steam lorries were seen occasionally in Govan Road proceeding to or from the docks, sometimes drawing up in our area to top up with water from a fire hydrant. A regular place for this was the quiet stretch in Renfrew Road between the Southern General Hospital and Hardgate Road. These unmistakable vehicles had rounded, open to the elements, waist-high fronts and a cab roof like the top deck end of a tramcar. Boiler and firebox was in the cab, the chimney of which passed up at the front through the roof, projecting above it for a few inches, and was capped with a counterweighted lid. Propulsion drive was carried from engine to back axle by an enormous unguarded chain running round small-to-large sprockets under the platform. Memory of them is fleeting as they were being withdrawn and disappeared from the roads during this time. I bet the crews were glad to see them go, with their open cabs, especially the Trojans with their solid tyred wheels. They must have been torture to endure running on cobbled roads, although the last of them had inflatable tyres, to say nothing of the disadvantages of the work involved with firing the engine.

The original Clyde tunnels

Another place of interest visited with Granda was the original tunnels under the Clyde, accesses to which were in the rotundas at Mavisbank on the south side and Finnieston on the north bank. Built for use by both pedestrians and vehicles and now disused and partly filled in, they provided the then unique thrill of walking under the river. The subway passed under as well, but sitting in the train you were much less aware of it. The rotundas covered a wide vertical shaft with 160 stairs for pedestrians, and lifts for vehicles which were probably operated by power supplied from the nearby hydraulic powerhouses in the form of pressurised water. This was also the power source for the dockside cranes. From the stairs I remember watching a carter having to calm his agitated horse disturbed by the motion of the lift, by standing close and stroking its nostrils while keeping a firm grip on the bridle. Still in existence, the powerhouse building, long since disused and the machinery removed, was the tram depot for storage and maintenance of the four trams which ran during the Garden Festival in 1988. Both rotundas are still extant.

Starting school

My school attendance commenced at St Anthony's Infants in Harmony Row in late summer of 1935. My mother and her sister had received all their education there, as there was no Catholic senior secondary in Govan in their time. St Gerard's did not open until 1937. My recollections of St Anthony's are slight due partly to frequent absences through illness. However, faintly remembered are making things with cut out pieces of coloured paper, drawing on thick dark paper with coloured crayons, and playing with plasticine. Using the sand tray is more clearly recalled. Each pupil was issued with a small shallow tray, about eight inches by six with wooden sides and a shiny tin base, which contained about a teaspoonful of very fine sand. When the tray was held flat and shaken gently a thin covering was spread evenly over the bottom. It was in one of these I learned to write figures and letters with a fingertip, the idea of the tray being economy, for after use a couple of shakes would give a fresh surface thus saving on pencils and paper.

Another learning-to-write aid was the slate and pencil. A

writing slate was a piece of ordinary slate about ten inches by six, with the surfaces on both sides polished smooth. One side was blank and the other lined off in squares for arithmetic. Each slate was set in a wooden frame with a hole in the centre of one end, the reason for which seemed to have been that, although collectively they were stored pile up, they could also be hung on hooks. The drawing implement was a thin rod somewhat thicker than ordinary pencil lead, made of some kind of hard brittle material which had to be used with care. A fairly heavy pressure was required, but not too much or it was liable to make a screeching sound which set teeth on edge. Why there were two different teaching aids in school for the same job isn't clear, but it may have been a time when a new system was introduced and the older one hadn't been discarded. The older one would be the slate for the pencil wasn't very efficient, the mark it made being rather faint and difficult to erase. Blackboard chalk would have been far better, but probably more expensive and certainly messier with chalk dust.

St Anthony's infants/primary school (and still a secondary as well at that time) had been built behind the church on a restricted site, and the playground was small. Seemingly having been crammed onto the space between the church and the adjacent Harmony Row tenement caused lower classrooms to seem dark and dingy. In those days, like most other regulations, lighting standards would be less demanding than now, and this is probably why the impression left in my mind is of a dull and gloomy place. However, that would be a wrong description to give. Cosy is a better word, as my time there from August 1935 to May 1936, when illness caused me to be confined in hospital for five months, was quite happy. Only one name stays with me from this school, Miss McGinty, a short stout 'ancient' lady probably in her early twenties. Visiting the building a few years ago it was found to be no longer used as a school, but has been given over to the business community for use by small companies from one of which I required a service. After being directed to the building and walking around inside, I became acutely aware of the historical significance of the place. Nearly fifty-four years had passed since I had enrolled, and twenty-nine years before that my mother had begun her education there. She and her sister would undoubtedly have walked these corridors and sat in the very room I was about to enter.

A journey into town

Travelling and visiting new places was a craving within me on a level similar to and complementing the fascination for railways. From an early age compulsion on any journey to look out from tram, bus or train at passing scenery was strong. How people could possibly be bothered to read or talk or play games during long journeys, except during hours of darkness, puzzled me greatly. My initial awakening to travel was on the frequent trips by tram into town from Govan, when soon every inch of the way became familiar. Even now, recollections of the thrill of anticipating features that interested me most remain. On boarding the tram at Howat Street, and at a later date at Holmfauld Road, Linthouse, pleas were made to whoever I was with to go upstairs, then with the request granted, dashing on up so that nothing was missed. Travelling from Linthouse, if I was quick enough and got up before the tram moved beyond the plots, it was possible to see over the fence which gave a good view of any shipping movements taking place on the river.

Beyond Drive Road, on the right was Elder Park and pond, while on the other side there were glimpses to be had over the wall bordering Fairfield shipyard, with farther along the strange sight of what looked like a range of 'doocots' set in the wall. They were a number of narrow doorways to time-clock offices through which workers passed to clock off or on. Later, an extension was added on to the west end of the office building which displaced the wall section with these entrances. Presently there were the interesting stone carvings round the main entrance to the yard offices, then excitement mounted with the faint chance of seeing Fairfields goods train, hauled by the English Electric steeple-cab locomotive used for this work. It emerged from the yard main gate a couple of times a day, and trundled along the tramlines for a third of a mile between the yard and Govan Cross Goods Station, with half-a-dozen or more wagons in tow. Because it was smaller, unlike the shorter ones of the double-deck trams, the locomotive had a tall bow current collector similar to those on single deckers, to pick up power from the overhead supply. I used to hope fervently that the main gate would be open which allowed a glimpse of any shunting taking place inside, with the possibility of seeing their steam engine. It too occasionally ventured out on a shunting manoeuvre into Govan Road, but that was a rare treat. Once in a blue moon it made the trip to Govan Cross Station. This was because it did not have a bunker, its meagre coal supply having to be carried in bags in the cab. That was the sight which made my day — a steam engine puffing along Govan Road with a train of waggons.

Living in Howat Street I was constantly tormented by the frustrating sight of clouds of steam pouring over the wall bordering the yard at Taransay Street, for at that time there was a roadway within the yard behind a high wall, long before the shed there today was built. Steam appeared occasionally during the day as the aforementioned engine, only the faint chuffing of which was heard from the street, worked along that section towards the east end of the yard. Travelling on past the Lyceum Cinema, the next landmark to watch out for was the 'Black Man' statue of Sir William Pearce. Then came Water Row, where a brief glimpse might be caught of the river. We were much closer to it here, and although the view was very restricted, it carried the possibility of catching a fleeting glimpse of passing shipping. Also, there was the faint chance that Harlands engine, a battery powered English Electric built steeplecab, would be spotted crossing over Water Row from one part of their yard to the other. Almost opposite Water Row was Greenhaugh Street with the entrance to the subway, then Govan Cross LMS Goods Station itself, with the Fairfield goods branch line leaving the tram lines, merging and curving away through the west gate to be lost among the many sidings.

Because the road was at a slightly lower level views of activity within the station itself were very restricted, but there was still the possibility of seeing a movement on the other extension, a second line of rails running out of the station. Harland & Wolf's shipyard platers' shed stood directly opposite, and their branch extension emerged from the middle one of three goods yard gates, passing directly across Govan Road into it and making a 90 degree crossing with the tram lines. Harlands fabrication shed lay to the west of the ferry and their line continued over Water Row into it. Although passenger services ceased here in 1921, the platforms were still visible on the west side of the goods yard until closure in the 1970s, and were still used in the 30s occasionally for excursion traffic. An occasion is recalled when passing, being amazed to see a train of passenger coaches and a crowd of people, of trying to find out what was happening and feeling exasperated when no-one could tell me. Perhaps it was a local works outing, or, if such a thing existed then, a visit by a train load of railway enthusiasts. On the west side of the goods yard was a cinema. While the Plaza was built around the middle of the 30s, there is no recollection of either the original building, the Old Govan Cinema, or of the Plaza being built in its place.

Continuing the journey, after scanning Orkney Street for fire-engine activity the next place of interest was the drydock, or docks for there are (at the moment) three of them side-by-side, with the largest next to the road. From a distance, of particular interest to watch out for was, is there a ship in for repair, and is it a big one? From the top deck of the tram everything could be seen over the high fence, except when the nearest basin contained a big ship. Graving Dock No. 3 was of sufficient length to take two ships at once and occasionally there were two in residence. It had a pair of doors at the mid-point, which allowed the outer basin to be flooded and a movement take place without interrupting work going on in the inner section. But two ships in No. 3 dock, interesting though they were and they were always studied intently, created the frustrating effect of obscuring the wider view of other perhaps more exciting activity behind. At this time of writing (1991) the dry docks are out of use and likely to be filled in and the ground used for other purposes. However, efforts are being made to preserve at least one of them, preferably the biggest, for use as a base in which it is hoped to place one or more of the old Clyde-built ships that exist in odd corners of the world, and are still in a condition to be moved. If that aim could be achieved it would make an excellent foundation for a museum to display the history of shipbuilding on the Clyde.

Beyond the dry docks the road was bordered on the dock side for

C

the rest of the way round by a high brick wall, and to see anything other than masts, funnels and cranes you had to be on the top deck. It made a sharp right turn then passed round three sides of Prince's Dock, a distance of rather less than a mile. Many ships sailing out east were crewed by Lascars from the Indian sub-continent. With their ship docked they took the opportunity to acquire items to carry home, heading usually for the 'barras', Paddy's Market and other flea markets located around the city. It was common to see groups of them returning loaded up with second hand domestic items, like furniture, bedsteads and bundles of clothing, and this stretch of road was known to locals as 'coolies' mile'. The problem with docks generally and this area in particular, was that there was always too much to see, which lead to much frantic scanning needing a lot of concentration in case anything of particular interest was missed, in the movements of ships, cranes, interesting road vehicles, or most of all on the dockside railway.

Various histories of the period state that it was a time of depressed trade. But what is remembered of the docks and river, is that they appeared to be constantly busy and full of bustle and movement. Quays seemed always to be lined with ships, with tugs invariably manoeuvering inwards the latest arrival, or another which had completed loading and was heading downstream. Of particular interest was the ship coaling stage then on the south quay in the canting basin area. Here, two of the many quayside rail lines rose on a ramp running west, from the lower level of the dock to above the level of the boundary wall, then made a sharp curve north through 45 degrees, to end at a gantry at the quayside at a high level. A ship due to have its bunkers replenished was manoeuvred alongside under the end of the ramp. A shunting engine then pushed a short train of coal waggons up the gradient to the edge and on to a tippler, which gripped the waggons singly and endtipped them, sending their loads straight into the ship's bunker. The empty waggon was then replaced on the other line to descend the ramp by gravity. (In writing about that ramp it is possible that it was removed before this time. My description may be based on photographs seen in the past which, because I found it so interesting, have lodged in my mind as being an actual memory.)

At the end of this straight stretch of Govan Road, where it turns the third of the four corners of the dock at Harvie Street, a bridge carried it over the concealed dock access line which, running in diagonally to the road from the Ibrox direction, lay in a cutting, and beyond this cutting was Govan Tram Depot. Located in Brand Street it was near Harvie Street, and as the tram went round the left hand curve, if you were in a convenient seat, by peering back round past the advertising hoardings which bordered the top of the cutting a glimpse into the depot yard might be obtained. My fascination with trams almost equalled that of railways, and although most of the 'cars on depot' were inside the shed, there were always a few to be seen with perhaps one or two of different design or in unfamiliar colours. However, because of the awkward position of the depot shed with its open end close to the adjacent tenement building, the view was very restricted. There was also the interesting layout of tramlines to give access to the branch through Lorne Street to Paisley Road West, as well as to Govan Road itself.

Sometimes, depending on which service the car we happened to be on was part of, a number 12, on peak-hour service to Mount Florida for example, ran via Lorne Street and on by Paisley Road West, turning right at the Toll into Admiral Street. But it was much more interesting to go the other way past the old tunnel rotunda. Here, though, was one of the most frustrating parts of the journey for me. Much of the dock railways were out of sight, even from the top deck, because they lay at a much lower level than the road and were mostly hidden by tall advertising hoardings and lower fencing. Still prevalent today, this habit of long ago of hiding the most interesting views of railways and industrial sites behind hoardings was a never ending source of irritation for me. Who on earth, I used to wonder, would rather look at advertisements than trains and docks and ships? The best sight to be obtained of them were the fleeting glimpses through gaps in the hoardings at each of the corners. But most frustrating of all was that the access line and marshalling yard in its cutting was completely out of sight, and if the amount of smoke and steam rising up from both sides of the bridge was anything to go by, there always seemed to be much activity here.

Beyond Princes Dock, having rounded the fourth bend, the tunnel rotunda at the bottom of Ferry (Mavisbank ferry) Road was the next thing to look out for. Also there was the goods tramway, which ran along the road running parallel with Govan Road next to the quayside sheds at Mavisbank, in the hope of seeing a shunting movement. This line was part of a loop formed by the Princes Dock and General Terminus lines, and an engine coming in from one side, from a section of line at Shields Road known to railwaymen as 'The Burma Road', could work its way round from, say, Shields Road low level, and go out via the line in the cutting mentioned in the previous paragraph, to join the Glasgow/Paisley line at Ibrox. Before reaching Paisley Road Toll there were Thomson's large premises on the right. They made and sold pianos and other musical instruments, and I had an unfulfilled longing to pay a visit to their showroom. Beyond the Toll the road becomes Paisley Road and at that time it crossed over the line running into General Terminus. That name used to puzzle me, but I found out ultimately that it was built around 1840 by an early railway company, the Pollok & Govan, for general cargo — hence the name. It was another location full of frustration because the interesting sights extended to both sides of the road, and I tended to be slightly neurotic in case something important was missed on one side, while I was busy scanning the other. It was rarely possible to dash from one side of the car to the other, or even to look by craning to see past other passengers, because the trams always seemed to be busy.

Past this point there were different things of general interest before crossing the river at KGV bridge. Besides masts of boats rising above the sheds lining Springfield Quay and especially those of Kingston Dock, nearer hand there was a stonemason's yard at an old villa type house set back on the left side, in a gap between tenements almost opposite Weir Street. It was probably originally a country mansion of the nineteenth century. Tucked away in an outside corner of the porch of the house was an object which seemed to be of stone but really must have been cast in cement, maybe fondu, of a model of rounded shape that looked like a big dolls house. It had the appearance of a kind of stylised Walt Disney's Snow White's castle in fact. The other, a peculiar memory to retain, was of a shop just opposite with a big frontage and 'The West Riding Wallpaper Co.' along the pediment. Both lay to the west of where the Kingston Bridge now stands.

Finally, before reaching the town centre there was another sight full of frustration. King George V bridge had been built in the late 1920s, and as evidence of this a garage business, which occupied the south west corner site in Commerce Street at the corner of Clyde Place up to the 1970s, was called 'Newbridge Garage'. Crossing from the south, in an age that was decades before the introduction of one-way streets, to the left the river was in full view, here in its upper reaches for shipping access, but still with plenty of movement to observe. Although boats coming this far up were smaller, they included steamers which brought on thoughts and memories of holiday trips downriver. (The expression 'doon the watter' was unknown then so must be an invention of a later age.) But the most frustrating sight of the entire journey was engendered by what was visible to the right.

Somehow I knew that the massive railway bridge (built by the Caledonian Railway and opened *c*.1900), the stone piers and orderly forest of girders of the underside of which was the only parts visible, held one of the most interesting railway vistas in all the world, where crack express trains hauled by famous engines were to be seen. And here I was passing glumly by unable to see anything except clouds of smoke and steam, and catching only fleeting glimpses of gantries with vast arrays of signals, any of which in the 'off' position might be signalling the arrival or departure of one of the many famous trains I longed to see. It is now clear that only local trains to Paisley and beyond crossed there, the really interesting traffic passed over on the far side, on the original (*c*.1880) bridge. That bridge was dismantled in the late 1960s leaving only the piers which can be seen there today. Other than within the station itself, the place to catch a glimpse of famous expresses was from the bridge on the east side, but the two-way traffic system of the time meant that our journeys to and from town took us only over KGV bridge. Consequently Jamaica Bridge (or Glasgow Bridge) was unknown territory.

If our destination was the Argyle Street shops we left the tram in

Oswald Street opposite Wilson's Zoo, which was owned and managed by Harry Benson, whose son is today a world famous photographer. The zoo was another place worth a visit, but I only succeeded in doing so once in the late 1940s, not long before it moved out of town. We than walked along Argyle Street, going under the 'Heilanman's Umbrella' to the sound of trains rumbling overhead. The question now asked of myself is 'why did I not pester Granda to take me to Central, or one of the three other terminal stations, on our many outings together?' It would surely have been the ideal place for both of us.

Early holidays

My parents nearly always took holidays away from home. Three summer holiday were spent at Aberdeen, 1932, 1933 and 1935, and there are enduring and fond memories of the sights, sounds, and smells of that city in 1935, for by that time I was old enough to take in and remember more detail. The pals I played with at home seemed less fortunate; none got to travel such a great distance to what appeared to be an exotic place. A feeling of importance was induced in being able to boast to them about it for they, if their parents desired or were able to afford a holiday at all, only frequented relatively nearby Ayr or Saltcoats or Helensburgh, places where we might go to on an evening bus run. One boy was quite proud of going to Rutherglen *by tram* for his holidays, while I boasted that we travelled on a Bluebird bus for all of 150 miles. The bluebird was then the emblem of the SMT Company's long-distance coaches, and was displayed on each side and at the rear of their vehicles. To a small boy who enjoyed every minute of it the journey seemed endless, lasting from early morning to late afternoon. It took many years to learn that not everyone's interests were the same as mine.

Travelling by train to the east coast with mum on one occasion (it might have been to Aberdeen, but could also have been to either Dundee or Arbroath), and going via the Forth and Tay bridges, was an unforgettable experience which provided ample material to boast about and bore my friends with. The journey involved changing trains at a station somewhere south of the Forth bridge, and searching the map in an attempt to identify it now, it may have been Falkirk. Somehow, a picture of that station remains with greater clarity than the actual crossings of the bridges. Situated on a curve it had a high stone embankment wall opposite the eastbound platform, which gave a restricted view of the line and surroundings, confining it to within the station itself. We had to wait for a time but I certainly wasn't bored, for what stands out is seeing other trains passing through with engines and carriages of unusual appearance. It is significant that in my juvenile state of ignorance, I was able to recognise features belonging to different railway companies. In other words I didn't know what types or classes they were, but was aware they were unfamiliar. Perhaps Mum, knowing my love of anything connected with railways, arranged the journey by that route for me benefit. Arbroath was a particular favourite because of Kerr's Miniature Railway which ran, and still does, along the sea front on the south side of the town between the beach and the main line north from Dundee.

Because times spent there were so enjoyable, memories of Aberdeen itself are prominent. They include travelling by tramcar from the town centre to the beach, passing on the way within sight of an amusement park and what we knew as a scenic railway, now called the roller coaster. This 'switchback' was one of only a handful encountered, and I have always regretted never having had the opportunity to ride on one. As well as being a busy commercial city and fishing port, Aberdeen was then a very popular holiday resort, and during good weather in summer the beach was crowded. There was a beautiful stretch of sand that was ideal for building sandcastles, backed by a promenade decorated with flags and bunting. Booths sold ice cream and buckets and spades etc., and a wide grassy strip behind the prom was great for games. Farther north were dunes tufted with marram grass, perfect hiding games territory. Like other people's childhood memories, mine are of weather which always seemed to be warm and sunny, and this probably contributes to the favourable impression retained of the place. No doubt there were plenty of cold wet and miserable days as well, but they never seem to be recalled in later years.

At the height of the season, during Glasgow Fair, crowds of holiday makers drifted back and forth between town and beach, a distance of perhaps a mile or two, and a frequent service of trams operated to transport them. At the beach, beyond the scenic railway, the tramlines curved to the north at Beach Pavilion Theatre, where Harry Gordon was regularly in the programme, then ran parallel with the promenade for a short distance. Layout of track at this terminus held endless fascination for me because of its seeming complexity. If it is remembered correctly it fanned out into a number of sidings with crossovers to cope with busy summer traffic. There was also something I hadn't seen before — lines of crush barriers to marshall queues.

During times spent on the beach, with its long row of neatly aligned wheeled changing booths, as well as paddling and building sand castles we watched the fishing boats, of which there seemed to have been a constant procession entering and leaving harbour. Those departing sailed out into the North Sea and, depending on visibility, could be observed until they disappeared over the horizon in a seemingly never ending line, while others returned from different directions, sailing into the harbour to unload their catches. They were known as drifters, with a very distinctive appearance which denoted their period, small steam engined boats with wheelhouse and tall thin black funnel situated at the stern from which clouds of black smoke constantly poured. Just aft of the funnel was a mast with a sail which might have started life any colour, but its position meant that it rapidly became black. Seeing photographs or film of them carries me right back with a powerful surge of nostalgia to that period.

Another fascinating place was the fish market and harbour. The area was in constant turmoil, with boats being moved about after unloading, and boxes of fish craned ashore and carried into the quayside shed for auction. But the market opened very early in the morning and most of the fish sales were over by the time we arrived. South of the harbour Girdleness lighthouse, where the two rivers, Dee and Don, come together and flow out into the sea, was a favourite place for picnics, as was Hazelhead, Bridge of Don, and Torry, and there are family group photos taken at Girdleness. Fog rendered lighthouses ineffective, so in the days before radar all important ones had a fog horn, usually mounted on the roof of a separate building that housed the equipment which produced the compressed air for the giant horn. We heard it in operation on one occasion, and the sound it produced would have wakened the dead. Duthie Park was another favourite place visited frequently, with its large pond with resident swans and paddle boats for youngsters to enjoy.

Another unforgettable feature of Aberdeen was the smell of the gas-works. In the days before natural North Sea stuff, gas was obtained from coal, and although there is a gasometer storage tank at Ibrox there was no gas works in Govan. The nearest production plant to us, Tradeston Gas Works in Kilbirnie Street, near Eglinton Toll, was quite distant and the strong sulphurous smell produced in the making of coal gas had never before been encountered. Aberdeen gas works was situated behind the amusement park, so the smell was very noticeable in the vicinity of the beach if the wind was blowing from a southerly direction. As coal gas is no longer produced that smell is never encountered now, but until North Sea gas arrived it was very noticeable, for example, in Eglinton Street, when it drifted over on the prevailing west wind. Eglinton Toll was passed regularly when travelling into town after we moved to Pollok, and each time that smell was encountered there, or anywhere else in later years, it immediately carried me back to Aberdeen and the happy holidays spent there.

Coal mines and a railway adventure

On journeys across Scotland in the 1930s, to the north-east and less often to Edinburgh and beyond, among some of the interesting sights then visible in countryside passed through were bings, the artificial hills which were a product of the coalmining industry. There being so many of them in some areas, coal mine winding machinery structures tended to merge into the landscape, but what caught my eye because of their height were the bings. They were once a common sight across much of Fife, central and south west Scotland as conical hills with seemingly precise geometric shapes.

I used to look at them with wonder, curious to know how, amid a landscape of such lumpy irregular outline, they came to have this shape, and what the machinery at the top was for. Apart from their shape, what made them look natural was that in most cases they were covered with vegetation, and seemed to be part of the original landscape. The possibility that they were man made did not then occur to me. Many coal seams in this country are narrow, two to three feet thick is about average, but the mining operation has to cut out working room of five to six feet, which means that after back-filling there is a lot of surplus spoil which has to be taken up to the surface and dumped.

A pit is a vertical shaft excavated down to a coal seam to which access was by lift, in effect the pithead gear, a pair of giant bicycle wheels mounted side-by-side a little way apart at the top of a truncated pylon, which turned back and forth in contra-rotating cycles carrying the lift cables. A mine is a sloping shaft down which a narrow gauge railway ran, usually cable operated on steep slopes, while the much less often encountered horizontal shaft into a hillside is an adit. The coal company's narrow gauge railway, considered as too dangerous for personnel, was normally only used to carry out coal and spoil, so that mining operations often had both types of access. Spoil was brought up in tub waggons on the mine railway and dumped. As the mound grew the railway was extended ever upwards until in some cases it was two or three hundred feet or more in height. A later age was to discover that these hills of spoil contained much material which was useful to the construction industry, in particular for road making. On journeys around the country in the sixties it was noticed that some roads were being resurfaced with a reddish material, referred to as 'red blaze'. Later it became apparent the term was actually red blaes, which came from a certain area, Midlothian I think, using material recovered from pit bings in that region. So, over the past twenty years or so nearly all of those conical 'hills' which intrigued me have gone, with most of the material used in road making, particularly for motorways.

An eventful journey by train occurred on an excursion trip to the east coast, a day return at a special reduced fare to a popular destination. Where that destination was is forgotten, but the return journey began late and due to a number of delays along the way the train fell more and more behind time. We had been due back at Buchanan Street Station around 10 pm, and as it was a mid-summer jaunt we should have been arriving at Govan as darkness was falling. The journey was punctuated by long periods stationary at signals, and after a particularly long wait, with much grousing among the passengers, the train started up with a jerk and everyone cheered — which ceased abruptly when it was realised we were moving backwards. After a short distance we halted again and there was another lengthy wait, during which there were other movements on the line, heard but invisible in the darkness, in which at least one train appeared to be passing on ahead of us. What stays most clearly in my memory about this episode was that the other passengers seemed a decent lot, and full of concern about me being kept out late for it was past midnight, obviously well past my bedtime. If the truth could have been told, bedtime went for nothing, for I was in my favourite environment. Eventually we got going again and arrived back at Buchanan Street after 1 am, but having fallen asleep there is no further memory of events that night. Taxis were still outside our scope, so I am curious to know by what transport? Were night services operated then by the trams?

In the light of later experience of railways, it is interesting to speculate and try to interpret what happened that night. Something leads me to think the incident happened between Perth and Stirling. The sequence of events seem to indicate that a breakdown had occurred ahead of us, causing traffic to queue up at signals along the section, with everything coming to a stand until the traffic controller sorted things out. Our train may have been at Auchterarder where there was a loop and sidings, and it was into a siding we were reversed, for the loop was probably occupied by another train, and the train that passed on ahead may have been a light engine sent to rescue the breakdown. Alternatively, perhaps the reason for the holdup was at Greenhill or beyond, a points failure perhaps?, and the line was cleared by our shunting movement to allow a train turning east at Larbert to go past, it having a clear road in the Edinburgh direction.

Of many sights connected with the working of railways which disappeared over the years, well remembered, curious, and one of the most dangerous jobs was that of wheeltapper. Dressed in dirty overalls and cap, he was active at all main line intermediate and terminal passenger stations, trudging along platform tracks carrying a torch, a canvas sack and a long shafted hammer with a tiny head. The long shaft was necessary for checking the wheels nearest the platform. His task was then regarded as vital, to check each wheel on all medium and long-distance trains to make sure the treads had not worked loose, and the wheels themselves were securely fixed on their axles. He did this by hitting them with the hammer which caused a clean sharp metallic sound, except on the rare occasion when he found a faulty one when, it is imagined, the noise would be dull and muffled.

The Italians

We were fond of ice cream and familiar with the products of all the cafés in our area. Favourite by a long way was made in a café in Golspie Street which seems to have been run by two Italian families. Noteriana's (the first part of that name is pronounced as in 'not') was midway up the lower half of the street on the east side opposite the Salvation Army hall. The other family connected with the shop was A. Fella (no kidding!). In the 1930s their ice cream was outstanding, to the extent that from Howat Street we would pass other cafés in Govan Road in the vicinity of Golspie Street to buy our favourite. Ice cream cones were called pokey-hats, and wafers were known as sliders. Perhaps the latter was an east coast term used by my grandparents.

Like many such establishments Noteriana's was fairly high class and very well run, and they operated one or two ice cream carts. Most such carts then were completely open, simply large barrows with a pillar supported roof, and in season vendors on three wheeled trike were still quite common. The big cool-box of the trike was mounted over the axle ahead of the rider, the whole lot pivoting for steering, controlled by a long bar handle fixed to the box in front of the rider. Other simple horsedrawn carts in which the vendor stood were windowless, but Noteriana's appeared to be of the latest design, then regarded as ultra-modern. The vehicles were totally enclosed with sliding windows at the sides, much like modern ice cream vans, but still horse drawn. However, they were soon to acquire a motor van the front end of which, from the cab forward, resembled a Rolls Royce and may have been one. But I fully expect to be proved wrong in this; it is likely to have been something much more humble such as a van body mounted on a light Albion chassis. The vehicle's external décor was similar to that of the shop, which was tastefully set out in pale yellow, with vertical black bars from a horizontal line at waist level down. We had a brown pottery jug of about two pints capacity which held up to six scoops, and this jug was always used when buying ice cream by the scoop. Although a bit chipped towards the end that jug survived use in kitchen and kitchenette into the 1980s, and was forever associated in my mind with the delicious product of Noteriana, because the smell seemed to linger in it.

The family doctor and pre-antibiotic treatment

Our family doctor was Dr Cummings. His consulting room (the term for 'surgery') was one stair up in the only close in the short stretch of tenement in Govan Road between McKechnie Street and Wanlock Street, opposite St Anthony's church. He had a good reputation and was well regarded in Govan, and is recalled as resembling my paternal grandfather in appearance in portraits during his later years. A faint recollection remains of his waiting room, with its spartan decor and naked light bulb overhead and rows of plain wooden seats. In those days doctors seemed to have a standard procedure, of questions which were asked sometimes even before you had a chance to say why you were there. They were preoccupied with bowels and temperature. The first question for patients was 'Have you had a bowel movement today?' posed as a thermometer was placed in your mouth! These observations are of course personal, in that when I appeared Cummings knew well enough my long-term problem and that using the thermometer would be required anyway. But bowels?

In preparation for his retirement from practice he had a house built in Mosspark Boulevard, overlooking the private tramway track at the corner of Bellahouston Drive, but died within a couple of years of moving there. In connection with the Garden Festival of 1988, a display to mark the 50th anniversary of the Empire Exhibition was set up. Among the exhibits were fine aerial photographs of the exhibition. One, taken from the west, shows two houses in this location which would then have been newly completed.

My worst illness was caused by three events which occurred at the same time. Had any one of them been absent I would have avoided most, if not all, of the subsequent ailments and thus been fit and well and perhaps still able to work today. The sequence of events which led up to it was as follows. My mother's parents originally came from Dundee. As well as returning often, some members of the families living there would occasionally come to Glasgow to visit them. It so happened Easter was late that year of 1936, falling at the end of April, and Grandma's younger sister and her husband had come for the holiday, bringing with them a model yacht as a present for me. I remember quite clearly the day they arrived and being taken to see them at Hutton Drive.

Entering the house the first thing to catch my eye was the yacht. Including jib it was a couple of feet long. It was a wee boy's dream, with a single tall mast and snow-white fore- and mainsails, and had been placed in a prominent position, sitting upright in a white enamelled pail to accommodate the keel. At first Uncle Jim and Aunt Mem pulled my leg a little, saying things like 'Some lucky boy is going to get that boat as a present, I wonder who he can be,' and 'Do you know anybody who would like it?' and so on, until desperation began to show on my face. After a time they relented and admitted it was for me. Having watched with envy as others sailed their boats in Elder Park pond I was desperate to try out mine, but was just then recovering from measles. The following day was one of bright sunshine but with a piercing cold wind from the east. I pestered mum to take me to the pond so much that, against her better judgement, she would say in later years, she agreed to do so 'Just for a wee while'.

Encountered together those three things, the measles, the yacht and the cold wind, were what brought me to within a whisker of losing my life. Had any one of them been missing I might have got away with it. During the days following a cold developed which became bronchitis, then pneumonia. Measles itself isn't a deadly affliction but the recovery stage leaves the body very susceptible to other much more serious diseases, and long-distance hindsight indicated that it would have been prudent to remain indoors for at least another week.

Chest illnesses have been a problem for most of my life, particularly so during the first five years. Although it was probably the best available, primitive treatment (by today's standards) administered in early years for bronchitis and bronchial pneumonia is certain to have caused bronchi and lung tissue damage, which left greater susceptibility to bouts of bronchitis up to the present day. Before antibiotics like penicillin arrived, the main treatments for chest infections were poulticing, applying a rub of camphorated oil to chest and back, and being dosed with sweet tasting syrup of squills soothing cough mixture and ipecacuanha wine. To an adult, poulticing would have been an unpleasant experience, but for a child of my age it was terrifying. Poultices were made up using a particularly glutinous substance similar in consistency to plaster, called kaolin, now identified as china clay. It was purchased in a tin which was heated by standing it in a pan of water on the stove. When it was hot, a piece of linen about 2 feet by 1 foot was laid out and held by the corners; then the kaolin was spread on one half and the other half folded over to form a sandwich. Two of them were made up, a quickly as possible to preserve the heat, then clapped on chest and back as hot as could be borne, and bound up with bandages wound round and round the upper torso as tight as possible, while leaving no room to breathe. That treatment seems futile now, giving the impression it was done only to induce in the sufferer the impression that some effective cure was being applied, really as a kind of placebo to create confidence in the young or ignorant.

Preparation of the poultice appeared to be carried out quite deliberately in front of the sufferer, the idea probably being that they would surely be grateful for the efforts being made to make them well. But the truth was that it was mental torture followed by physical agony, the judging of temperature of the poultice tending rather on the hot side. My mother said in later years this went on three times a day for about three weeks. Considered now, it was the most severe illness of a number to afflict me during those early years, probably exacerbated by poulticing. However, it is realised that these thoughts are being set down in ignorance of whatever curative properties the kaolin did have, and if it hadn't been used I might not be here today. An event remembered quite clearly, and certainly among the very earliest of my recollections, is that when recovering from an earlier extended period of being bedridden, truly confined that is, it was found that I could not stand on my legs. Mum proved to be correct when she said, though probably in jest, 'You'll need to learn to walk all over again,' for it took a couple of days of continued recovery and effort before I was able to go unaided.

Fog used to be a regular feature of our winters, and while weather patterns are less severe in recent years than they were then, most of the prime causes of fog formation, smoke and dust particles present in the atmosphere, have been eradicated. We seldom see fog now and never smog. It may not be possible today for young people under the age of 30 to imagine what a pea-souper was like, but this is what had to be endured often during the course of every winter. Every house had at least one coal-burning fire going, and industry, such as Dixon's Blazes, south of Hutchesontown, Tennant's chemical works at Sighthill, where there are now blocks of multi-storey flats, and Beardmore's at Shettleston, were only three of many old-style large industrial complexes continually pouring out smoke and other pollutants into the atmosphere. Other contributors no longer around today were railway engines, gas works, electricity generating stations, ships, tar boilers (torry bilers we called them) and steam road rollers for road mending. As well as these, there was much other heavy industry around the city using power in vast quantities, and most of the larger ones, if it was economically beneficial, produced their own in coal-burning boiler houses. I was fortunate, if that is the correct word to apply to an ordinance that saved the lives of a large number of people including my own, in that smoke-laden air in winter which aggravates chest ailments was greatly reduced over the following decades and eradicated completely after the introduction of the clean air act in 1956, although it took twenty-five years or so to become fully effective. Unfortunately the greatest improvement was caused by the loss of virtually all these labour-intensive industries. But developing countries have inherited the health problems as well as the work.

A number of deadly diseases were still encountered at this time that are now rare or non-existent, such as polio, meningitis, scarlet fever, rheumatic fever and pleurisy. Even smallpox epidemics occurred occasionally, brought in by seamen from abroad. The most feared and one of the most common diseases around was tuberculosis, then commonly known as consumption, and by late summer, with recovery delayed, it was feared that I had contracted it. Mearnskirk Hospital had been built in the late 1920s for treatment of chest conditions, and specialised in treatment of TB. Although not definitely diagnosed as suffering from it, towards the end of September I was sent there for an extended stay, in the hope that if I did have it I could be kept under close observation and receive treatment. An aspect of needing to call on the services of the doctor so much then, no recollection of which now touches my memory, is the fees which required to be paid for his consultations and call-outs. How on earth did my parents manage, for I think the cost was something like one-and-threepence ($12^{1/2}$p) for a surgery consultation, and two shillings (20p) for a home visit? They obviously must have been able to cope with the financial drain on their resources. Was it solely out of whatever small savings they had managed to gather, or did my father have a stake in, perhaps, a trade union organised insurance scheme? The after-effect of pneumonia, in the 1930s a disease with a high fatality rate, was a lifetime of susceptibility to chest complaints.

CHAPTER 3

Linthouse

Prior to 1930 Skipness Drive was called George Drive. Indeed my parents and other older people invariably called it by the old name, as they did with other streets similarly affected. The original plan, when the area was being laid out for building in the late 1880s, was for the drive to run between Drive Road and Moss Road, and at the beginning tenements were built at each end, but the intention must have lapsed after a time. Then a continuous line of tenements was built up on the east side of Burghead Drive, which effectively cut George Drive in two. This led to the two halves being renamed George Drive East and George Drive West. Also, a large electricity sub-station was built in Holmfauldhead Drive, partly across the two halves, making the division final. In the 1930 street renaming, George Drive East became Skipness Drive and George Drive West became Peninver Drive. Most of that information was uncovered by studying the set of Post Office Maps held in the Glasgow Room of the Mitchell Library, which go back in almost annual stages to near the beginning of the nineteenth century.

Having newer tenement buildings than those in the rest of Govan, Linthouse was regarded as an upmarket area, with tenement facades in the 1930s showing a fresher less weatherworn aspect. Only a tiny percentage of houses had a bathroom, and some of these even had no hot water. But there was no such thing as a 'dunny' here. Some older tenements elsewhere in Govan had a basement apartment below ground level, with access from the back-court down a flight of steps. While familiar with them, I never saw one used as a dwelling. Any I knew of were empty, either door- and windowless and a haunt of dogs and cats, and sometimes of derelict human flotsam who had to be ejected by the constabulary, or boarded-up. Children spoke of them with awe, regarding them as places where ghosts and evil men lurked. Any who went 'doon the dunny' to play (presumably 'dunny' is derived from dungeon) were regarded as being extremely brave, or reckless and liable to be the object of chastisement by their parents.

Skipness Drive

Being rather timid by nature as a child, because of a feeling that Govan was a rough place, the prospect of living in Linthouse had strong appeal. To have to walk along a strange street in central Govan by myself would have filled me full of apprehension of unidentifiable dangers, so the move to the 'Garden of Eden' (as it was known to Govanites) was a relief. The front section of closes here were tiled to dado (shoulder) height, while staircase walls were painted dark brown to the same level. Above that height walls and ceiling were whitewashed. Tiling a wall to shoulder height was the most effective way of delaying the scruffy appearance caused by age and the passage of people, of innumerable shoulders and arms brushing along them, to say nothing of the effects of children's games, for a painted wall in a close would need re-coating frequently. In evidence of this, look at the walls of buildings along busy pavements of street scenes in many old photographs. In particular look at the earliest ones dating from last century and note how, in densely populated areas even plain stone coursing along walls and passageways has a scuffed, dirty and greasy look from shoulder level down. This is especially true where pavements and closes are narrow. Closes in some old buildings dating from the days before properly paved roads became general had mud scrapers set low down in the wall at the entrance. These were simply an iron bar with a roughly sharpened edge, fixed horizontally across the centre of a deep hole cut in the stone. Other places, mainly back courts, had them set in the ground, only the rusted remnants of which were left by the 1930s, and these were a detested hazard liable to trip people up.

Direction of ascent of the stairs at number 12 was anti-clockwise when viewed from above, and as before there were three houses on each landing. The middle house was similar in layout to the one we had left at Howat Street, an 'all' to the front two apartment with an outside toilet on the half landing. Our new house was on the top flat, in the position known as 'three up on the right', with layout of the house opposite being a mirror image. It was again a two-apartment room and kitchen, but with an 'L' shaped lobby. Its main advantage was that it had an inside toilet, the door to which was the first one on the right inside behind the main door. Through this door was a small narrow third room about 8ft x 4ft called the cloakroom because one wall was lined with coat hooks, which was perhaps originally intended to be a bathroom but quickly became the junk room. At the rear was a partition reaching to between 6 to 7 feet high, in which there was a second door with a large pane of frosted glass in the top half. Through this door was the small toilet cubicle with the standard high chain-pull cistern, wooden toilet seat, a shelf, and a window to the outside overlooking the back court, the lower panes of which were frosted.

About this time, because of the move father away from his work, Dad had acquired a cycle. At first, keeping it in the house caused a problem, because the only place it could be parked was in the cloakroom. But people brushing past to reach the toilet frequently caused it to fall. Cloakroom walls were faced with nicely varnished bevelled tongue-and-grooved panelling, and after a time it was showing signs of scoring, so he installed a pulley which allowed him to hoist the bike up above head height. Later, at the beginning of the war, when a cousin of Mum's, who had a racing bike of the latest design, was called up to the army, he offered it to Dad at a very good price. Having recently learned to ride I was starting to agitate for a bike, so he took up the offer and installed another pulley for it. Walking through the cloakroom with that mass of machinery hanging overhead was rather intimidating, but the fact that it was possible serves to illustrate how much higher, compared to modern housing, ceilings of older tenements were.

The term 'through and through', which may have been a local expression, was applied to a house with one apartment overlooking the street and the other the backcourt. The usual kitchen fittings were laid out as follows. Entering the apartment the double window faced you, here in the centre of the outside wall, with the range and mantelpiece in the middle of the left hand wall of the same design as in the Howat Street house, but with fireplace and oven positions reversed. The sink and its associated cupboards were the same too, but laid out on the opposite hand — here the sink with its crane on the left side of the window bay. However, with the coal bunker located in the larger lobby, the dresser stood alone but with shelving above it the same as in Howat Street — on the right as the kitchen was entered. Family furnishings moved with us and were as previously described.

A four-bar pulley stretched from above the door to near the outside wall at the window, with a cleat for the rope on the window facing. Adults entering after a washing had been hung up to dry found that if they didn't duck, their heads might be brushing through damp dangling sheets and shirts sleeves. A pulley for drying clothes is something not often seen today because modern houses have a ceiling height of only about 8ft, compared with the old tenement minimum of around 10ft. In a modern house a pulley has to be installed away from where people walk, or the hanging clothes would make things difficult. Every old tenement house had a pulley in either kitchen or, if it was long enough, lobby. Originally, they consisted of a single 4" x 3" wooden batten 8 or 9 feet long, but a newer type became available having 2 or 4 spars held, well separated, at each end by a cast-iron frame, with a loop on top to which the rope was attached. There were the usual bed recesses in each apartment, and the one in the kitchen was again curtained off and used for storage purposes. Apart from the advantage of the house having an inside toilet, great benefit was derived from the bunker being in the lobby in that if all internal doors were kept shut during a delivery of coal, it confined the scatter of coaldust there. Upper shelves of the kitchen cupboard, situated here in the corner between range and outside wall, were used as a larder. Lower shelves held dishes, while at floor level bulkier items like potato and vegetable storage boxes etc., were squeezed in.

Room sleeping arrangements were the same as before for my parents, but I had progressed to a single bed placed against the right hand wall between the low fireplace and bay window. (Did I actually sleep in a cot until six years of age in the previous house? There is no recollection of having anything else.) Alignment of the building was such that the wider central oriel room window faced slightly west of south, and because it was on the top floor it had a view of a greater expanse of sky. In that situation, my bed position near the window provided a first look at the night sky when there was time and inclination to study it. One night in winter, without knowing the identity of what I was seeing but aware of the first stirrings of interest, three stars of roughly similar magnitude, in line and evenly spaced close together were observed. Much, much later they were identified as Orion's Belt. My bed was placed against the room press, which was inconvenient as it did not have castors or even glider-domes. It had to be pulled out each time access to the cupboard was required, which caused severe wear to the new waxcloth in that area. That floor covering seems to have been purchased in standard patterned deep bordered 12 feet by 9 feet pieces, having the same variety of designs as a carpet of that size, which, when laid, left an outer border of exposed floorboards. That area would normally be dark-stained, and varnished regularly when the apartment was decorated. The high-level view from the windows was dominated by the roofs and a multitude of smokey chimneys of surrounding buildings.

The fireplace here was the normal bedroom installation — a broad low coal-burning grate with an adjustable cast-iron ornamental hood, a tiled or cast iron simulated-tile surround, and a mantelpiece of dark varnished wood rising to a shelf at adult waist height. That fire was used only during winter cold spells, and after the first winter coal capacity of the grate was considered too great, so, as an economy measure, shaped firebricks were purchased and installed in the nest corners. I never saw gaslight in this house because, although it was gas only when he took over tenancy, Dad had it wired for electricity before I arrived. However, a memorable feature of this house for me was centred round the fire, for that room was the last apartment slept in regularly that had a coal fire. While it was seldom in use, only occasionally during winter, it is impressions of lying in bed close to the fire which had been lit to dispel the chill, and drowsily watching the flickering light of the flames on the ceiling before dropping off, that remain in sharp focus.

Communal chores

Number 12 was near the middle of a side of the block, so the stair landings were small, with double flights of stairs having about six inches of separation between flights, and a half-landing between each main landing. Each half-landing had a toilet, and a window with large centre panes of plain glass and long narrow stained glass border panes with a marbled surface on the inside, overlooking the back court. Keeping staircase and close clean was the responsibility of tenants, who had to take a turn every three weeks to sweep and wash them. According to a local by-law sweeping was supposed to have been done daily. Most closes, and some stairs and landings, had ground edging embellished with lines in pipe-clay, usually just two-inch deep borders marked with this chalk like substance. Pipe clay cakes were ground down and mixed with water to a thin paint-like consistency, and applied with a brush, but it was often done by simply rubbing the cake along the wet surface. Some housewives with artistic talent, and many who thought they had, embellished their borders with elaborate designs of whorls and/or blocks, especially those living in closes where their efforts were likely to be seen by passers by and not just the neighbours.

Washing floors in houses was always done on hands and knees with a scrubbing brush, rag, a bar of washing soap and bucket or basin of water. (Bear in mind that any utensil mentioned on these pages, like that bucket and basin, which today is made of plastic, would then be of either wood or metal). Stairs and closes were also done this way, with powdered pipe clay added to the water. An enduring memory is of my mother and other women doing this work, kneeling on a pad of sacking or rolled up piece of old carpet to protect their knees, work which caused the affliction 'housemaid's knee'. There were mops then but no-one seems to have thought to use one for the job, and the impression now is of degrading, laborious and time-consuming work. Usually in each district there were women who did other people's stairs for payment, who sometimes became notorious for paying for their messages with small change from their earnings, the coins of which were caked with pipe clay from being handled by contaminated fingers. Some women advertised the fact that they took in washing, ironing and mangling for payment, while certain rather illiterate stairwashers advised prospective customers that they 'took in stairs'. As the name indicates, pipe clay was the material used to make cheap pipes for smoking, an essential requirement of an earlier age so that working-class people could afford it. A good pipe of wood could cost pounds, the making of which was a highly skilled profession often using rare and expensive wood, but a clay pipe, while it was fragile, cost only a few pence.

Pipe clay, in the form used for stairs and closes, was sold in hardware stores as cakes about the shape and size, but perhaps twice the thickness, of a 2oz. bar of chocolate, I remember being sent to buy it by Mum, when each cake was individually wrapped in newspaper, probably by the hardware shop owner who had bought it in bulk. It was usually too hard to crumble by hand, so it had to be broken up very carefully with a hammer in a box, or covered over with newspaper because, like breaking coal, fragments flew around with each blow. After being washed with the cloudy mixture, when dry, stairs had a dusty whitish appearance. That use of pipe clay was sometimes resented by houseproud women, because the white powder was carried into houses on the soles of shoes, so that they strictly enforced wiping of feet on the doormat. Where borders were painted on, this was done with enough pipe-clay or whitewash added to make a separate mixture of about the consistency of today's cheaper quality emulsion paint. In a later development, in an effort to find a more durable treatment white oil based paint was tried, but even with it frequent touching up was required.

The chore of 'doing the stairs' was undertaken by housewives each in their turn, as part of the weekly Friday ritual of cleaning the house, which included beating the carpets, sweeping, washing and polishing the floors, work which often extended into late evening. Floor polish was used with pride and not a little danger on linoleum, which tended to make the surface slippery. After stairs, the most important tasks were cleaning the fireplace, blackleading the grate, and doing the brasses. All houses had some brass in the form of ornaments, such as candlestick holders, letter rack, companion set, fender and coal scuttle, even some sections of gas piping, particularly the lighting supply pipe at the 'swans neck', etc. All main doors had the array of brass fittings previously described which custom, and fear of criticism by neighbours, actually fear of being talked about behind their back, drove most housewives to keep shining. Cleaning a lot of brass-ware using 'Brasso' polish, as well as being sore on the hands was laborious and time-consuming, and any young person today would scorn such work as needless drudgery. Today these items are made from materials of the fix on and forget variety needing no maintenance, or if they become disfigured or get broken they are usually cheap enough simply to throw away and buy a new one.

Fresh surroundings
We lived in this house until the summer of 1945. Much of the rest of the book is concerned with Linthouse and the surrounding area, and readers with an interest in topography can study the frontispiece map. However, anyone in possession of an old large-scale street and transport plan of pre-1965 vintage, as produced for Glasgow Corporation Transport Department would find it ideal, as construction of the Clyde Tunnel, and later redevelopment to the east significantly altered the locality after that time. Other excellent large-scale maps of the district can be examined in the Mitchell Library.

Most street frontages of the Linthouse tenements had a railed off section along the front between closes. In Skipness Drive it took the form of a rough concrete aggregate plinth standing about six to eight inches above pavement level, which projected out into the pavement for six feet or so. The plinth was bordered round the three outer sides with decorative cast-iron railings rising to adult waist height, which had harmless flat-spiked capping of the same material. Elsewhere, in Hutton Drive for example, the fenced-off area, with the railing embedded in an edging of stone capping, was earth and beaten-down grass haunted by dogs and cats. An occasional plant, stunted bush, or shrub showed briefly in summer where in the past a tenant living low down had tried in vain to indulge in gardening. During the war these railings were removed with cutting torches and taken away, in an all-embracing drive to collect as much scrap metal as possible for the war effort. Recent accounts of this operation suggest that most of the material recovered was quite unsuitable for any purpose other than railings, and had to be dumped.

The close entrance to Number 12 was a little to the right of a line down the west pavement of Kennedar Drive and extended across Skipness Drive. Linthouse Church of Scotland, still standing at the north end of the Kennedar Drive/Hutton Drive block, was diagonally across the street from us, so that from the high elevation of our room window we had a near eye level view of the bell in the belfry in the west tower rocking backwards and forwards when it was rung on Sundays. At that time there was a railed-in grassy area on the west side of the church (since built on), in which the church officer's wife, from her house in Hutton Drive next to the church hall, hung out her washing. Elder Park, at the eastern end of our street, was an ideal place for children. It had large level grassy areas for group ball and other games, a swing park and paddling pond, putting and bowling greens, tennis courts, a model yachting pond with a clubhouse and sailing club, and a permanent resident, a one-legged swan called Jock. The putting green was a favourite when I grew old enough, but tennis courts and bowling greens were just becoming accessible to me age-wise when we moved away to Pollok. The park and its amenities in the 1930s are described in detail in Chapter 5.

Nearer hand were the back courts with their dykes to climb. They, and the closes themselves, provided a variety of concealments necessary for hiding games. Nearby, there was a football ground, the Maxwell Park, known as the Maxy Park, in the middle section of Holmfauldhead Drive (Humflheed in localese) between Skipness Drive and St. Kenneth Drive, a small section of which, including the goal posts at the northern end, was visible from our room window. Junior and amateur teams played here, changing in the British Legion pavilion in Holmfauld Road, known to us as 'ferry road'. An ornate single-storey timber building owned by the Legion, it was situated on the east side about half way to the entrance to the shipyard of Alexander Stephen & Co. It had one large hall big enough for dances and other functions, and side rooms for smaller meetings. Along the side facing the road there was a covered verandah reached by two or three steps, which ran all the way along the frontage, from the un-made-up pavement.

Having visited the building once I recall most clearly the lovely smell of the wood. In 1938 it was burned down during the night, and provided another vivid memory in being awakened by my parents and told to 'Come and look at this!'. Viewed from our kitchen window from the opposite side of the block, the fire itself was out of sight. But it was still spectacular, with the plume of smoke illuminated by flames rising up beyond the roof opposite; it was a preview of something we were to see rather a lot of in cinema newsreels within a few years under wartime conditions. In the days following the fire and before the charred remains were removed, we boys used to rake through the ashes hoping to find something of value. Each time the smell clung to us and gave the game away, initially without my being aware of it until reaching home, when Mum noticed it immediately and went on at length, demanding that for safety sake I keep away from the site.

The Coup

Behind the British Legion building, the plots lay at a lower level than the road and covered the area above where the south portals of the Clyde tunnels now lie. They took up the southern quarter of the long narrow strip of land running from Govan Road to the river, between Holmfauld Road in the west and Fairfield shipyard boundary fence in the east, and were bounded on Govan Road and part of ferry road by a high clap-board planking fence having a saw-toothed top. Access was by a doorway in the fence almost opposite Clachan Drive, beyond which plotholders descended a flight of stairs. All that stretch of land to the river, and much of the rest of Linthouse, belonged to Stephen's. The central section of the strip, which was lover than the rest, was used by the yard as a coup for their rubbish, and, being unfenced, the area was treated as an unofficial adventure playground by children of the district. It was a great place to explore. Part of the enjoyment of playing there was because every concerned parent absolutely forbade their children from going near it, for it was full of hazards which today, if it was permitted to exist at all under modern environmental regulations, would have to be securely fenced off. Some of the dangers present were broken glass, lengths of nail-studded and splintered wood, pools of permanent standing water that were ideal for rafts, smouldering material, supposedly empty red lead and other paint tins, and oily cotton waste, the oil of which was of a particularly enduring type. Getting it on hands, clothing, or shoes, it was impossible to remove and was a dead giveaway when you went home. Newly-tipped rubbish often contained previously burned material, from the supposedly extinguished embers of which fires could be conjured up with oily waste and wood splinters.

The carters who brought the stuff out were probably supposed to reduce it by burning as much as possible. But like most work of this kind if it was unsupervised it was done in a careless way, which left more than enough material to give us our fun. In the tipping area the ground at the lower level had a height difference of about ten feet, which was gradually being filled in over the years. The tipping face advanced only a little during the few years I frequented the place, for the volume of dumped material wasn't great, and only about half the total area had been filled in since it began to be used for this purpose, probably last century. The lower level was most likely the original level of the land on the river's flood plain, having poor drainage, for there was always standing water of up to six inches in depth over much of it. That was sufficient to float a raft without the danger of anyone suffering anything more serious than a soaking and getting covered in mud if they fell in. Rubbish was brought out from Stephen's in horse-drawn single-axle wooden carts with large iron-shod wooden wheels, of a very common general-purpose design in use everywhere. They carried out the same function as tail-end tipping lorries of today, but their capacity was only a fraction of the load of modern vehicles. Built very solidly with outward flaring sides and front, they were about four feet high from the load bed above the axle. When preparing to unload into the tipping area the horse was made to back up to the edge. Harness and tailgate fixings were then released and the cart was allowed to tip up, controlled by a rope held by the carter, and fixed to the forward end of one of the shafts.

Manoeuvring the cart might appear to be a simple operation but it had its perils particularly when reversing, a backing up as it was called in those horse-powered days, over the uneven elevated surface of the already infilled part of the site. With a docile horse it was comparatively easy but a lively or fidgety one made it a risky business, and the carter needed good control. In particular, a young horse might display much agitation when required to back up, with mincing steps and much head shaking and swinging from side to side as it tried to see round the blinkers to check for danger. The man had to persuade it to stop and stand perfectly still at exactly the right spot, without going too far and allowing the cart to go over the edge, taking the animal with it. There may have been a brake but there is no recollection of seeing one. After tipping the load the carter hauled on the shaft rope to pull the cart down level, and re-connected the harness. A well-remembered sight is of a carter swinging on the rope with one foot up on the wheel tread for leverage to get the shafts down. My great-grandfather, Alexander McFarlane, was a carter, and worked with horses all his life. Indeed during the time he lived in Govan he is reputed to have worked on the horse trams, when the depot was in Greenhaugh Street.

The rest of the coup northwards away from the tip, stretching almost to the river, consisted of a series of low grassy hillocks known as 'the sunny dumps'. They were at a higher level than the coup, effectively preventing any drainage from it, and were probably built up from river dredgings during last century. The whole area was ideal for games like cops and robbers, hide-and-seek, cowboys and Indians, or plain simple 'sodgers'. These and other games were supplemented by acting out our fantasies generated by the current film being shown at one of the local cinemas, the Vogue, Lyceum, Plaza, or, the smallest of the four in Govan, the Elder. Many were the arguments on the coup pond about who could be Clark Gable or Errol Flynn on board the pirate ship we fondly imagined our rough lash-up of a raft to be. Or Leo Gorcey in the Dead End Kids, or George Raft and James Cagney as gangsters, as he stealthily crept around the sunny dumps, trying to catch members of the 'other side' unawares. Another cinema hero was Johnny Weissmüller as Tarzan, but really the most popular were cowboy films, of Tom Mix, Gene Autry, William Boyd as Hopalong Cassidy and the mysterious Lone Ranger. A series of films which provided ideal role models for us was based on what were called 'G' Men, and featured stars like Cagney, Raft and Pat O'Brien as special American law enforcement officers. G Men were, I think, Government agents of the 1920s and 30s.

Like anywhere else, children in Linthouse played in groups that formed spontaneously in a given area. The one I associated with mainly gathered its members from the west end of Skipness Drive and nearer ends of the three adjacent streets. Rivalry occasionally broke out, which sometimes developed into hostility between groups from adjoining areas, but this was usually confined to shouting insults at each other, with plenty of boasting between members of what they, the group, could do in a fight with any other. Competition between them for possession of the coup for a play area could on occasion become fierce, and it wasn't unusual for one group to chase off another. There was no special pecking order between them, with the single exception of the large number which formed the group from the dead-end street called Linthouse Buildings, who were known as 'The Linties'.

Linthouse Buildings lay within the area of land occupied by the yard, and had been built before the 1880s to house their workforce. It was a single long tenement building, with closes which went up to number 42, running north from Govan Road almost opposite Burghead Drive, only a short section of which survives. Its residents had the reputation of being rather a rough lot, and their street was regarded as deepest enemy territory by all children in the surrounding area. Among our group they were talked about with bated breath, and according to those who actually knew them they were unbeaten in any so-called fight they were involved in. So-called because I never actually saw them, or any other group for that matter, actually fighting. This kind of talk was a favourite subject with us, as no doubt it still is with all children in a similar environment anywhere, but it must be stressed that it was almost always confined to talk. The only exception encountered was a battle which drew blood between two members of our own group. The odd thing about this set-to was that it involved two boys a little older than me, and searching my memory about them now, both were decent, sensible and popular, but the cause of the quarrel is obscure. Any encounter between rival groups (I use that term in preference to gang) was almost invariably confined to stone-throwing or chasing each other, usually ending with a few youngsters suffering nothing more serious than a fright.

There were two occasion when the Lintie's reputation for toughness was put to the test. The first happened on a day I was invited by Dad to go for a stroll. After walking with him into Govan Road, he said he had to visit a customer who lived in Linthouse Buildings in connection with *The New Leader,* the political newspaper which he delivered. I was worried by this and thought that surely he must know it was a dangerous place, and that if we went in there we might not get back out again. He must have noticed the look of apprehension on my face. No doubt he was fully aware of the reputation the place had among the young, for he laughed and then said 'Come on, you'll be safe with me'. Although aware of his amusement I wasn't so sure. But he must have recognised what was going through my mind because he took a few seconds to reassure me, so that after a little while I was able to go with him. Not with any confidence at first. But as we walked farther and farther down the street and nothing happened, passing through groups of playing urchins and lounging youths whose territory this was, who regarded us only with curiosity, my peace of mind slowly returned. By the time we reached the house he was heading for the feeling of panic had almost gone, and far from being a lions' den it proved to be an ordinary dwelling inhabited by friendly people, who were amused but not surprised when Dad told them about my fear of entering their street.

The other encounter at a later date had a more ominous beginning but ended in farce. Some of us were playing in the coup when a crowd of Linties, better described as an army that seemed like the Mongol horde of historical legend as depicted in a then recent film about Kubla, or Khubilai, grandson of Genghis Khan, which really should be Chinggis, came down ferry road towards us. Because of the dead-end nature of the area the only way out, other than by the ferries, was by ferry road itself, so we were panic stricken, believing we were trapped and would be 'in for it'. In a tight knot we left the coup and moved on to the road, then across it to the pavement on the west side, all the while trying to make ourselves look inconspicuous and unconcerned, as we slunk along by the platers' shed wall towards Govan Road. At the same time we kept an eye on the other mob with furtive glances, hoping they would ignore us. No doubt they were boys much like ourselves, though to us they appeared menacing, and for a while they kept pace with us, keeping to the other side of the road and making no move to cross over. They outnumbered us by about four to one, and in the way they eyed us they seemed to be out for trouble — or fun, we fervently hoped. But they were obviously planning something.

Presently an older boy among them, evidently their leader, began directing others of his group to cross over and pick out, one at a time, individuals from our group and take them back across to join their group. This continued as we walked, outwardly brave but inwardly quaking, towards the relative safety of the main road. We sensed that it would be unwise to start running too soon because that might provoke a chase, and there wasn't enough distance between them and us to be sure of out-distancing them, for if that happened we were certain to be overwhelmed by their numbers. As we neared the corner there were only two of us left, me being one of them, so the instant we judged it safe the pair of us took to our heels and ran as if the devil was after us, across Govan Road, along Holmfauldhead Drive and into the safety of our own street. Who the other boy was I cannot recall, but we paused there in an agitated state to discuss what to do about the situation. Should we sent for the polis or go round the mothers of those 'captured' and tell them what had happened, and let them organise a rescue party?

We hung about near the corner for a few minutes in indecision while slowly calming down, then decided, before doing anything, to have a look back round the corner to see what was happening. On doing so we were amazed and relieved to see all our chums who, in our juvenile fantasy world, we half expected never to see again, strolling towards us with smug expressions on their faces. My fellow survivor and I were agog to find out what had happened to them, but this story was too tame for us to accept after the fright we had endured. All were dismissive of the event, passing it off lightly by saying they knew nearly all the Linties from school. Indeed, when I thought about it, a few of them were known to me as fellow pupils at St Constantine's.

That adventure must have occurred not long after war began because two air raid shelters, brick built, and with a flat reinforced concrete roof like most of those buildings, had been put up in Holmfauld Road, spaced out beyond where the Legion hall had been and set back at the rear edge of the pavement. Our friends had been taken into one of these and made to obey orders like stand up, and sit down, and run round in a circle, and a number of other tame (to us now) demands, while their captors switched off and on the light for effect, before letting them go. It was a great let-down to the two of us who had escaped, and almost made us wish that we had been taken as well. It seems odd now that that shelter had lighting laid on, but they were solidly built structures with no opening but the door. There was an entrance passageway at each end before a turning led into the main area, which was almost pitch black inside. But these two shelters were probably there for a special purpose, built perhaps to accommodate members of Stephen's workforce, for they were the only ones known to have lights installed.

The fence which separated plots from coup was of dense wire mesh that seemed impervious. But it could nevertheless be penetrated by enterprising youngsters who were able to slip underneath unobserved if it was done at the right time, and in the right area with no plotholders about, concealed among long grass. Bravest of the group would venture in and crawl away through the dense border of summer greenery and disappear from sight, then return with their pockets full of potatoes for baking on a wood fire. This method of cooking was new to me because, as already related, Mum found that using the fireplace oven at home was too difficult. The one and only time I took part in this coup potato roasting operation proved to be very successful, and despite being sceptical

D

about it initially, the spuds turned out to be delicious.

Holmfauld Road had a tram terminus, the rails of which ran down quite a distance from Govan Road to accommodate the extra vehicles turning there during peak periods. It had three crossovers to enable them to shunt about and depart in correct order, but something that intrigued me was that on both lines, where they terminated, there were signs of where a vehicle had gone beyond the rail ends and the wheel flanges had cut grooves in the granite cobblestones for a few feet. A burning curiosity developed to know how this had happened, and for years I kept an intermittent lookout in an effort actually to see it occur. Wheel-flange grooves were a phenomenon seen at other termini but I was fated never to witness it actually happen. The most likely reason was that it would have occurred during the night, when the permanent way maintenance squad was working with their specially adapted work vehicle and trailer which, in the gloomy street lighting of the period, had been propelled too far. Or perhaps a fall of snow had made it difficult for service drivers to judge their position. It might have been harder for an ordinary tram to have managed to do this, except by coasting, because it would have run out from under the overhead cables carrying the electric power supply, and suffer a loss of power.

River traffic and industry

The river, though farther away, was more accessible than from Howat Street, and continued to be a source of endless interest. The regular traffic of ships and boats passing up and down could be observed from the riverbank path next to the ferry berths. This activity was supplemented by frequent movements back and forth of the two ferries, plus constant shipbuilding work and occasional launches from the three yards within sight. Despite being well past the peak of maximum activity, which occurred during earlier decades of the century, the 1900s still saw plenty of movement even with the country in a depression, although, as the threat of war loomed, activity was very soon to pick up. Set down in the following paragraphs are some recollections of interesting sights to be seen.

At the foot of Holmfauld Road, the section of riverbank path of compacted gravel upriver from where the two ferry terminals lay was peculiar, in that for a path that led nowhere it was broad and substantial. After a couple of hundred yards or so it ended at the boundary fence of Fairfield shipyard. However, from reading historical accounts of river development, J.F. Riddells' among them, it seems that it was, and it may still exist there today if perhaps inaccessible, the last remaining stretch of the original tow path used in the days before steam propulsion came into general use. This would be before 1820, when the steam tug arrived and could be used as a means of towing sailing ships, when horses were employed to haul them up or down river during periods of contrary or insufficient wind. Because of the prevailing westerly wind, direction of tow would have been mostly downriver, but the question is, how did they cope with the difficulties this practice would involve? Was there a towpath on both banks for example, for illustrations seen of horse-towing operations show only a path on one side, presumably the south bank. If that is correct, because of complications caused by tow lines the only practical method would be a convoy system, with a string of boats going down river then another lot coming up governed by the state of the tide. Otherwise, how would boats pass one another safely as one lot of lines would have to be cast off? And how did they cope with a wind getting up and blowing the ship, depending on size of course and perhaps not yet under control, away from the bank and maybe taking the horse(s) with it? But of course ships then would have been tiny, and the tow would only need to be in one direction at any time anyway, except in calm conditions.

In the 1930s the path was bounded on the side away from the river by the sunny dumps of the coup, and separated from the river itself by high spiked iron railings. The bank at that point below the railings, in common with most other reaches of the river away from docks or quays, slopes down to an angle of about 35 degrees and is laid with large squared off stones with smooth faces set flush. This gives least resistance to wash thrown up by ships and waves generated by stormy weather, which would otherwise be liable to cause erosion. One of the sights keenly anticipated by young ship watchers like myself, was a high tide and a tug passing at full speed, so that the wash would come right up over the path. But this was likely to happen only during spring tide, when the path itself might be under water and the ferry service suspended.

Tugs were the most common craft seen on the river. There must have been at least a couple of dozen owned by to or three towage companies, because all ships above a certain tonnage needed the assistance of at least one tug, up to the very biggest that came up past the Clydebank reach, which required four. Movement of ships above a certain size was regulated by tidal ebb and flow. This meant that large vessels coming up had to begin their journey about midway through a rising tide, and any departing would set off at high water, in case they should touch bottom and stick, hence the term 'catching the tide'. If that happened on an ebb tide the grounded ship would remain there for a few hours, until the water returned to the previous level and lifted it off, and it was vital to avoid this because of the risk of damage to the hull. It follows that while bigger ships tended to pass in procession, small boats could move about at any state of the tide.

A big ship passing at high tide was quite awesome. The high water level and narrowness of the river made them really dominate the scene as they went past. Liners on the North American services of the Anchor Line, the *Cameronia* and *Transylvania* and the Donaldson Line's *Athenia*, were the biggest of a number that ran a regular service across the Atlantic to New York and the St Lawrence river. The Anchor Line's terminal was at Yorkhill Quay, and that of the Donaldson Line was at Queens Dock, where the Exhibition Centre is today. When anything of that size passed, whether passenger liner or cargo ship, everybody within sight with time to do so would pause to watch, and at night the sight was even more spectacular as they were lit up like giant elongated mobile Christmas trees. Today there is so little river activity that even a rowing boat will make people stop and look. In the past the bustle of more or less continuous ordinary river traffic would not merit a glance, much like the attention air traffic of the present receives from disinterested members of the public. My fascination with ships was closely linked to a growing desire to travel and see the world. Cargo vessels watched so keenly were off to, or returning from, exotic places like Africa, India, China, Canada, America, etc., places I longed to visit. That longing was partially fulfilled when at the end of the following decade a year was spent by the Suez Canal. While many were lost during the war, a few of the ships seen in the 30s were still passing through the canal in 1949, when the number to be seen with 'port of registration Glasgow' on the stern, was amazing.

Merklands Quay on the north bank, with the lairage behind, was in full view of anyone looking towards the river from Linthouse, from Govan Road, that is, and it frequently had the medium-size ships used to transport cattle from Ireland berthed there. But one thing that constantly frustrated me was to see this arrival or departure actually taking place. How I used to envy people who lived in the other side of our block with an unrestricted, if somewhat distant, view of all river movements, fondly imagining that they were all like me — keen ship watchers with all the time in the world to indulge in it. My permanent bad luck meant that I would often turn the corner of Holmfauldhead Drive and Govan Road and see a new arrival moored there, or the ship that had been there for a few days had gone. On these occasions, resolving that in future I would be more vigilant had no success.

Another interesting sight was watching a dredger at work, with its buckets on an endless chain clanking round the boom set at an angle which could be altered, allowing it to be lowered to the depth required for the reach (section of river) being worked on. The top of the boom was at an elevation well above superstructure height so that buckets, having scooped up their load of silt from the river bottom, carried it up and over the top. In going over, at the start of the return journey, the contents spilled out onto a chute angled to carry it to one side, where a hopper barge would be moored to receive it. When full the barges carried their loads away downriver and out to the outer firth beyond Bute and Cumbrae, to be deposited through bottom-opening doors off Garroch Head. Barges were nameless, seemingly identified simply by a number painted on the side — *Hopper No. 11*, or *Hopper No. 12*.

In summer pleasure steamers passed daily at certain times during the holiday season, on their regular run down to Dunoon and Rothesay and other destinations, returning later in the day. Lovely little ships like *Eagle III* (*Eagle the Third*) on the 11 a.m. departure from the Broomielaw to the Kyles of Bute, calling at Dunoon and Rothesay — *Queen Mary II* and the turbine steamer *King Edward*. While the latter was a beautiful ship, there as something odd about it which made it different from other steamers that took me a little time to resolve. It was observed that it moved almost silently, there was no rhythmic beat of paddles churning up white foam. My initial reaction in perceiving this was faintly hostile, in that, here was a ship with no visible means of propulsion like other steamers, so what made it go? Then came the realisation that no ships other than steamers had paddle wheels. After lines, speed was the main attribute of any boat. Performance of each steamer was studied closely by most people who used them regularly or who frequented the Firth. Eventually, when it became known to me that turbine steamers were faster, it was recognised that the spectacular visual attraction, and beat, of paddle wheels did not indicate a fast boat.

Most ships then were coal-fired to produce steam for propulsion, which caused them to put out thick plumes of black smoke from the tall thin smoke stacks common to almost all of them up to this time, which added the thrill of anticipation to ship-watching, in the same way as it did to train-watching with steam locomotives. Under favourable conditions ships could give advance warning of their approach while still out of sight upriver beyond Govan, or down past Shieldhall. From the riverbank, on days when weather conditions were suitable, with little or no wind, we would be on the lookout for distant smoke rising from a vessel coming our way. If there was a lot of smoke it might mean a tug or tugs in attendance and this, of course, indicated the possibility of a really big one, but we were seldom on the spot for that. Generally we heard about it later on, or at best saw it from a distance. When writing 'we' I really mean me, for few of my pals showed anything other than minimal interest in river activity, other than when a big boat was passing.

The smell from the river was unmistakable. While large amounts of untreated sewage were still being poured into it from the two plants nearby downstream, and while it didn't quite smell like what you would expect, although by no means fragrant it had a certain, almost attractive, salty methane/sulphurous tang of its very own. It was an aroma which quickly became associated with the interesting sights likely to be encountered by its banks. The gas works smell had a similar effect on people, in that when its not quite rotten-egg-like pong was first encountered, it caused wrinkled noses and exclamations of disgust. But soon, some undefinable element in it made one begin to sniff in earnest, to draw in and 'enjoy' (if that is the correct word to use in this context) it as much as possible, before passing out of its range. Another smell with the same effect was encountered in the underground or subway. Before the tram service was properly established, before electrification. Cluthas were the almost legendary boats which, from 1884 until the turn of the century, operated a passenger service between the city centre and Govan. Reading about them in later years, it seem likely they would have been disposed of decades before my time. However, the Clyde Navigation Trust had a number of hulks which were used in the course of maintenance work, and it appears that one or two of them were in fact old Cluthas, and one of them was still in use in the 30s.

Shipyards

Cranes of various shapes and sizes dominated the skyline at many places along the river, as a working requirement of docks, quays (pronounced keys), and shipyards (which were always referred to as 'yards'). Docks and quays had what today would be regarded as cranes of conventional design, with a jib which stood up at an angle from a central pivot where the cab was located. Most yards had hammerhead cranes, with horizontal jibs pivoted near the centre on top of a vertical support, of the same design as Yarrows, Kvaerner/Govan basin, and Finnieston heavy lift cranes of today, but of lighter build to suit hull construction loads. The cab was at one end of the jib while on the opposite side beyond the central pivot, the carriage carrying the lifting gear could travel along most of its own half. (Not long after writing the foregoing, it was announced that the Kvaerner/Govan crane alongside the fitting-out basin is to be dismantled because it is no longer needed, as ships are launched with all their heavy equipment already installed).

Until welding became the norm in ship construction during the following decade, noise was the most prominent feature of this, or any industry working with steel plates secured by rivets. Boilers for steam engines, whether for ship, rail or other uses, were constructed using curved steel plates riveted together, work which took place in what was called a 'boiler shop', a name synonymous with deafening noise, the din being made worse for the workers by the confines of the building. In days before ear defenders became available (and now mandatory), deafness afflicted everyone who worked in one of these places. A complaint sometimes directed at noisy children by adults was 'Yer makin' mair noise than a biler shoap'. I certainly heard my own mother use that expression to me often enough. Another saying heard occasionally at that time seems to have come from a bible story, the only likely explanation for another expression that has long passed out of common use. It was employed in describing an event in which someone created a din by shouting loudly in pain or anger, as though a child had fallen and been badly hurt. In re-telling the event later it was said that they 'bawled like the bull of Bashem!'. Later reading seems to indicate that what was meant was the 'Bull of Bashan', Bashan being a town in pre- or early biblical times in south-eastern Turkey.

In the open air of yards there was some relief from noise for those in the vicinity of riveters' hammers, except for the riveters and their mates themselves, in that the racket was dissipated somewhat. But in travelling farther afield it could still be heard over a wide area. The sound itself has been compared with that of a machine gun, but having experienced both I would say the riveters' hammer was marginally the more penetrating and least tolerable of the two. Living as we did within earshot of four yards, although the nearest riveters would have been working at least five hundred yards away, the noise they made was an ever present feature of life in the area during working hours. In addition there was the intermittent clang and clatter of steel plates being moved about. Evening and week-end silence was to be savoured, with drowsy summer Saturday afternoons the most peaceful time of all.

A longing for familiar experiences of the past is common with many people, even noises which were regarded as annoying at the time. Because of the possibility (more like certainty) that it may trigger other memories of a more sentimental nature, how about someone setting up a working mobile display that could be taken round old shipbuilding areas? Experiments with a few pre-bored steel plates of the correct size, a compressor, a riveter's hammer, a supply of rivets and a means to heat them, if it could be arranged, would surely bring expressions of wide-eyed amazement to the faces of many older people within earshot, with the comment 'Ah huvnae heard that racket for mair than fifty years'. However, at best that would be only a pale shadow of the noise produced in the past by dozens of rivet guns working at the same time along the riverside.

The actual building of ships itself was a natural source of interest, induced by watching activity in the nearest yards into which it was possible to see from our riverside vantage point, Stephen's and Barclay Curle. The easternmost slipway of the former was so close to Holmfauld Road, and lay at such an angle to the river, that the bow of any medium-size ship under construction, complete with scaffolding, overhung the pavement, so that walking beneath it was slightly intimidating. A similar situation was found on the north bank in Ferryden Street at Barclay Curle's yard. Part of this fascination was in seeing in close-up, and hearing close to, riveters busily engaged in assembling the hulls, which grew up from a skeleton of ribs and stringers. Next, the hull plates were riveted in position, and work progressed to the application of the first coat of paint, red lead, indicating that launch date was coming close. When the final coat was applied the launch might be within a week or so. Then one day it was gone, and within a few weeks the skeleton of the next one began to rise up in its place.

Local launches seemed to take place apparently without ceremony because we seldom heard about them in advance. Boats built in the two nearest yards at this time, on the slips nearest the road anyway, were usually no larger than a few thousand tons, and being fairly insignificant (except to the builders or prospective owners), they attracted little or no publicity. It was bigger ships, especially passenger liners like the *Queen Mary* and the *Queen Elizabeth*, and the larger naval vessels, which received most attention from the media. While there is no recollection of witnessing a launch during this time, I feel strongly that with a grandfather so immensely interested in such things and he knowing I was also, he probably did take me along. Although it must be remembered that he worked on weekdays, and launches almost invariably took place during the week. In considering that last point, the *Queen Elizabeth* was launched after I came home from Mearnskirk, but there is no recollection of the event. Regarding the other 'Queen' there is the most fleeting of memories of being on the riverbank opposite when she entered the water in September 1934, but the impression may stem from seeing photographs or film. Contemporary accounts of the launch speak of flooding of that field by the stern wave produced when the ship took to the water, but this does not help bring it back fully into my recollection. It would be gratifying to be able to say I saw her, fitting out completed, being taken downstream in March 1936, for that sight must have been the wonder of the decade.

Fairfield yard, lying east of us in Linthouse, was less easily seen because of the lie of the land. G. & J. Ingles and D. & W. Henderson, whose yards were on either side at the mouth of the River Kelvin opposite Water Row, were too far away to see their operations. On the east side of the coup was the fence, behind which was an embankment covered with trees and bushes, with more ground between it and the Fairfield basin. Even from the north bank ferry terminal nothing could be seen because of fencing bordering Meadowside. The only opportunity afforded, and that briefly, was during a ferry crossing. Fairfield usually built bigger ships, and it was a permanent source of annoyance that we couldn't watch construction work going on there without taking a trip, for although the ferry was free it wasn't always convenient to do so. Some ferrymen were intolerant of adolescent travellers who might be intent on mischief, or who might lark around and be in danger of falling into the river. Another sound that was part of the river environs was that of ships' sirens. These ranged from the higher-pitched whistles of tugs and smaller boats, to the deep blare of bigger vessels and occasional rising hoots of smaller naval vessels, such as destroyers, although the latter were uncommon until the war. Just how wide-ranging that sound could be is well illustrated by the fact that when we moved to Pollok, about four miles away from the river, when weather conditions were suitable, for example, at the New Year with industry shut down, we could still hear the ships' horns sounding midnight.

Another sound, equally distinctive but of greater significance, was works' horns, a phenomenon people of later generations might find incredible. In those days, before personal transport like car ownership became common, most men lived near their work or just a short tram trip away. So an obvious way of alerting them to the fact that starting time was near, was to blow a horn or whistle which sounded like a ship's siren, loud enough to be heard over a wide area. The horns were blown two or three times at measured intervals, the usual sequence being a half-minute-long blow at fifteen and five minutes to starting time. At two minutes to, the final blast began and was continuous until a few seconds past starting time. At that period a 48-hour working week was in force, with starting/stopping times something like 8 to 12 a.m. and 12.40 to 5.30 p.m., although among local companies times were staggered to ease the burden on public transport. While home from school at dinner (lunch) time, a horn might sound. Mum would say 'There's the (quarter-to-one) "bummer", you'd better get a move on or you'll be late' (for the 1 o'clock start of the afternoon session).

At starting and finishing times the surrounding streets were thronged with crowds of men dressed in caps and boiler suits or overalls, streaming towards or away from their workplace. At starting time, when the two-minute horn sounded, those outwith a certain radius, at a distance learned through experience, took to their heels in an attempt to get into the gatehouse and stamp their timecards before it stopped. Starting time was strictly observed. Any workers clocking in after the whistle stopped were 'quartered' that is they lost fifteen minutes' wages, and anyone later than fifteen minutes was half-houred. This was a practice considered necessary in order to maintain discipline in companies employing large numbers of workers. At teatime Govan Road between Elderpark and Elder Streets, and Homefauld Road, were a mass of dark-clad men surging out to the waiting ranks of trams, or beyond, to spread out through the surrounding streets. There were no works' washing or changing facilities then, and other reminiscences tell of toilet arrangements that were very primitive to the extent of being almost non-existent. Men engaged in dirty work went home as they were, so that travellers other than workers had to be careful to check seats on public transport after the works came out. The chance of coming into contact with oil, grease or paint if a workman sat beside you, or had previously deposited it on the seat, was real.

Although confined to morning, mid-day and evening, works' horns were a major contributor to the general din in our highly industrialised area. For most women with a husband or son rushing in for a meal it was an excellent way of knowing the time. It saved the distraction of clock-watching. Also, not everyone had a wireless from which time checks could be had, and cheap clocks could be undependable, especially if the daily winding had been forgotten. Company horns had to sound quite different from each other so that workers knew which was which, and of course everybody else got to know them as well. Another good reason for them was that it avoided disputes about whose time was the correct time. Familiar sounds of those times, from the clip-clop of hooves and rattle of cart wheels over cobbles, whine, screech and clatter of trams, the general din of industry, their horns and ships' sirens, and noises made by vendors, while some are a relief to be without, all are but a memory. Even the sound of church bells is rare now. Sunday mornings and afternoons of the thirties were briefly enlivened by them ringing out at different times. A glance at a map of the period will show almost a dozen churches in west Govan, the bells of most of which were within earshot of Linthouse.

Normally my father didn't come home for the three-quarter hour dinner break allowed, preferring to take a 'piece' for lunch and have his dinner in early evening. Dinner in working-class homes always referred to the mid-day meal. When he did come home, with his work a mile or so away in Helen Street, the sequence in our house, and numerous others around mid-day, might have gone something like this. Stephen's horn would sound at ten to twelve and mother put the potatoes on to boil. After ten minutes had elapsed Fairfield's horn was heard, and mum would know they would be boiling and salt could be added and Dad would be leaving his work on his bike. After a further ten minutes a third blow from another yard indicated that the potatoes should be ready for pouring, and Dad ought to be in the street or coming up the stairs. As he finished eating, yet another blast, in this case the 'ten minutes to go' start warning of the first in the earlier sequence of blows, told him he had another five minutes before he needed to leave on the return journey. He worked regular overtime and the early evening visit home for his tea was a hectic operation, with a shorter break of half-an-hour, which, with ten minutes' travelling each way, left little time for eating.

He usually carried his bike up the stairs to the top half-landing and left it under the landing window where it was fairly safe. Once or twice he risked leaving it in the back court parked under the wash-house window, in full view of our kitchen window, although from rather high up, an action that would re regarded as the height of folly in the present day, until one day it disappeared. We all rushed downstairs to look for it, but it transpired that it had been taken by a boy not much older than me, who had no thought of stealing it; he only wanted to try riding it up and down the street, but of course it was much too big for him. The bike was quickly recovered with some harsh words said, and a long time passed before it was left in the back-court again.

As a way of indicating they were in the close and that their arrival was imminent, some people would whistle a brief tune of a few notes to alert anyone in the house. Dad used a four note tune for this which I, too, quickly adopted. It was handy to be able to signal from the bottom of the stairs that you were on your way up, so that the door was open for you instead of having to wait after knocking. Obviously neighbours used different tunes, and once or twice I must have caused a neighbour's husband's dinner to grow cold, as I caught myself absentmindedly whistling 'their' tune as I went up the stairs. Passing a lower landing door lying ajar I realised what had happened and crept past silently, listening for the mutters of complaint from below as the woman inadvertently fooled into thinking it was her husband figured out what had happened. Acoustics on tenement staircases were ideal for whistling, and, reckoning I was pretty good, I did it all the time with current favourite tunes. Every staircase had a bannister of decorative cast iron uprights topped with a broad handrail of polished wood, conveniently shaped for gripping, that was ideal for sliding down. Some handrails had a gap of about six inches where it made the 180 degree turn at each landing, as ours had, allowing bannister-sliders to slide all the way from top to bottom. Other banisters had a gap which was too small to permit sliding, other than the open mid-sections between landings. Some handrails had brass studs, peaked but with the tops rounded off, to deter bannister sliders, although these were mainly confined to the lowest flight. Growing up meant that I could no longer do it; it was too painful, later realising it was because I had reached puberty!

Public transport

Travelling on public transport within Govan to the city centre or Renfrew was always by tram. The only bus service along Govan Road was Western SMT's red buses between central Glasgow and Renfrew and beyond. The shade of red used was one which, because of defective colour vision, I found impossible to identify. Many years were to pass before it was realised that the 'red' buses people talked about, were those Western buses. The shade was wine red. There were no bus terminal stations as such. Any convenient street or roadside was so designated. Western's terminus for the service passing our way was at that time in North Drive alongside St Enoch Station, opposite the entrance to the North British Hotel, which was narrow and had an inconvenient steep slope. This is clearly recalled because at holiday time and bound for the Firth, when the service was busy with no-one getting off before the city boundary at Merryflatts, to make sure of getting on, my parents travelled in to the terminus and joined an enormous queue there. That terminus endured until road traffic increased after the war, when it moved to Clyde Street for a number of years. During the latter period, some SMT services from north of the river to destinations to the south used Clyde Street as their terminus, while those proceeding to destinations on the north side used Carlton Place. Because of the low bridge between Langbank and Finlaystone, with its Z bend where the road passed under the railway, services which proceeded beyond Bishopton were operated by single deckers. The old bridge can still be seen on the alignment of the old A8 road, beside the new bridge.

In those days an odd public transport regulation was in force (introduced in 1930 to protect the Corporation Transport Department's revenue) which applied to Glasgow. Only Corporation trams and buses were permitted to carry passengers on journeys that began and ended inside the city boundary, and as the boundary was then at the Southern General Hospital (the above-mentioned Merryflatts) we were unable to use Western buses on journeys to and from town. That apparent restriction was in fact no restriction at all, as their frequency of service was poor compared with our 'caaurs' and their fares were higher as well. The latter fact meant that when travelling to Renfrew regularly to visit an aunt over the year near the end of the decade, we still used the tram. When we did travel by bus it was in the happy atmosphere of holiday time, going to Gourock to take the ferry to Kilcreggan, and a few years later to Lochgoilhead, but the rest of that story (of events after the 1930s) belongs to other reminiscences planned for the future.

Until the allocation of service numbers late in the decade, tramcars had broad coloured bands painted all the way round the outside at mid-height, between the upper and lower decks. Colour was assigned as far as possible to a service, a rule fairly consistently followed, given that there were over thirty services citywide. When standing at the car stop at Govan Cross goods station for example, at the corner of Greenhaugh Street, known as Morris's Corner because of the large newsagent and tobacconist's shop of that name there, it was possible to see for a half-mile eastwards. Along that straight stretch of Govan Road a car could be seen turning the corner at the dry dock, when its colour immediately became apparent, allowing intending passengers to know well in advance if it was the one they were waiting for. Advantage of the link between service and colour was best appreciated in the town centre, where at peak times vehicle ran virtually nose to tail. Trying to determine the destinations of cars in a line in Argyle Street, Sauchiehall Street, Hope Street, or Renfield Street, was often impossible, because running so close together the destination screens were hidden by their proximity to each other, so the coloured band was a good guide,.

Two services operated through Linthouse. One by blue cars, which became the Number 4 service, went as far as Sandyford (where the M8 passes between Renfrew and Paisley) showing *Renfrew South* on the destination screen. Green was the colour of the service later numbered 27 which turned at *Hillington Road*. For us there was the complication of a yellow car service, the Number 7. This turned up Golspie Street and went on to *Craigton* where the terminus was at the Cleansing Department destructor plant, but was soon to be extended over the newly widened bridge over the railway line to Jura Street, with the destination *Bellahouston*. Travelling from, say, Govan Cross to Linthouse, it might be thought that there was no problem in boarding the correct car, blue or green. But this was a mistake made by nearly everybody at one time or another. Westbound travellers sometimes boarded cars at the Cross or points east without paying proper attention to what was shown on the front, or the colour, most often at night or in fog when these indicators were least visible, to find themselves being whisked up Golspie Street, and having to scramble off, walk back to Govan Road and wait for a 4 or a 27 and pay again. A service extended during our time was the Number 12. It ran originally from Mount Florida, threading its way along Allison Street, through Pollokshields to terminate in Admiral Street at Paisley Road Toll. During the war it was extended to Linthouse at peak times. Instruction given by residents of Linthouse to visitors to the district was, 'Take a blue or a green car, but whatever you do don't go on a yellow car!'

Peak hours saw a large increase in the number of cars turning at or passing through Linthouse. As well as the dozen or so extra vehicles turning in Holmfauld Road morning, mid-day and evening, a similar number proceeded to Shieldhall. These turned in Bogmoor Road, where a terminus was established in 1937. A large number of workers, including dockers and other travellers from KGV dock nearby, numbering thousands, had to be carried to and from the SCWS works, so at busy times a procession of vehicles trundled out and back along Govan Road. Vehicle width standards of the time meant that layout of seats was lop-sided, but only on the lower deck. The top deck had, as on present-day buses, conventional double seats down each side, while at each end of tram lower decks there were three-person longitudinal seats on each side, on which passengers sat with their backs to the window. Between these end seats, on one side was a row of four double seats, while on the other there was the same number of *single* seats for which there was much competition. All double and single seats were set transversely with passengers facing forward. Except where a reversing loop had been provided, vehicles could not be turned at termini, so there was a mechanical arrangement which allowed seat backs to be reversed, by pulling a chromed open-loop handle on each top corner on the side nearest the passage. Ten standing passengers were allowed, on the lower deck only, and grab-rails with dangling straps were fixed to roofs, extending from front to rear on both decks, as a steadying aid when the vehicle was on the move.

It might be considered by people who have never been on a tramcar or were too young to recall the experience, that details described here are unnecessary when they can be studied at first hand in the Museum of Transport. But how many would realise the necessity of reversing seats at each terminus, or having to lean out of the top deck window at the end of the car and haul on the rope which hung down there, to pull over the current collector on the roof for proceeding in the opposite direction? It is likely that the same young people might think the saying 'off his trolley', suggests that someone who does something stupid has fallen off a wheeled barrow of the type used to move patients around in hospital. Whereas it's quite likely to come from the analogy of a derailed tram losing power by running out from under the wire, which picked up power via the trolley on its roof. Actually, the type of pickup used on Glasgow trams was termed simply a bow current collector.

Traffic staff uniforms were dark green and workers were known as 'the greenstaff'. Seasonal wear was winter coat or summer jacket, and uniforms had to be pressed and kept clean and tidy, with buttons and shoes polished, cap badge gleaming, and collar and tie worn. Crews worked under a strict régime, with many inspectors prowling around looking for infringements of rules and regulations. Such simple things as not wearing the uniform cap or smoking on duty, or more seriously, running late or early, showing the wrong destination on the screen or route or service number, or infringements in issuing tickets, were severely dealt with. In my time during the 1960s and early seventies as a bus driver with the transport department (I left just before it lost its old identity to Strathclyde in the reorganisation), an inspector finding an infringement had to confront the guilty party and obtain from them their name and number. But in the 1930s it was standard practice for inspectors to report, without needing any corroboration, infringements observed from a distance. If a driver was spotted fleetingly driving past, without having his hat on for example, or smoking, he could be reported. That seemingly oppressively strict system could have been the reason why the transport department was so well run and highly regarded up to around the 1940s. After the war, as the tramway system contracted and buses were substituted, because the latter were not 'confined' by rails to a set route in the same way as the cars, flying squads of pairs of inspectors of the more efficient and aggressive type were formed. They drove around in small green vans to keep track of malingering crews, and their skulking, spying, and hard-nosed behaviour earned them the name of 'The Gestapo'. The author has tales of this and other aspects of life on the buses during the 1960s already set down, which may one day be seen in print.

On the top deck of the older type of tram, at each end there was a compartment with a sliding door. At the leading end, to prevent a through draught when the vehicle was moving, the door was kept closed, so that five passengers could occupy it and be in a little closed off saloon by themselves. The window at each end above the destination screen box was a 'droplight', and opened by the same system as was then current on railway carriages, a simple arrangement which did not use counterweights. A heavy leather strap was fixed to the lower edge of the moveable section of the window frame, to hang down inside the saloon. While it normally rested in a seating in the frame, to open it the window was lifted by the strap and lowered down a slot within the bulkhead. Railway carriage windows could be set at a variety of heights, because the strap had a series of holes punched in it which pressed over a stud fixed to the inside door facing. However, it's not recalled now whether trams had that facility. Of course, during warm weather both windows and doors could be left open to allow a cooling breeze to blow through.

In summer conditions were ideal for tram drivers, for anyone young and fit, with the then relatively traffic free roads and no steering demanding constant attention. According to those who worked on them, the open platform gave a fresh air feel when driving in the suburbs on warm sunny days. The sliding door between driving compartment and lower deck passenger saloon, which was normally kept closed, could be wedged open to allow a through draught. A temporary barrier in the form of a spar 'T' piece (perhaps with another crosspiece at mid height to keep children out) of dark varnished wood, was fixed across the opening. In winter it must have been hell for drivers, having to stand constantly with an icy blast coming through the doorless entrance and whipping round the wide cab. Such exposure during a winter freeze-up caused them to dress up to resemble early versions of the Michelin Man. Very occasionally a driver would have a seat, simply a round piece of polished wood set on a metal rod which plugged into a hole in the cab floor. They must have had an infirmity, perhaps due to ageing, and long service behind them to qualify for it. But a less comfortable perch could hardly be imagined, on which a driver would be more likely to fall off than nod off.

In place of a horn trams had a bell, operated by stamping on a plunger in the floor at the driver's feet. It may not be obvious to the museum spectator that trams have a form of cowcatcher. This was a slatted wooden platform carried flat underneath the cab, set back from the ends. In the raised position the catcher was held just above the road surface, and when the gate at the front struck an object, it swung up and allowed the obstruction to pass underneath. In doing so it released the catcher, the leading edge of which dropped onto the cobbles and scooped the object up, in the case of someone knocked down and run over, not perhaps unharmed but with a considerably better chance of being alive.

Employees approaching retiral age who found the strain of driving becoming too much, weren't discharged. Easier jobs were found for them, such as point-changer at peak-time at a busy intersection, saving drivers of older vehicles from having to stop. (The newest vehicle had an on-board device for doing this.) Another was going round all junctions and cleaning dirt out of the chamber below the moving blade of the point, which was done with a flat rod having a sharpened bent-over section at the tip, and a flat brush with long stiff wire bristles. The gentleman (for so he seemed) who did this in our area in the thirties, was a tall thin individual of military bearing, with white hair and walrus moustache.

Conductors had a simple form of ticket dispenser, a punch, and an extremely heavy, even when empty, cash bag to cope with. Tickets were in pre-printed thick bundles of 50 or so, stapled together and held in a row by powerful coilspring clips on a wooden tray mounted over the cash bag. The bundles, of different colours representing various values from $1/2$ penny, penny, $1^{1/2}$ penny (expressed as three-halfpence) and so on to 3d, were of thin cheap-type card or heavy coarse paper, oblong shaped and numbered sequentially with the numbers along the top. Other numbers along each long edge corresponded to the stages along the route. When purchasing, the request was for a ha'penny-one, or a penny-one etc., and a ticket of the requested value was plucked off the top and punched at the stage number to which the holder was entitled to travel. As the bottom of the bundle was approached, to free them from the staple the few remaining tickets had to be plucked out with a jerk from under the spring, in doing so causing a well remembered and surprisingly loud snapping sound. Each ticket had in its centre the legend — The Glasgow Numerical Ticket Company & CPB Co. Ltd., Finnieston Street, Anderston.

Worn over the breast bone, the ticket punch was suspended by a strap which passed over the right shoulder and under the other arm. It was a flat four-inch square of shiny metal about an inch thick, with GCT embossed, entwined within a slightly inset section on the front. On top, to the right of centre, it had a narrow peaked extension, with a slot between it and the main part of the unit into which tickets were inserted. Below was a thumb operated lever which, with a ticket in the slot with the stage number aligned, when thrust sharply down punched a hole in it, causing a bell to ding with a gentle high-pitched tone. (A waggish member of the greenstaff used to tell the apocryphal story of a rather simple fellow newly recruited as a conductor, who wondered if the department employed people to add up the punchings to check against ticket money he paid in.) The sound of that bell encountered today would bring a tear to the eye of many older people, including me, although it could become monotonous on a busy car. Along with the rumble and swaying movement, they are among sensations redolent of the age.

The cash bag, with the strap over the opposite shoulder from the punch, was deep, front to rear, and had a rounded bottom. It had a division across the centre to keep silver and copper coins separate, and a flap, in the form of an upward extension of the rear panel which came down in front to be held in place by a short punched strap, the hole of which pressed over a stud. Memory of the bag centres on the material it was made from. So heavy and thick was the leather it might almost have been stood on round the edges without distorting. Empty, it was quite heavy, but after a busy shift it must have been back breaking to carry. As a child I had a conductor's set, consisting of hat, cash bag with strap, rack of tickets, badge, and punch formed from sheet tin with strap, all very similar to the corporation's, and a bell which rang in a most realistic way, just like the real thing.

Destination screens were different between trams and buses, although both used the same style of roller blinds which might hold up to thirty or forty place names. On older trams it was in the form of a box with two screens giving a double over-and-under display, the lower one indicating a place passed en-route, to which the prefix *via* was later added. Located on the ledge above the driver's windscreen at each end, the box was accessible from the top deck end compartment for changing by the conductor, whose responsibility it was. Screens were scrolled independently by two crank handles on vertical shafts, one at each end of the box. If, like us, you happened to live near a tram terminus it was a familiar sight to see, as Linthouse bound cars approached the turning point, conductors with long service leaning nonchalantly half out the window in order to see the screen (and read it upside down), while expertly twirling both handles. This of course had to be done at both ends of the vehicle, and it caused a succession of places, familiar and unknown, to flash past so fast that only an occasional name could be picked out.

Service numbers were an innovation introduced towards the end of the decade, which caused service colourcoding to be phased out, although it continued in use for some time. Service numbers were displayed on a large white board mounted in a bracket at the top of the top deck nearside hex panel window at each end. After changing screens the conductor remained in the front compartment until the end of the line was reached, for he had to pull over the bow current collector by hauling on the rope attached to it, which looped down from the roof of the vehicle at each end.

Earlier in the decade the Corporation Transport Department acquired a most unusual vehicle, an AEC Reliant double-decker bus. While never fortunate enough to have a ride on it, it was seen occasionally in Langlands Road when on my way to school, on either the 4 or 4A service. It always fascinated me, with its double rear axles and large bar resembling a pram handle at the front, curving up in front of the open radiator. All local bus destination screens, whether on double or single deck vehicles, were single aspect with the service number above and set within the body. Cranks for changing them projected down from within the bodywork on the front nearside, just within the open 'half-cab' compartment above the engine and quite high up, so that the driver, whose job it was in this case, had to stand on a step provided low down on the side of the radiator block to reach them. All trams had on their platforms (I'm not sure now about buses) a little red box, about 4" square and 8" high, fixed to a wire frame on the outside of the saloon window. It had a locked lid, which sloped steeply, with a slot for coins. On its front was a notice inviting you to 'Please place uncollected fares in this box'.

A device long gone from internal combustion vehicles is the starting handle. Virtually all vehicles had them up until the 1960s, although by then they were kept stored away from the engine, in cars usually in the boot. In the thirties, however, they were a permanent fixture at the front, usually positioned behind the bumpers of cars. On commercial vehicles and buses they projected out in front in line with the crankshaft, through an aperture in the radiator, with some held off-centre by a strap. While I am unsure if electric starter motors were common then, it was a regular occurrence to see vehicles having their engines started by their handles. Heavy commercial and public service vehicle starting handle cranks were spring loaded, to keep the 'dogs' on the business end out of contact with those on the forward end of the crankshaft when the engine was running. When starting, the handle was pushed in to engage the dogs, using the heel of the hand pressing on the large centre of the blind tube end, and the handle turned until the dogs engaged. Then the serious work started. The operator turned it a little against compression and allowed it to return to compress the other way. Using the momentum gained, he turned harder once more in the clockwise direction. Return swing this time was usually enough to enable a full turn to take place and, hopefully, the engine would start. With certain makes of engines extreme care had to be taken in case of kick-back, and broken arms, and worse, were an occupational hazard. Cold starting heavy vehicles often involved two strong men, and the effort required for the first start of the day in winter in sub-zero temperatures, conjures up the vision of a special breed of he-men.

Street and backcourt hawkers

A young person today transported back in time to the streets of the period being written about, and looking around to see what the greatest differences were between them and those of the present, might be amazed, not so much by the lack of traffic during the day (private vehicles mainly but also commercial other than horse and cart), but by the absence of parked vehicles. All side streets away from upmarket residential districts were quite empty during evenings and at weekends, except for the occasional horsedrawn ice-cream cart. Even during the day, when there would be the normal occasional passing commercial traffic and a fair number of hawkers doing their rounds, it didn't amount to a great deal. Hawkers had mainly hand barrows or horses and carts, such as the sellers of coal, briquettes, fish, fruit and vegetables, and milk and buttermilk (by different vendors), who were the most common. Less frequently seen were the scrap iron collector, who would take away any metallic scrap, paying a pittance for it, the crockery seller, and cheap clothing flea-market type seller/buyer — the rag and bone man. Not seeing the candy rock men after the move to Linthouse was a great disappointment, for I had grown up a bit and could have coped with the rush. There was a certain amount of passing traffic in Skipness Drive we didn't have in Howat Street, mainly because drivers preferred the rumble-free ride away from cobbles. But it could also be used as a through route south and east, for vehicles to thread their way from docks or ferry to the Craigton Road and Helen Street area. This traffic still mostly consisted of horses and carts, but the proportion of motor vehicles was growing. Nevertheless, streets here were almost perfect playground for children, particularly after working hours. Except for house windows, which were vulnerable to ball games.

With their horsedrawn vehicles or handcarts, or carrying their wares in baskets, perhaps 'humphed' on their shoulder, hawkers provided interesting, or irritating if it wasn't the one you were waiting for, diversions in a constantly changing daytime scene in streets and back courts. Most common of these were coal merchants, with their low sided four-wheeled carts with a four-foot high tailboard, above which metal flags on rods displayed grades and prices. An example of this might be *Best House Coal* 1/10d (per cwt. bag) or *Nuts* (coal graded to a small size convenient for shovelling straight on to the fire) 2/-d (two shillings = 10p) per bag. Side edges of this type of cart were really just a three-inch deep, thick metal-clad ledge, on which the outer edge of the outermost row of bags of coal rested, causing them to lean inwards which helped stabilise the load. One or two merchants displayed signs which indicated that a particular consignment came from a named mine or pit with a reputation for high quality coal, at a correspondingly dearer price of course. Those names are hazy now, but there is a feeling they might have been in Fife, although one that comes to mind is the Lady Victoria pit at Newtongrange, Midlothian. Tailboard of the cart and outer edges of the platform were lettered, sometimes quite colourfully, in scrolled and perspective lettering with the merchant's name and depot address in large letters. The local coalman in Linthouse was portrayed thus — *Daniel Morrison and Sons, Coal Merchants, Shieldhall Goods Station* — and in smaller letters — *Home Address: 1 Skipness Drive, Linthouse,* and their Govan exchange telephone number.

Thinking now about the carrying capacity of these carts intrigues me. General dimensions of the load bed were, at a guess, roughly about fifteen feet long by six feet wide. It was mounted on two sprung axles with spoked steel-tyred wooden wheels. To the leading axle, set in a truck which pivoted at the centre to enable it to steer, were attached the shafts between which the horse was harnessed, so that the cart should follow the horse whichever way it might turn. Over the horse's neck, and fitting snugly on its shoulders, was a large padded heavy-looking collar, to which the main trace straps of the harness were attached, often decorated with a finial, or a pair of curved finials which stuck up to form a V. Many collars had an additional embellishment in the form of metal tracery rising to a point between the finials. Inset near the top was a small hole with what looked like a ruby (?) fixed in such a way as to pivot at the top. As the animal walked along its head nodded, causing the stone to swing back and forth through the hole so that it sparkled in sunlight. The collar was the device by which horses were able to handle the weight of a fully laden cart, by spreading the strain evenly over a large area of their shoulders. At rest, the shafts themselves were supported by a chain attached to them, which passed over the horse's back, to lie on a form of saddle having a groove to confine it.

Layout of the load would be something like three bags across by ten along the length, which is 3 x 10 = 30 bags, each of 1 hundredweight (cwt). In addition most carts when fully loaded would have another lawyer with a slightly lesser number of bags, and there are vague recollections of seeing one or two with another part layer. Even a roughly estimated total of sixty bags, which is three tons, seems rather a lot for one horse, always one of the heavy breed and generally a Clydesdale, to manage. Topography of Govan and the surrounding area was mainly flat and level, so this may account for the heavy loads seen in our area. Carts operating in hilly districts, mainly in the north side of the city, probably had to commence work with lesser loads to compensate for hills. Nearest slopes steep enough to cause difficulty in Greater Govan were at the top of Craigton Road and Moss Road where they cross the railway line, but handling a load like that on the level did not seem to cause difficulty to these powerful animals.

Feed in the form of oats for the horse, was carried in a nosebag slung under the rear end of the cart, where it swung gently to and fro as the cart rolled along. Feeding and watering was done at a fire hydrant, and the carter carried in his toolbox a watermain key to operate the hydrant tap. The name burlap, sacking of heavy dense canvas, comes to mind and this might have been the material. The bag, which had a wooden base, was suspended by a double loop of rope over its head, one loop behind its ears, the other in front, so that it was enclosed up to its eyes, making it snuffle and sneeze constantly as it ate because the oats were always dusty. In having to eat in such a suffocating way, I always felt sorry for horses.

As this was before there was regular treatment of roads with salt and grit, winter brought big problems for horses and carters. When a horse slipped on ice and fell, a fairly common occurrence in that period of lower average winter temperatures, the first thing the carter had to do was unhitch the cart and have it pulled clear, then sacking was put over the horse's hooves. If any kind of grit could be obtained, like sand or a shovelful of earth from a garden, or even sawdust, this was spread around. Then the horse was encouraged to stand up, which led to agonising and traumatic scenes. Sometimes the struggle would go on for quite a long time, with the horse slipping and sliding and suffering repeated falls if conditions were particularly bad. In one observed incident the animal had to be lifted with a sling round its belly by some kind of mechanical means, and set on its legs, probably by a hand-wound crane mounted on a motor lorry. Very occasionally a horse would break a leg in a fall and if that happened it was the end of the horse. It was killed on the spot, how I'm not sure, but disposal with a humane gun would be the most likely method. One lay in Drive Road covered by a tarpaulin after an occurrence of this nature, awaiting the arrival of the knacker's cart to take the carcass away. In icy conditions, the transverse ridges on horseshoes, one at the front and one on each wing at the rear, gave a better grip in the slots between cobbles on main road surfaces than the treacherous smooth surface of asphalted sidestreets.

The number of coal carriers travelling with each cart varied. Usually there were two men but sometimes there were three or four or more. They must have been a strong and stout-hearted lot to survive travelling on an open cart in an icy downpour and freezing wind, and getting covered in coal dust, then having to carry hundredweight bags on their backs up three and sometimes four storeys of a tenement. A lumpy bag (actually a sack but never in my experienced called that) weighing a hundredweight on your back would be an intolerably painful experience, so regular workers wore a substitute, and they had to be carefully watched when a householder was taking delivery of say, four bags. It wasn't unknown for an strong stiff leather studded round the edges with shiny steel rivets, and braced with narrow horizontal strips of steel held in place with brass rivets, and deep enough to cover the wearer from neck to below the small of the back. Casual workers used an empty bag as a substitute, and had to be carefully watched when a householder was taking delivery of say, four bags. It wasn't unknown for an inattentive housewife to be a bag short, when a 'padding' sack was slipped onto the empties pile to be counted in front of her for the final total. The carter in charge kept his takings in a bag slung round his neck, to hang down at his hip in the same manner as tram/bus conductors. One is recalled as having an identical transport department type bag of that very heavy leather.

A regular coal carrier handled a full bag with deceptive ease, carrying it standing upright high up on his back near the neck.

Others less practised would struggle laboriously to climb up flights of stairs bent almost double, clutching the lip of the bag with their forearms braced against their forehead and the bag trailing down to their backside. Sometimes this caused a spill on the stairs whereupon the wife taking the delivery would be down 'at the toot' with a brush and shovel, as every bit was precious, as well as to clean up before any neighbours saw the mess. Of three methods of tipping coal into bunkers, two were used by the strongest men. In the first, the bag was carried across the shoulders with one hand gripping the tail end and the other holding the neck firmly closed, for they were never tied, until it was in the correct position over the bunker. Then it was a simple action to lean over and release the neck allowing the contents to shoot straight in. But this was disliked intensely by householders because it produced the greatest amount of dust. The second method was to drop the bag straight in and wrestle it empty. But the favourite and the most skilful way was to throw the bag horizontally off the shoulder, so that its mid-point landed on the edge of the folded down bunker front with the mouth inside. This would put half the contents straight in, and a deft movement of the hand could catch the tail to throw it over and empty it. However, if the catch was slow some of the contents might end up on the floor.

Wear was constantly occurring on the edge of bunker and flap, causing a slot to develop which gradually widened over the years. Eventually, a stage was reached when, with the flap in its normal raised position, young children found it a convenient place to 'post' small household articles. In my case it was cutlery. Mum used to talk about the time she could not understand why she was so short of spoons, and the mystery was only solved when, as consumption of coal progressed the spoons were revealed at the bottom of the bunker. I had posted them through the slot just before the previous delivery of coal had arrived.

Try to imagine what it must have been like having to trudge about all day, carrying heavy bags of coal from which gritty dust or dampness percolated down your neck, for the cuirass didn't provide protection from that discomfort. All carriers wore a cloth cap, usually reversed with the peak down the back to give a small measure of added protection, steel-toed boots or clogs, and had their trouser legs tied with string below the knee as a guard against rising dust. Except when touting for sales the crew would travel on the cart, driver on the front nearside reins in hand, and whip carried vertical conveniently placed in a socket alongside him, the top of which jiggled about with the motion, seated on a pile of empty bags which became higher as the load diminished, with one leg dangling and the other resting on the cross-tree between the shafts. A second man occupied the opposite corner and the others spread themselves out over the load. Their sales technique was to walk along the centre of the street with the horse clip-clopping behind, and bawl their distinctive cries through cupped hands, going through one close in each block into the back-court and calling again, constantly scanning windows for prospective customers. Sometimes inconsiderate fellows would bawl while passing through the close, and if you happened to be on the stairs just then you were deafened. A device used in an attempt to enhance volume of shout when calling, was to place one black hand horizontal with fingertips on the ear, flat against an almost as black cheek.

It has to be emphasised that coalmen or other vendors were not in constant attendance. They all had calling days and had to make their rounds, so that if a housewife needed any of their wares she had to be alert. This was even more important if she wanted to buy from a particular coalman, for if she happened to be preoccupied and missed him, if her stock had been allowed to get too low it could mean no fire in the house that night. So it was vital to keep a sharp lookout and listen for his call, and here another annoying problem was occasionally encountered. Like others in the same situation, Mum found that certain men who were lazy, could, if their boss's attention was elsewhere, be deaf and blind to calls and signals requesting a delivery to anyone living up three stairs. Of course their favourite customers lived low down. Some merchants issued regular customers with a card about four inches square with their initials on it, for them to display on the sash of the window upper casement, which saved householders from being tied to their window watching and listening for them.

Another street vendor was Vennard the fishmonger, whose horse and cart were of a lighter breed and similar but lighter design to that of the coal man. As well as the usual haddock and whiting he sold Loch Fyne herring, Fynnan haddock, Arbroath smokies, and Aberdeen kippers. Apart from the usual filleted white fish, what puzzled me for a long time was something called line-caught haddock. Having fished on Loch Goil in the 1940s, I began to understand that net-caught fish were generally bruised in the crush when caught in a trawl net, and line-caught fish was always in better condition and therefore dearer. The fishman carried his wares in, and sold from, flat wooden boxes swimming with melting lumps of ice spread out over the bed of his cart, just as they had come off the boats. It was weighed on a Salter dial-scale suspended from a gallows-shaped bracket clamped to the cart side, the large shallow stainless steel pan of which sat in a cradle slung beneath the dial, making it easy to slide the fish onto newspaper for wrapping.

The milkman, Johnnie Owens, came round twice a day driving a cart of quite distinctive design, a two-wheeler with panelled high sides and front. At the top of the front, in the centre, there were a pair of short thin metal rods which matched the finials on the horse's collar, about a foot apart projecting upwards, between which passed the reins, to confine them when the driver put them down or should he accidentally lose his grip on them. Churns of milk were carried in the body of the cart above and forward of the axle. At the rear there was a low shallow partly enclosed platform stretching from one side to the other, on which the driver and his assistant stood to drive and sell from. A picture of that cart that remains with me is of it approaching along the street with the horse at a smart trot, with only the head and shoulders of the people on the platform visible. It will be understood that the platform skimmed along only a few inches above the ground.

Milk was dipped from the churn with metal pint and halfpint measures shaped like the bean or soup can of today, to which a long handle had been fixed as an extension of the side, with the other end bent over in a tight 'U' to hang over the lip of the churn and down inside. Most people still had milk cans of universal shape holding a quart, miniatures of a full size churn, while others brought along jugs. Small cans had wire handles forming a high carrying loop from one side of the neck to the other, and most had lids. Large churns for bulk transportation, were round with a variety of girths from tall and narrow to short and squat, but all had a conical section shoulder near the top, and a further straight extension into which a mushroom shaped lid fitted. That body design was evolved to reduce spillage when being moved. The youthful assistant looked after daily orders by carrying an armful of cans up each close to regular customers. As he climbed to the top flat he paused at each main landing and hung cans over customers' door-handles, and knocked on doors so that he could collect the empties on the way down.

Bottled milk was a fairly recent innovation which quickly became general. Early bottles had wide necks, sealed with round waxed-cardboard stoppers which pressed into a recess within the neck after filling at roadside or creamery. School milk came in one-third-of-a-pint capacity bottles of the same shape, the smaller stoppers of which had a partly punched hole in the middle which was pushed in to insert a straw. The pushing in had to be done with a degree of care — more care than was present among any generation of school children, because the whole stopper frequently popped in causing splashes of cream to shoot out, ruining many a jacket or gymslip — not always those of the pusher. As there were no fridges or freezers in working class homes then, there was no way to make perishable food like milk, fish and meat last, so they had to be purchased daily.

A blast on a trumpet or cornet signalled the arrival of the rag-and-bone man, a title which puzzled me for a long time because he was never seen to collect any bones. In retrospect it was probably a worthwhile function of his before this time and the name persisted. At one time bone was a more valuable commodity than it is now, although the bone lorry can still be seen today collecting from butchers' shops. Anyone who doubts this need only cast their mind back to the last time they were walking in the street, and caught a whiff of a really rotten smell as an open low-sided lorry passed by. That was the bone lorry. Bone was ground down and made into fertiliser, and used by farmers and gardeners in the days before the manufactured product became widely available. It was also melted down to make rather smelly glue. When the rag man arrived in the street, a few brassy notes from his instrument was the signal for every child to disappear up their close, to pester their mothers for rags to exchange for a balloon or a celluloid windmill.

Among many hawkers we used to see two are remembered in particular who pushed handcarts. One sold sour milk, or buttermilk, as it was otherwise called. His was known as the 'soor mulk cairt'. My dad drank it, as it was supposed to be good for chronic indigestion sufferers, although it's possible he actually liked it. It was dispensed from a distinctively shaped enclosed olive green barrow, quite small and narrow with shelved compartments inside, and mounted on a single axle with large diameter spoked wheels. It had a spar supported roof with sharply curved side edges, rather like a bus. Buttermilk was packaged in dark green square waxed-card halfpint cartons, similar to today's plasticised milk cartons. Soor mulk is still with us as yoghurt.

The other barrowman sold coal 'briquettes' (usually pronounced not with the accent in the centre of the word, but unstressed — more like 'brikits'), which were used to economise on coal. Coal came in various grades. It could burn well or badly. It was liable to contain stones, or in large lumps or have a high proportion of dust known as dross. Unless the graded stuff called nuts was bought, it was generally a combination of these. Good burning coal gave off plenty of heat. An estimate of its output would be equivalent to about four kilowatts for the average kitchen fire at its most efficient (much of which was lost up the lum!). As graded coal tended to burn up quickly, a way to make it last longer was to put in a briquette; these were intended to slow down combustion and therefore would not burn on their own. But one placed in the centre when replenishing the fire, with coal heaped up around it, could extend the life of the average fire by between 50 and 100 per cent. Briquettes then available were slightly smaller in size than a half brick, and most people used them except perhaps in very cold weather when maximum heat output was needed. They were made from dross with a little binding, cement or plaster, added and mixed

The author's parents, the witnesses, after their wedding at St Constantine's, Uist Street, Govan, on 13 October 1927. From left to right: Molly Chambers 1903–70; Agnes 1901–93; George Rountree 1898–1981; Alec Rountree 1903– *(Page 2)*.

No. 7 Howat Street, April 1986, with grandson Paul at the closemouth. The author was born in the room immediately above, with kitchen windows to the left *(Page 2)*.

No. 56 Queen Street, Govan, 1924, six years before it became Neptune Street. Grandfather William Rountree with son Alec and two customers. In the Lyceum window bill the *Govan Press* is advertising the film *You Can't Fool Your Wife*, for the week beginning 15 September.

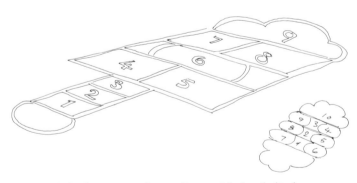

Peever beds. The two games illustrated here are fully described in the street games section on page 152 *(Page 154)*.

Reconstruction in heavy-duty card of a tenement kitchen by Govan Reminiscence Group in 1989. Note dresser and coal bunker with bunch of sticks. The frieze would have been higher up and the shelving deeper and heavier, and would have extended farther (*Page 4*).

A realistic impression of the window and its outlook. Observe the boxed-in sink with cupboard and crane tap, kitchen press (cupboard), minus door for convenience of viewing, Singer sewing machine and range. The single-leaf table was a common feature — often a product of the SCWS furniture factory at Shieldhall (*Page 2*).

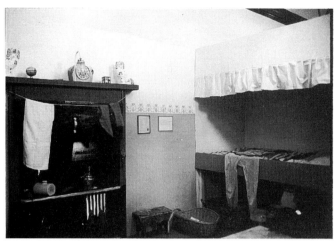

'Hole-in-the-wall' or recess bed. The garment looks like a man's 'combinations' — combined vest and longjohns in one piece, and a boon to shipyard workers in the winter. The range would often have a gas-cooker frame occupying the position of the 'pig' hot-water bottle on the left of the fireplace. Other notable items are the wickerwork basket for carrying the washing, large galvanised bath and the 'chanty' (chamber pot) on the floor *(Page 5)*.

St Anthony's School, Harmony Row, *c.* 1934, with part of the church showing on the right. My mother was born in the close (No. 12) which used to stand on the left against the school building *(Page 53)*.

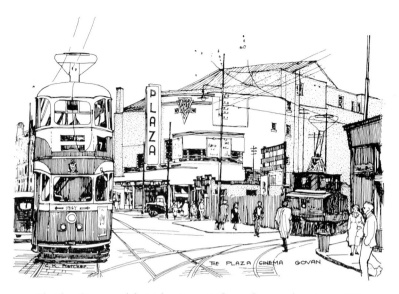

The Plaza Cinema and the triple entrance to Govan Cross goods station *c.* 1950. Note the bow current collectors on tram and locomotive *(Pages 55–57)*.

Left: Fairfield's two-axle electric powered locomotive, by English Electric (*c.* 1940), which hauled trains of wagons along the tram lines between Govan Cross goods station and the shipyard. In a 'shipyard' type modification, the bow current collector was changed for a dual pole type when trolley buses took over from the trams. This loco is not in the care of the Scottish Railway Preservation Society at Falkirk. *Right:* Harland's battery-driven locomotive (*c.* 1960) *(pages 55–57)*.

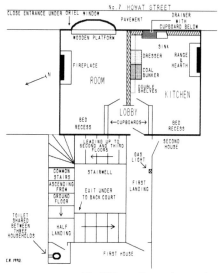

Plan of our house, one-stair-up at No. 7 Howat Street, showing layout and basic fittings. Not to scale *(Page 2)*.

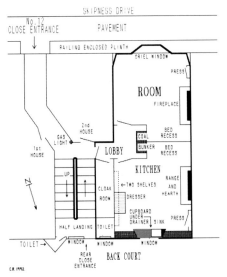

Plan of No. 12 Skipness Drive, with a bold line outlining the house (in both plans). The triangular projection on each half-landing housed the toilet used by the 'middle house' tenant. Not to scale *(Pages 75–78)*.

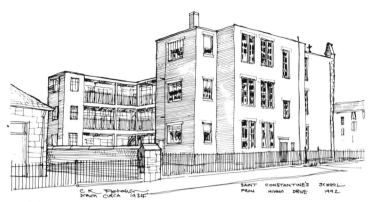

St Constantine's Primary School, Uist Street, as it was in the 1930s. Note the open verandahs and staircase (*Pages 175–178*).

St Constantine's Primary School, 1938. The 18 identifiable faces are, according to the indelible numbers: (10) Robert Watson; (2) J. Lawson; (4) Sergio Innocenti; (5) ? McMenamie; (6) J. Farrell; (8) H. Murphy; (11) ? Mulligan; (13) Gerry Belton; (14) Michael McAuley; (15) Francis Sharp; (16) The author; (18) Alec Shades; (19) Pat Sloan; (25) James Campbell; (26) James Fox; (36) Jean Flanagan; (40) Bridget McAvoy. Gerry Belton (No. 13) lived at 40 Rigmuir Road (*Pages 174–178*).

LINTHOUSE CHURCH FROM
12 SKIPNESS DRIVE CIRCA 1938

C.K Fletcher '92

Linthouse Church of Scotland in Skipness Drive in the 1930s. Where the new hall stands today there was a drying green with poles where the church officer's wife hung out her washing (*Page 82*).

The Vogue Cinema (1938) stood at the corner of Langlands Road and Crossloan Road and, as represented here in Chris Fletcher's drawing, it had a novel mechanical system of displaying 'stills' from the 'Film Now Showing' in the windows on either side of the entrance (*Pages 187–190*).

with water to a thick pouring consistency, then cast in moulds and dried in a large oven or kiln. Other briquettes which appeared later were about the size and shape of duck's eggs, and could be shovelled up like coal. In Govan we used to see carts loaded with the first type passing along the street in winter trailing plumes of steam. Obviously carrying a batch just out of the oven.

Coal merchants usually sold briquettes, but a few individuals specialised in them. One was a local man. Sandy was his name, as I was reminded some years ago on reading reminiscence stories by another Govanite, Jenny Chaplin, latterly of Rothesay, of life in Govan at roughly the same period. Sandy had certain characteristics which made him an extremely comical figure. He was very short in stature, probably under five feet tall, with the worst example of bowed legs I ever saw, which gave him an ape-like gait. He must surely have had rickets as a child. If he stood erect with feet together his knees must have been about eighteen inches apart, and his face was always so black with coal dust that his eyes and teeth flashed like beacons. He gave the impression that he never washed, because I never saw him any other way. Summer and winter he wore a bunnet, coat and scarf, all of which were thoroughly impregnated with coal dust. He wore his bunnet, or cap, in a quite distinctive manner. The age had ended when every male, old or young, seen in period photographs, was wearing a hat or cloth cap. Where later the top part of caps was normally kept fixed to the skip by a press stud, in the fading fashion of the time Sandy wore his with it open, with the skip pulled down over his eyes and a little to one side, which gave him a very period look — Victorian almost, or Edwardian. His barrow was the usual single-axle, large-spoked wheels, flat platform type, with a six-inch-high board edging extending round three of the sides, and a pair of legs at the shafts. The near end was open for handling the briquettes, which were usually purchased in dozen lots and carried up to customers' houses by a boy, on a short length of wood with feet that allowed the fingers to slip under the ends to pick it up when loaded.

All hawkers required a way of bringing their presence to the attention of householders. As mentioned before, some had an instrument like a trumpet, a cornet, or a bugle, while others used a handbell, a whistle of the rattling pea type, or a rickety. One man came round with a horse and cart selling cheap crockery from crates well stuffed with straw. He would cry out and rattle two plates together in a most effective way, so that I used to wonder how many he broke. Others used their voices. Coalmen in particular always possessed remarkable stentorian shouts. Sandy, our briquette man, was equally distinctive, calling, if I can put it down as it sounded — 'Coalbrikates' (rhyming with dates and the stress on the second-last syllable), and the price: 'A penny each or tenpence a dozen', frequently adding, without bothering too much about the truth of the statement, 'Big scarcity!'. That picture of Sandy is laden with nostalgia, just one more clear memory of the period.

Other itinerant callers, some of whom were women occasionally accompanied by children, went round the doors selling a variety of items, which might be crochet work like table doylies, or sewing, knitting and darning needles, bobbins of thread, buttons, hanks and balls of wool. As well as the ragman with horse and cart, there was the ragwife. She went round the doors collecting, and carried her gatherings wrapped in a blanket or sheet, which she 'humphed' like the coalman but with the sheet-ends enclosing her round the upper arms. Usually accompanied by a child, who was left in the close to guard the bundle to save the woman from having to carry it up the stairs as she made her rounds, she was a sight so reminiscent of the age. Rag women were of that class who picked from what they collected to wear themselves, and the ones I remember appeared to be past middle-age and were invariably stout. It was no uncommon sight to see one bent double, trudging along the road with her bundle which could reach massive proportions, balanced on her backside, with her 'helper' similarly laden struggling along somewhere behind.

Other vendors sold round back-courts, and a child was sent up the stairs with any item ordered by people calling down from their window. Still others had factory rejected or even 'mended' cast-off clothing collected from ragstores, candles, matches, Murray's Diaries or Old Moore's Almanacks. Murray's Diary was a small book of time-tables, about the size of a present day Wee Red Book popular in recent times with football enthusiasts, which gave the times of all train and out-of-town bus services. That book was a very popular and necessary item for anyone who needed to travel, in that age when few had their own transport, when there were few phones and much ignorance of how to use them. There was always a current Murray's in our house, and somehow it was used regularly, particularly in summer.

Usually, hawkers were male, with many different items of the very cheapest kind used in the home which needed to be replaced frequently, such as sweeping and scrubbing brushes, mops, washing cloths, clothes rope, buckets made of ungalvanised iron that quickly rusted away, pipe-clay, floor polish and dusters. A point stressed elsewhere has to be made again. It is that virtually all these utensil items are still available today made from that ubiquitous material, plastic, in various forms. Some callers had firelighters and sticks, or kirbygrips and hairnets. The latter items is generally unknown today, but may still be available for older women. All women wore their hair long, some keeping it tidily confined inside a hairnet, while among men, only tramps and oddities let their hair grow long. They were generally a target of ridicule in the street. At that time only a very few women of the 'arty' class began to wear their hair short. This was considered very daring, and if they smoked as well they were regarded as being 'fast'. Begging was common, from soliciting of spare coppers (pennies) round the doors, of which there was little to spare, to men and women singers, one of whom had the bearing of someone in poor health who, with his singing, generated an uneasy feeling that overwhelmed me. When he appeared, accompanied by children, who may or may not have been his, I had to run off out of earshot. I was avoiding him for a reason that only now, examining it more closely am I able to identify, as it comes to mind for the first time in more than half-a-century. It was simply a desire to help without having the means. All hawkers, beggars and entertainers were subjected to the inevitable indignity of scrambling about on the ground for coppers thrown down to them, although usually money was wrapped in a twist of paper.

In local slang the midden was 'the midgy', and among the lower elements of society, at the stage before being consigned to the poorhouse and lower even than beggars, were the 'midgy rakers'. These poor souls, often the most physically disabled to be encountered, were subjected to much scornful abuse on their rounds of back-courts, and regarded with revulsion by everybody. They were invariably either mentally impaired, or crippled in some way, such as having only one arm or leg, or a withered limb or a hump, or one of many other physical deformities like dwarfism or obesity. One character had a most frightful squint and such a wide-eyed stare that children, and some women, were terrified of him. When he appeared the backcourts cleared as if by magic. Most came round in irregular rotation, from one or two who passed through daily whom you could almost set your clock by, to the occasional or once-only figure. They carried a sack or bag and were, of course, looking for anything of value, like scrap metal or returnable bottles, and some more than likely wouldn't turn up their noses at discarded food raked out from among the ash. Their like are never encountered today round the domestic rubbish containers, but is it because people do not need to do this, or because modern methods of rubbish-gathering in high- and low-rise buildings render access to it difficult? There are possibly some folk in the lower levels of our present society who would liken this activity to prospecting for gold, and would welcome the opportunity to indulge in it.

Another caller, one who usually kept to the streets rather than back-courts, was the knife sharpener. He appeared at infrequent intervals with his unique equipment in the form of a single-wheeled work-bench. To describe it will be taxing, but it has to be attempted because of the period interest. The grinder who frequented our district had an open spar timber structure about 4 feet x 4 feet x 1 foot. Inside it was mounted a single relatively small spoked cart-type wheel, which was the means of moving the bench about. With it lowered off the wheel onto a side, the drive for the grinding wheel was provided by a foot-operated treadle working through a push-rod to a crank on the large wheel shaft. On the same shaft was a large pulley round which a belt passed, which drove a smaller pulley at the high speed needed on the grinding wheel shaft. The grinder parked his barrow/bench at each close or shop, such as butchers and provision merchants, in turn, and went round asking for knives and scissors to sharpen. He then worked away busily on the treadle sending showers of sparks from his grindstone.

A curious pedlar we saw only occasionally, one of the seldom encountered foreigners, was the 'onion Johnny', or in the east coast form of my grandmother I knew him by, 'ingin Johnny', from France. They probably kept away from working-class areas because of the necessity, if they had to go round tenement doors, of leaving their wares unguarded in the street or back court. I certainly remember seeing them in the thirties, and they may have returned after we moved to Pollok at the end of the war. Perhaps they sold mainly to retailers such as greengrocers, although they were seen regularly calling round villas and terrace houses. Those I saw were short, wiry and tanned dark brown, of odd bucolic appearance, complete with beret, a kind of waistcoat, smock, neck-cloth and gaiters. They apparently came from Brittany, a region of France reputedly renowned for the quality of its onions. They travelled around on peculiar bikes, obviously foreign models, festooned with pleated strings of onions, which hung in long strings all round from handlebars and panniers. Both mudguards had stiff netting strung over them and fixed tautly to the spindle to keep the onions from getting caught up in the spokes. Just how they operated and acquired replacement stock remained a mystery to me until recently. I used to imagine them selling all their stock in a morning, and having to cycle all the way back to that impossibly remote and foreign place called France for a fresh supply later in the day. Recently, an elderly knowledgeable friend indicated they had only to go as far as Fife, where they rented a store.

CHAPTER 4

Domestic Chores and Street and Backcourt Games

Enclosed back-courts which formed open wells within a tenement block, like the two on the north side of Skipness Drive, were somewhat more sheltered than those in other incomplete blocks, although that shelter was confined to reducing wind force. As far as drying a washing was concerned a breeze will dry it quicker than no wind, so our situation was a mixed blessing. In a strong wind the worst effect was reduced but on days of light winds which would be considered ideal for drying, there would be hardly a breath of air within the block.

Sometimes there was a conflict of domestic cleaning chores between different households, an example of which is one woman putting out a washing while another wanted to beat her carpets. It will be understood that those two tasks couldn't be undertaken in close proximity. Mother used say about a neighbour 'I wish she'd hurry up and take her washing in so that I can get the carpets done', and the converse complaint: 'Look at her in the next back(-court) beating her carpets and letting the dust fly over my washing.' Before the arrival of the suction cleaner, or before working-class families could afford one, for they were long since available to the wealthy, carpets had to be taken down weekly to have the dirt beaten out, another of the many Friday cleaning jobs. Energetic and houseproud women did this daily with kitchen rugs from the area of heaviest traffic. Few households could afford a Goblin or a Hoover cleaner, but mechanical carpet sweepers were cheap enough. Mum had an early Ewbank which was good for lifting surface dirt, but would have been useless long-term on fitted carpets, or in place of an almost permanent cleaner like a Hoover. (Chapter 5 contains a description of the layout of the back courts, and how they were divided one from the other by chest high spiked iron railings.)

To protect carpets slung over railings for beating, most back-courts had a piece of hardwood 3 inches by 2 inches or 2 inches by 2 inches, four or five feet long, which had probably been fitted by the husband of a community spirited resident in the past. It was hammered over the top of a section of spikes in a convenient position away from low-down windows, and tied down by a loop of twisted wire at each end, over the spar and under the top horizontal of the railing, to prevent it being stolen. To this spar, which had the corners and edges worn down and polished by probably decades of use, housewives brought their carpets. Rugs were thrown over it to have the dirt beaten out with a carpet beater, then finished off with the carpet brush. Carpets, perhaps fortunately, were not all that common. Our house had what was probably an average number, about a half-dozen rugs, none bigger than 6 feet by 3 feet. The day of a room-size (12 feet by 9 feet) carpet did not arrive for us until after the war, and fitted carpets, unknown to us until the 1960s, were looked on initially with suspicion because of the impossibility of taking them out and beating them! The reasoning was: how could you possibly keep a big carpet like that clean over a long period? But experience proved that the suction cleaner was up to the job.

A carpet-beating implement could be any handy stick, a walking stick even. However, it was usually a device made for the job from cane, with a business end shaped like a tennis racket, which could be bought in any hardware shop. Mum's beater had a large dinner plate size head, with the cane, made up of as many as six strands, basket-woven on a flat plane into a decorative but functional disc, with open loops round the edge. The strand ends were gathered together and wound tightly and, strengthened with wire in the centre, formed into a handle a couple of feet long with a loop on the end for hanging on a nail. The beating job was finished off by removing fluff, threads and hair still adhering with a carpet brush of the type still used today. The beater was sometimes pressed into use as a disciplinary tool on naughty children, and although I can't remember being beaten with one, it might just be a subconscious desire not to want to remember.

Another item used in the home, which could also be made to

perform a disciplinary role, was Dad's razor strop, called, with a certain menace, the strap. For about twenty years, until he died in 1926, Grandfather William Rountree had a barber's shop at 56 Queen Street (Neptune Street), and as the son of a barber my father used an open cut-throat razor until he acquired his first electric shaver in the early 1950s, although it was long after this time before he finally gave up using the cut-throat. Safety razors were available and most men used one, but some preferred the open razor. Cut throat users' tackle consisted of razor, strop, shaving brush and shaving soap (cream was in the future), styptic pencil, mug, and a sheet of newspaper to wipe the razor on. The soap was round, like a section cut off a rod, could be purchased as a refill, and was kept in a hexagonal bakelite container having a round screwed end with a recess into which the plug of soap was pushed. To perform successfully the delicate job it was used for, an open razor has to be made from the finest steel and be precision ground to get the cutting edge exactly right. Although Dad had a grindstone for this job I never saw him use it. In fact, because he seemed to lack the skill needed for some ordinary jobs which crop up around the house, I would be surprised to know that he ever did use it; but his razor was carefully stropped before every shave.

The strop was a length of thin leather about three inches wide by eighteen inches long, with a teardrop-shaped leather covered plug-of-wood handle at one end, and a hole with a metal eyelet at the other, by which it hung permanently from a cup-hook screwed in at the side of the kitchen sink cupboard. Standing at the sink and holding the strop taut, he carefully flicked the razor back and forth along it, always with the cutting edge trailing. After soaking the shaving brush in the mug of hot water, he would rub it on the soap until he worked up a good lather. Then, after rubbing a little soap directly on his chin, he applied the brush, working it all round up to his side-boards, rubbing it vigorously in for a few minutes to soften the growth and generate a good dense froth.

The actual cutting of the stubble caused the blade to collect a lot of lather with each stroke, but strangely enough it was simply wiped off on a piece of newspaper. Even in barbers' shops that was the practice. Why did they not just clean the blade under a running tap, I used to wonder? It was so obviously a quick and simple way, but would have meant drying the blade between each stroke. However, the cutting edge was so delicate that no matter how carefully it was wiped, the wiping always removed some of the keenness from the edge. But that should also have applied to wiping off on paper. Queuing in the barber's shop for a haircut, I used to watch fascinated as the service was performed. With the customer tilted back on the adjustable chair, a square of newspaper, or in better-class establishments, tissue in a form somewhat different from today's - the crisp rustling kind, resting on his shoulder convenient for wiping the blade on, the barber worked away with deft strokes. Eventually the piece of paper was covered with the now dense foam, darkly streaked with whorls of hair, which at home was disposed of in the fire, or by barbers into a bin. The styptic pencil, a small white rod not unlike a thick sweetie cigarette, was a treatment used to staunch bleeding which, like iodine, stung like fire. It was required more often when using a cut-throat than with a safety razor. Iodine, in a small bottle of dark glass, was always kept at home for dabbing on cuts or scratches with cotton wool. Because it nipped like a burn I hated it, despite assurances that 'It was good for you!' but the stinging didn't last for long. Further fascination, tinged with apprehension, was induced by the word 'Poison' with a skull and cross-bones sign moulded on the bottle, which conjured up thoughts like 'Was this really the stuff that murderers used?'

The function of the leather strop on the blade was as a final polishing medium, to remove any minute nicks and rags left by honing, or by previous use or misuse. Never having dared to try using an open razor I have no experience to quote from. As suggested before, an alternative function for the strop was that it could be used to frighten me into behaving when I needed it. But like the non-existent memory of being punished with the carpet beater there is no memory of actually being beaten with that strap. My father said that as a youngster going into his teens, and one of his younger brothers after him, he helped his dad in the shop as soap boy. He prepared customers by soaping their faces, for his dad to perform what is after all a very delicate service. This seemed to have been the main function, or at least one equal in importance to cutting hair, of barbers' shops at that time, borne out by the old sign outside, the red-and-white stick-of-rock-like barber's pole. Red represents blood, and white bandage, or so I was told. Before the arrival of the safety razor, and subsequently the electric shaver, a surprisingly large proportion of men were dependent on barbers, probably because of the expertise required with preparation and use of the open razor. Thank goodness for the present-day convenience of the safety razor and electric shaver, for I do not fancy one bit allowing a stranger near me with a cut-throat at the ready, even some I've had shave me daily for years, because mental instability can surface without warning.

The lamplighter

Side-streets and closes in older districts, like the two tenement areas we lived in during the 1930s, were gaslit and each light required to be lit at dusk and extinguished at dawn. Pilot lights were unknown and the work was done by men employed as lamplighters. The lamplighter was a figure in a green uniform with peaked cap employed by the Corporation Lighting Department, who hurried round the streets evenings and mornings at a brisk walk carrying a lighting pole. Side-street lights on their low cast iron posts were twelve to fifteen feet high, with a pair of decorative/functional horizontally opposed arms below the lantern aligned parallel with the street. The lantern was a square-section metal box frame with glass sides, which flared up and outwards from a small base, above which was a metal cap surmounted by an ornamental finial.

In view of the large number of old photographs in various collections in which street lamps can be seen, the above description is almost superfluous, although explaining how they worked may be desirable. Street lamplighters carried a long pole on the end of which was the brass lighting unit. The tip had an arrangement for turning on or off the gas tap, a recessed slot in a slim extension at the business end of the pole, and a cowled naked flame to light the mantle. At the top of the post, under the lantern, the supply pipe emerged suitably bent to shape for access, with the tap fitted inverted like the domestic gaslight described earlier. A hinged glass flap in the base was pushed up with the tip, allowing the unit access, and the light applied to the mantle. Lamplighters' work included keeping the lantern glass clean and replacing mantles when required. He did this during the day by carrying around with him a long ladder which reached the crossarms. In some areas lamps carried street names in white letters on a narrow blue strip at the top of each glass face.

It may have been the same man who did both jobs within a district, but the stairlight man carried a shorter thicker pole and a short narrow and rather neat ladder on his lamp-maintenance visits. My mental picture is of him hurrying along intent on daytime cleaning tasks, carrying his ladder with an arm through a rung, with dusters hanging out of his bulging jacket pockets. Stair lights were glass faced cubes with a shallow-domed top, the sides of which were about eight or nine inches square. Usually mounted out of reach from ground level, they were fixed on the outer angles of corners in closes, to spread their meagre illumination as far as possible, and on each main landing upstairs. They were lit in the same way as street lights. Gas lights and stoves were subject to an irritating fault involving the airvent. Sometimes the flame travelled back along the pipe and landed with a 'plop' at the vent, burning with a muted roar and the white flame of pure gas, which gave off a pungent smell. This was liable to occur if the vent had been opened too far in trying to obtain the hottest flame, or could be caused by a draught. Street and close lights were often affected in this way in windy weather, which left the light very dim and the close reeking with the sulphurous smell.

The lamplighter's portable light was a naked flame inside a brass cowl generated by the chemical reaction between carbide and water, which produced acetylene gas. The broad part of the brass fitting on the end of the pole had two compartments; one held carbide and the other water, and a hole between them, with the aperture controlled by an adjustable screw, allowed water to leak by the required amount into the carbide. From there the gas produced was piped up to burn in the jet. Acquiring some carbide was a signal for a great deal of excitement among us street urchins, because it could be used to make loud bangs.

For this prank, in addition to carbide an empty tin and a little water were needed. But the escapade was only made possible because at the end of an evening shift some lamplighters would empty out the residue left in the container at the pavement edge. Amounting usually to something like an eggcupful, it may have been discarded because if left in the container perhaps it had a corrosive effect on the metal. Carbide is a greyish white powder which had been used in vehicle lights before battery-powered systems of lighting were developed. When damp it cakes into lumps, and in lump form it was easiest to collect, and in disposing of it all the lamplighter had to do to disperse it and make it impossible to gather it up in a usable form, was draw his foot through it. Maybe some 'leeries' were aware of this who were still boys at heart, and deliberately made it possible for us to have our fun. Today carbide is probably treated as a dangerous chemical with a list of regulations governing its handling, and even at that time there probably were instructions issued to lamplighters about its use and disposal. Some disposed of it as I've described, and it was known for boys to surreptitiously follow the man on his round in the hope that they would spot him in the act of doing this, and so be able to acquire the small amount needed.

Second item required for this game was an empty tin with a lid of a particular design. Certain brands of such grocery items as cocoa, baking powder, Creamola Foam etc. were sold in tins of this type, with a tight-fitting round lid that pressed into a recess. Other kinds with lids which fitted over the outside of the top were less safe for the job, but could be pressed into use if none of the correct kind could be found. Finding the right kind was usually a rather sordid tale of midden raking, a practice made necessary when the first line of endeavour, going round our houses and asking our mothers if one of the required type was available. This ploy was usually unsuccessful because the mums in question knew perfectly well what it was wanted for, and being a forbidden game because of the chance of injury, the answer was invariably 'NO — and don't let me catch you playing with that carbide, it's dangerous and if your dad hears about it you'll be for it!,' and so on. We nearly always had to fall back on the only other source, the back court middens. Which meant that the least fussy of our group would have to climb in and rake through ash, rotting food and other unmentionables to find one. If our luck was in and a suitable tin turned up, the next comparatively minor difficulty was to find an implement to make a few small holes in the bottom. That accomplished, there was the problem of the availability or otherwise of matches, lack of which might scupper the game. However, they were in constant use in every house and a box was normally kept on the mantelshelf or at the side of the hob, so it was usually easy to acquire a few from the kitchen, using a chair to reach them on the shelf when our parents' backs were turned.

With those items gathered and the tin holed, a few lumps of carbide were dropped into it. Then a little of the fourth and final and easiest to acquire element needed, moisture, was added. It was sometimes provided by the nearest puddle, group members spitting into the tin, or even by someone pissing in it, then the lid was quickly pressed tightly in place. At this stage the carbide could be heard fizzing away inside producing the gas. Then, with the tin lying on its side, perhaps on the ground but often held out at arms length by one who could be described as the bravest, never me, I hasten to add, with face averted, eyes screwed up tight and a finger stuck in an ear, even although the other one was going to be closer to the bang. The moment we had all been waiting for with mounting excitement had arrived.

A match, perhaps the only one we had, was carefully struck, and being too short for safety the flame was transferred to a piece of paper screwed up into a long taper, which was then held against the holes in the bottom of the can. These preparations were well out of sight of adults, who would have put a stop to it at once, usually in a corner of a back court or in the angle of washhouse and midden not overlooked by windows if possible. Such a location wasn't easy to find in a quadrangular tenement block like ours, so it was sometimes done inside a midden. The resulting bang was surprisingly loud, like a thunderflash in fact, and unless the lid was directed against a wall it was propelled for quite a distance. If there was enough carbide left for another 'go', one of us had to climb over the railings across several back courts to recover it, then we all scampered away from the scene to another location. This activity was infrequent, but how we escaped injury because of the careless way it was handled, and how, among the large crowd of youngsters which invariably gathered for the event, we avoided being hit by the flying lid is a mystery. It never failed to cause windows to be thrown up and heads pop out looking for the cause, and this meant that a different location had to be sought if a repeat performance was possible.

Games variety

Of many games we played in streets and back courts, most seem totally lost to the children of today. With entertainment so well provided they don't need them. Strenuous games, like the half-dozen or so ball games as well as hide-and-seek, leave-oh, kick the can, cops and robbers, gird and cleek, whip and peerie, skates, bogies, stilts, skipping ropes and cowboys and Indians etc. were just some of the many we indulged in. To-days dominant game, football, was less popular than some of those mentioned. It could be put at about the same level as cricket among our group anyway, just one of many games played with a ball. Other marginally less strenuous games such as ball-stoting and beds (peever) were played, like skipping ropes, mainly by girls. Still others, those involving singing or chanting a rhyme and moving in a circle with linked hands, like ring-a-ring-a-roses, were almost always played by the girls. The words of a couple of them and dim memories which conjure that scene, are of half heard rhymes retained without really being fully conscious of them at the time, as chanted by a large group of girls in a nearby back court. 'There's a big ship sailing through the Eeely Ally O!' was one, and another, set out in full in Maureen Sinclair's booklet '*Murder, Murder Polis!*', *Glasgow Street Rhymes and Songs*, begins 'Down in yonder meadow where the green grass grows', with names of individual participants inserted through the verses.

Various activities came and went in an irregular cycle which partly depended on season, so that for a time bools were dominant. Then it was the turn of whips and peeries, or girds and cleeks, followed perhaps by roller skates, pedal cars, trikes (tricycles) and fairy cycles. These latter cost more money than most people could afford so only a few children had one, and even then they were generally second hand or well used hand-me-downs. Other crazes came and went never to be seen again. One of them was the Hi-Li, a thick plywood table-tennis type bat, with a solid rubber ball smaller than a golf ball fixed to it by a length of elastic. Players hit the ball away for it to return. A lot of practice was needed to master it but some children became really skilful. (After writing that last description my grandchildren appeared one day with poor plastic imitations of the hi-li.)

Ball stoting (bouncing) was a skill that looked easy when played by someone who was good at it, and although I tried often to improve my skill it proved too difficult. It needed a quick eye and accuracy in throwing that I just didn't possess. The game needed a tennis size ball, took different forms and was played solo, with a partner, or by a group. Possessing a suitable ball, the next require-ment was a wall, preferably smooth and without windows or at least well away from them, at the back of a pavement with an even surface. Some tenements in Linthouse had stonework with a horizontal angled ledge at waist height in their street frontage, a decorative feature that allowed us to play a local version of this game. The solo game in its simplest form was a matter of standing at the pavement edge and throwing the ball at the wall, aiming to hit the ledge, a strip about three inches wide which lay at an angle of 45 degrees.

If the aim was good and the ball, pitched with the right amount of force, landed square on the ledge, it would return to the thrower in a high curve without a second bounce off the pavement. This seemingly simple pastime sometimes became so absorbing, like today's computer games, that long periods would be spent in continuous pitching by individual boys and girls, in trying to achieve the greatest number of throws without the ball touching the ground. All done, needless to day, much to the annoyance of passers-by. A little bit of frustration was added to the game by the wall having an uneven surface of rough cut stone from about four inches below the ledge which, if the aim was exceptionally poor and the ball landed low enough, could cause it to shoot off to one side so that the player would have to run along the street after it. If played near a house with tenants at home the constant thud of the ball could be very annoying for them, but that was just another difficulty to overcome.

Another form of that game didn't need a ledge. It was played mainly by girls with the player(s) standing near, almost within touching distance, of the wall. The aim was to bounce the ball in a sequence, first off the pavement in a throw angled towards the wall, to bounce off it and return to the thrower. The second throw and double bounce off pavement-and-wall was made standing side on to the wall, with the ball again stoting off the pavement under a leg held out. Third, repeat with the other leg, fourth, standing legs apart facing the wall the ball was thrown from behind to pass between them. Fifth, with back to it. Sixth and seventh, rotate the body once one way and then the other, ending the sequence with a straight throw. Finally, through the sequence again with throw, bend-down-touch-the-ground and catch. Then the sequence began again, and some girls could perform two or even three rotations of the body between the throw, double bounce and catch. I vaguely remember seeing it played by two girls in close co-operation with one ball and sharing the sequences. Ability to throw accurately with the right amount of force and catch well was really the main requirements of the game.

Rounders

While knowledge of the rules and conduct of baseball is minimal, our game of rounders seems to have been similar, though played with, for preference, a tennis ball and racket. We played it in the street, much to the concern for their windows of those tenants whose houses overlooked the chosen pitch. Because of constrictions, layout of bases was in the form of a long diamond, with the long axis along the centre of the street. A square sewer manhole (a 'grater' in local parlance) was a perfect home base, while the half-way base was the next manhole, the distance between them being ideal. The other two bases were marked out mid-way on opposite pavements. The term 'base' wasn't known to us. We called them 'dults' but where that originated isn't known. Rounders was one of many games for which sides had to be chosen from among those wanting to play, so a counting-out rhyme was used.

Once this was done a coin, or more often some other flat object, even a piece of slate or a tin lid, would be tossed to decided which side went in to bat first. The winning side lined up to take their turn, while members of the other side spread themselves out along the street to act as fielders. While hoping for a catch, their main purpose was to retrieve the ball, and throw it back up the pitch to another member of the side better placed for a hit on a runner caught between dults, and knock him out. When someone once produced a genuine baseball ball we were full of enthusiasm about it. Until we came to handle it. When we felt how heavy and solid it was no-one fancied being hit with it, so it was never used. Of course the major difference between real baseball and our game of rounders was that in the former, the ball arriving at a base in front of a runner would knock him out, whereas in the latter, in addition a direct hit on a runner between dults had the same effect.

Strengths and weaknesses of each of us quickly became known, so that some in an obviously weak team would suffer from apathy and fail to try, which could become a source of friction between them and the more determined players on the same side. Generally though, sides were evenly balanced and many good games resulted. While the police seldom harassed us, occasionally a resident would complain to them about a game they considered annoying or dangerous. Football and rounders played in streets or backcourts were two which were liable to come into that category. At rare intervals the 'polis', in the form of a single bobby, with his period high-peaked helmet and tunic buttoned up to the neck, would walk into the street and everybody would take to their heels and vanish up the nearest closes, running through the backcourts and over dykes without stopping until they were a few streets away. The only time I ever saw anyone 'nabbed' was during a season of bogies.

Building and riding on bogies was a favourite with us and a description of this activity will be given presently.

One form of police presence everyone dreaded was the Black Maria, a period van of a type which is sometimes glimpsed on old film and photographs. The crime rate then was lower and it was seen only at rare intervals, and I would not be surprised to discover that the Govan division had only the one vehicle. It was comparable in size to those of today's capacity of two tons. Its main feature was its ominous black forbidding appearance, windowless except for narrow darkened strips high up along the sides. During all of my childhood up to the time I left school, there is no memory, except on that one occasion of the bogie riders having their names taken, of witnessing any police activity other than a foot or cycle patrol passing by. Today, the police presence is almost constant (except when you need one) with their patrol cars regularly seen, and the occasional appearance of foot patrols. In the Linthouse of the thirties a policeman was seldom seen, and when any did appear it was nearly always a single individual, sometimes on a cycle. You really felt you were in the presence of someone in authority when the bobby was around.

Football

Perhaps the true reason football seemed to be less popular with us was that a proper ball was seldom available, for in trying to play it with a tennis ball the game lacked something. Real footballs of the time were in two parts, a rubber inner and a leather outer, similar to pre-radial motor tyres, called 'a bladder'. That probably derived from a time in the past when a bladder from a pig or a sheep was used. The inner was made up of elongated oval strips of rubber stuck together to form a reasonably accurate round shape. Two drawbacks with them compared with a modern plastic ball, was that even when new their ability to hold pressure was less enduring, and they were more easily punctured. Secondly the valve arrangement was similar to a car wheel tube but without the non-return valve, simply a straight-through tube about three inches long. The bladder was encased in a stout outer made of pieces of leather, sometimes oblong shaped, in others hexagonal, stitched together in the form of panelling. On today's expensive plastic footballs that panelling is simulated by embossing, while the cheaper variety usually has them simply printed on.

A three inch long slit in the outer, with a line of holes along each side for lacing, allowed the deflated inner to be forced inside. The difficult part now was to blow it up hard using a cycle pump for preference, failing that by mouth, which was the most common state of affairs with us, by the strongest boy, or preferably by an adult if one could be persuaded to oblige. However, asking an older boy or adult was something to be avoided if possible, because they invariably wanted to play and usually finished up monopolising the game. When the inner was blown up as hard as possible the tube was folded over, the cock we called it, and tied tightly with string so that there was no escape of air, which needed strong fingers. Even with this successfully accomplished it was by no means the end of the work. Against the bulging pressure of the inner the valve had to be forced inside the outer casing and underneath the protective tongue, tongue as in shoe, and the slit laced up tightly while ensuring that no grit or anything likely to cause a puncture got inside.

Each stage of preparing a bladder for play was difficult. No matter how tightly the tying up had been done, because of a natural loss of pressure the ball seldom remained playable for long so that the whole process had to be gone through fairly often. It is recalled faintly that at official games a supply of freshly prepared balls had to be kept ready, and frequent changes made. Actual lacing of the ball was often the cause of trouble because a lacing implement, a special large needle with a broad flat curved section near the point, had to be used to make it possible to thread the lace through the holes against the pressure of the inner. As can be imagined, in careless hands this operation could cause a puncture, and laces had to be kept short so that no loose ends flapped about. Although it might appear possible to lace up before blowing up, it couldn't be done because with the lacing in place there was insufficient room to force the cock inside. That description assumes a bladder and outer was available, but this was seldom the case with us, so when we did play football it was usually with an unsuitable ball.

Wide ranging games like football along with rounders, cricket, kick-the-can, leave-oh, and others, needed a proper pitch, and back courts were generally unsuitable because the dividing railings made them too cramped for anything except a gentle kick-about. As well as that they were overlooked by many windows which lay directly in the line of play, so these games were normally played in the street where, hopefully, any hard kicking, hitting, or throwing would be directed along the length. In out street pitches, the goals were usually located in the width of the pavement between a lamp post and the building. Normally lamp posts are staggered, set diagonally on opposite pavements, so our games were played at an angle across the street.

A curious aspect of the football scene was that I don't remember many of my pals being enthusiastic supporters of any team, other than the usual tribal allegiances of Rangers and Celtic in which football was of secondary importance. Which seems to confirm what I have suggested elsewhere about a local apathy towards big time clubs. There is, however, a memory of seeing one or two pals going off to games with their dads, carrying that fiendish period noise maker, a rickety. Here's another implement of former times worthy of description. Entirely made of wood and operated by hand by being swung round in a rotating motion, it produced a most penetrating racket. It was a short stout baton-like stick with a flag on it, but the flag part was a heavy frame able to rotate round the stick. In the centre of the frame was a length of tough springy wood held rigid at the outer end of the flag, with the other end bearing firmly on a ratchet that was part of the handle. When the flag part was whirled round the handle fast, allowing the braced strip to flick off the teeth of the ratchet, it gave off a continuous series of loud snaps a little like drawing a stick along railings.

Not long after we arrived in the district the Maxwell Park became unavailable when the ground was taken over for housing. In the mid-1960s about half of those built in the 30s were demolished during clearance work connected with the building of access roads for the Clyde Tunnel. Those that can be seen there today, plus the row at the top of Kennedar Drive on the west side, were all part of this same development.

Headers, header-football and dodgie-ball

The ball games heedies and heedie-footer, and closes, were made for each other. In those days there were no closes with entrance doors, for controlled entry did not arrive until after the 1960s. The first few yards of the majority of Linthouse tenement closes from the street entrance, were straight, high and narrow, until the first house door was encountered. Beyond this point were the stairs to the upper floors. Others were straight through from front to rear of the building with the staircase lowest flight inset to one side. Most closes, however, made a double right-angle turn at the point where the stairs began, and this was the best kind to play in because on scoring an inward goal the stairs were a barrier, stopping the ball from running on into the back-court, avoiding a delay while it was recovered. A youngster of about twelve stretching out his arms could just about touch each wall with finger tips, so here was a ready made pitch for these popular games. The rules were that in headers only goals scored with a header counted, but in header-football a kick was allowed in certain circumstances. Conditions of play had to be agreed before play started. Such as did heights (a high ball) count as a goal? How close could you be to your opponent's end when you hit the ball? If your hand touched the ball during a save in heedie-footer you weren't allowed a kick.

Playing this or any other noisy game in a close (not your own if you could avoid it because of the greater risk of being reported to your parents) was always accompanied by apprehension, for grumpy tenants would be out smartly to chase you off. Ideally you waited until those tenants went out before starting, but even then people from upstairs would be liable to complain if the game was particularly noisy. Usually you took a chance and started quietly in the hope that no-one would notice, or that only the more tolerant tenants would, giving a longer spell of play. The best closes to play in were where the bedrooms of low down houses were next to the close, and hopefully, anyone at home would be in the kitchen and maybe far enough away, so that any noise generated would not bother them too much. Another not insignificant problem was that the ball hitting the upper whitewashed section of wall and roof sometimes dislodged flakes which made a mess. This further increased residents' resistance to ball games in their close.

Dodgie-ball was simply a form of tig played in the street with a ball, though with one other difference. The ball, tennis size, was used by whoever was counted out to be 'het' to hit others, and anyone they managed to hit had to join them in trying to do the same to the rest, and last one hit was het for the next game. Another game, a variation of dodgie-ball, required a big expanse of blank wall up to three storeys high. We were fortunate in having just such a wall in Skipness Drive, to the west of Clachan Drive, that can still be seen today. It was a peculiar result of the design of the building, which had at this point a broad chimneyhead (since removed) built flush above the wall at roof level, giving it about eight feet of additional height above three storeys. Layout of houses in the close nearest in Clachan Drive must have been such that all flues ran up the outside wall here. False windows had been built into the stonework to maintain symmetry of the facade, which added interest to the game. I suspect it might have been a spontaneous invention by the children in our area because of the almost uniqueness of the wall feature, for there is no recollection of seeing one like it anywhere else.

After a counting out session, the winner among those taking part selected the minimum level to which the ball had to be thrown. Usually it was to full three-storey height to allow sufficient reaction time, but sometimes, to generate greater tension, a lower height was chosen. This, however, tended to cause bunching, and throws to one-storey-up meant that the concentrated rushing about of the tight-knit group resulted in accidents, and induced in us what is now recognised as neurosis of the 'Get-oot-ma-road-you' type, while giving a violent push against someone you think is going to be in your way. This was likely to be answered by an aggressive retort of the 'Who d'ye think yer shovin' variety, usually accompanied by an agitated glare. Then the 'dukes' were up, Dukes being fists, presumably after the Duke (Marquis?) of Queensberry. Winner of the count had first throw and pitched the ball against the wall above the level chosen, at the same time calling out the name of a fellow player. This named player had to be in a position to catch it before it touched the ground, and if he missed or dropped it, he then had to field the ball, chase the others and try to hit someone and knock them out. The excitement generated could be quite effective, with the surge of the crowd as a throw was taken and a name shouted, and the collective subconscious question in every mind, 'Should I run out of range now in case the boy named misses it — but what if he catches it then throws and calls my name?, I might be too far away to catch it!'. It was the essence of the game for the thrower to call the name of the person he thought least likely to catch it.

It wasn't always possible to play unhindered because there were house windows nearby and people did complain, but they were room windows and the game could usually go on without tenants noticing. The full height of a three-storey tenement over the roof ridge was just about the limit of our throwing ability, and attempting this sometimes caused the ball to lodge in the gutter or behind a chimney head. When that happened it was truly lost — until a chimney sweep or slater went up on the roof to work. If a long time had elapsed since anyone had been up there, a few balls might have gathered, and he would throw them down. In those days balls weren't ten a penny, like they appear to be today. They were treasured because they cost money and money was scarce, so a roof visit by a workman and a consequent rain of balls was treated as manna from heaven.

From what I've observed of the activities of the current generation of children, only a tiny handful of the games we played are indulged in today, in fact the only two that come immediately to mind are tig and football. One of the many bat-and-ball games was called French cricket. The batsman's legs were the wickets and guarded by the bat, preferably a mini cricket bat. If the ball hit a leg or he played a catch, or if he moved his feet, he was out. What made it tricky was having to keep his feet firmly planted on the same spot, and be bowled from whichever angle the ball happened to lie in, so that if he missed a shot from the front the next ball came from behind.

Leave-oh and kick-the-can

Leave-oh was like dodgie-ball played without a ball, with sides chosen by two 'leaders'. Whichever side was het had to chase after and catch the others and put them in a den, usually a marked out section of pavement. The den needed to be watched carefully thereafter because anyone still free would be hovering around watching for an opportunity to run through it shouting 'Leave-oh,' releasing any 'prisoners' confined there. Playing kick-the-can in Skipness Drive at the corner of Clachan Drive on a warm summer evening with a group of up to a dozen pals, is a powerful memory. This game was similar to hide-and-seek, except that an empty tin was used as primary control. Again, an area of pavement was designated as the den, and if chalk or pipe-clay was available it would be marked out and the tin, recovered from the nearest midden, was placed at the outer edge next to the suiver. (Suiver, the first syllable pronounced as in sigh, is the gutter. It was an old term always used by my father and older people even today).

After counting out, the same system was used for kick-the-can as for hide-and-go-seek, as we called it. Whoever was het had to cover their eyes and count up hundreds by fives, five-ten-fifteen-twenty, twenty-five-thirty and so on according to how many were taking part, six hundred if there were six for example, while the rest rushed off to hide. Covering of eyes was taken very seriously indeed. With the simple hands over eyes method, it was considered too easy to cheat by squinting through fingers to see where the others were heading, so a more effective method was devised. Anyone het had to stand against the wall, the usual location of a den, hold an arm up so that it formed an upside down U and lean with their face buried in the U. A short cut in counting was permitted by saying five-ten-double-ten, five-ten-a-hundred once for each partici-pant. He then went off to look for the others, and on spying someone had to run back to the den and shout out the correct phrase incorporating the boy's name, at the same time banging the .

tin on the ground. Wording of the phrase was important in that if it was said incorrectly the boy named took no notice. It was '(Boy's name) IN DEN ONE-TWO-THREE'. The person so named had to return to the den and sit on the pavement with his back against the wall hoping for release.

The het boy continued to seek out the others, while keeping a sharp lookout for someone sneaking out of a close, or even shadowing an adult by walking close behind, in an effort to get near enough to perform the release. When he thought it was safe to do so, if he was close enough and the het boy too far away to stop him, he ran forward and kicked the can as far as he could. Those held in the den could then run off, and a fresh phase of the game began when the het boy had recovered the can. Next one het was the last to be spied, but this system, as applied to all games, came to be looked on as flawed when it was realised that the craftier players were seen to be not really bothering to hide, and were thus able to avoid what was regarded by some as the stigma of being het.

One peculiar and amusing feature of chasing and hiding games was a device for calling a temporary halt to the game. If the robust physical activity became too much for anyone, if for example they ran out of puff or if someone had been hurt, or for any other reason real or imagined, they held their clenched fists out with the thumbs up and shouted 'Ah'm keys'. Billy Connolly uses this phrase occasionally in his comedy routine, and I sometimes wonder how many know where it came from, for he never bothers to explain. Observance of this depended somewhat on the amount of authority possessed by the caller. If it was a younger boy frequently no-one paid any heed and the game would roll on over him, but if it was an older boy, someone able to command attention, then everybody else was supposed to freeze until the emergency was over. It will be seen that it was open to abuse, which of course did happen but not often.

Many of the counting-out rhymes referred to will be found in the book, mentioned previously, first published in 1986, with another edition in 1989, by Maureen Sinclair, some of which I had never encountered before. Most others had some variation in words from what we used. Copies will be found in libraries or in the Glasgow

Collection room at the Mitchell Library. Almost all of the rhymes remembered: 'Dic-dic-tation, Corporation'; 'One potato, two potato, three potato, four' (using clenched fists held out in front), etc., are there.

Marbles

Marbles, bools or jauries, names for the same activity, were a favourite game. They are seldom seen today, and those that are, are never used for the games we played. They are regarded simply a curiosities by modern children who have little or no idea what they were for, and they will surely disappear altogether. It might therefore be a good idea to put down a full description, or as much as can be remembered, of them and of the three games we played with them in the late 1930s. Marbles then were clear or shaded glass balls roughly five-eighths of an inch in diameter, usually with coloured blotches or twists in the centre giving a pleasing effect, and bestowing on particularly attractive ones a reputation for being lucky when used as a plunker. Ball bearings of similar size could also be used although they were sometimes frowned on because it was felt their weight gave them an unfair advantage. The best and most highly prized and rarest kind were white, made of a porcelain-like material with a finish similar to that on a pottery sink, with two thin twists of red on the surface running from pole to pole. These whities, which had a name that cannot be recalled, were regarded as luckiest of all and if you had one you always used it as a plunker.

'Plunking' was the word we used to describe dodging school. The first time I heard the modern term 'dogging' in this context was when my sons were at school three decades on. It also described the action fundamental to games with marbles, the single exception being the initial throw. Unless you were caurie fisted (left handed) plunking was done with the fingers of the right hand formed into a hook, and held down so that the first joints of the fingers beyond the knuckle rested on the ground. Then, with the hand held vertical with a bool gripped in the curl of the index finger and thumb braced behind it, when the grip was released suddenly and the bool flicked with the thumb, it would travel a distance and direction according to aim and the amount of pressure used. Another style of plunking was employed by those regarded as being highly skilled, for shots needing more force than usual. It was done with the bool braced between the tips of first and second fingers and thumb, with hand held flat knuckles down. In trying to demonstrate these actions to my grandson, Paul, it has been impressed on me just how much skill it required. The ability I seemed to remember so well just could not be recaptured, probably because of the passage of fifty years since it was last tried, and no doubt a touch of arthritis has something to do with it also.

There were three basic games of marble, ringie, moshie and the third, I think, was called rollie. This latter game was played most often. It involved each participant rolling their bool down the camber from the middle of the road, the surface of which, of our local streets, had that silky smooth asphalt surface described elsewhere in these pages, to see which one stopped closest to the kerb, the owner of which then had first go. The object thereafter was for each in turn, determined by proximity to the kerb, to hit, by plunking, someone else's bool with their own for an agreed number of times, and if you succeeded you kept his bool. The best games were those with the largest number of players, but the exact form of the rules of this particular scenario are now very hazy. Anyway, it involved the usual dilemma. Should you roll down in close proximity to the others and risk being second (or worse) in order of play, giving those with turns ahead of you easy shots, or farther away and winning first shot that was made more difficult by distance?

Rules seem to have been variable by agreement among players before beginning, whether it was (1) a free-for-all (which allowed you to aim for the nearest bool) or were you confined to aiming for either the bool of the player in front of you or the one behind?, or (2) how many hits you had to make to claim a bool. In the latter case it could be as many as six, and if there was a large number of players you had to keep your wits about you in keeping track of your hits on the others and theirs on yours. If a needle match developed the number of hits might be reduced to one, causing a fast turnover of bools. But this was unusual because it was unpopular with the less skilled, who lost most. Those who were good at it quickly learned it was better to play a long game and win a few marbles, than agitate for a short game to win a few, which the losers very soon tired of and called 'The gemme's a bogey', citing some imagined infringement of the rules but really indicating they were fed up losing.

Moshie, or moashie — with the first syllable sounding as in motor, was played on a piece of bare earth by selecting a flat area and digging a tea cup size hole. Then, from a distance measured by three long juvenile paces, roughly 10ft, the bools were thrown to roll towards the hole one at a time. The owner of the bool which finished closest to the hole, and the others in rotation, then tried to roll, by plunking, aiming to put the bool in the hole. At that point the resemblance to golf ceases. If you succeeded you were free to hit another bool, then into the hole and another hit and so on for the agreed number of times. The final game, ringie, was different from the other two in that it didn't involve hitting your opponents play-bool. Each player contributed a certain number of bools. These were placed round the circumference groove of a circle scored on the earth or chalked on a hard surface, and made big enough to hold all the bools, well spaced out, by all participants. If six took part and they agreed that each should put in three bools, then at the start there would be eighteen on the ring, and if its diameter was about six inches, spacing between them was such that a plunked bool could roll through the ring without hitting any.

When the ring was set up with the staked bools in position, and after counting out for turns and marking the point from which to throw, each player tried with their initial throw to get as near the ring as possible. With this first throw you weren't allowed to knock any out the ring. If that happened, any displaced had to be put back on their original position and the throw retaken when the next turn came round. Then, in turn by plunking, you tried to knock as many as possible out the ring, which you kept. Various disagreements arose with the three games, the most common of which was called moodgying, meaning picking up your bool for a shot and attempting to play from a position nearer the target than the spot where it had rested. Another was moving your hand forward when plunking, giving more momentum to your shot than you could otherwise put into it. In ringie, if you were snookered from the ring you were allowed to move round in an arc for a clear shot, and yet another ploy was fiddling the angle of arc to shorten the distance.

At this distance in time it is difficult to say whether or not I was good at bools, but I never had to buy any. By the time I reached school leaving age a fair collection had been gathered, most of which were given away to the younger ones. Other skills, or lack of them, are easy to recall. At football I was among the last to be picked when sides were chosen, only just ahead of the smallest boys. The situation with certain other games was different, because I could achieve good long distance throws, in rounders for example though not with any accuracy. Occasionally there was the 'honour' of a turn of picking a side for rounders, dodgieball or cricket.

The expression 'The gemme's a bogey', usually followed by 'The man's in the loabey', the latter or no apparent relevance that I can think of other than it rhymed, occasionally heard echoing round the streets emanating from among groups of playing children, was commonly used to indicate a temporary abandonment of a game. If, for example, one of the players was subjected to the ultimate indignity of being called up by their mother to go a message, usually for a pint of milk or a loaf of bread, or it was their bedtime, or someone was detected cheating during a game. In particular it was used during hiding games like hide-and-seek, to alert those out of sight of what was happening, with loud calls of 'The gemme's a bogey, The man's in the loabey.'

Ropes

Ropes was the word applied to the game of skipping ropes. It was regarded mainly as a girls' game which took a number of different forms. One, called wee ropes, was played with a short length of rope just long enough for one child to play, which gave the freedom to run about while skipping. If bought it had wooden lollipop type handles. These could also be operated stationery by two 'ca'ing' while a third performed the jumps. Amazing skill and dexterity could be acquired in skipping so that it was entertaining to watch, making it look easy and beguiling the novice to join in in order to show off. After attempting it once or twice and making a fool of myself, I gave up and had to be content to watch as others, mainly girls, displayed their skill. Probably because of this, few of the names of the various ropes games register in recollection. Some girls, and a few boys, could work the ropes with skilful timing, whipping up such a speed of rotation that two and even three 'turns' of the rope might be made for each hop. A lone player could alternate with crossed arms, if done with the rope turned at a suitably slow speed and if it was of the correct weight, suitably supple and kink resistant. Otherwise, as it whirled round another person could, by a well timed approach, join in and jump close too in unison with the original skipper. If they were an exceptional team a third could take part as well, by joining in with one in front and the other at the rear of the rope operator.

The best ropes game, big ropes, was the one in which an unlimited number of participants took part, using a piece of rope as long as was manageable, a length of clothes line for preference. Life expired clothes rope or pulley rope was the easiest to acquire, but really the best was window cord, with its slightly oily texture when new giving it just the right weight, if a piece of sufficient length could be acquired. At its height, the ropes 'season' saw teams strung along the street, with players in each forming a crocodile which moved in a figure of eight, with members awaiting their turn to join in with a well timed lunge. The long rope was turned in majestic slow motion, while each player in turn hovered beside an ender, and swayed backwards and forwards in synchronisation as the rope passed by their nose. Then, at the critical moment, he or she darted in within its arc and began the timed jumps, hopping their way along to the opposite end. Nearing the end they swooped out and passed round the back of the 'ender' there, as the person ca'ing was called, and joined the queue of individuals awaiting the end of the crocodile to pass, to begin the next sequence. Anyone fouling the rope and breaking the rhythm had to take a turn as an ender.

One form of the game was 'wavy', but recollection differs between contemporaries of how it operated. One school maintains that the rope was simply waved with a gentle rhythm from side to side, rather than ca'ed in full circular loops, while jumping took place in the same way as above. The writer recalls seeing the game start like this then, when a certain stage was reached, the speed of the wave was increased until the rope went over the top and continued as full speeding-up turns. This may have been the game accompanied by the rhyme which began — salt, pepper, vinegar, mustard etc. The other school say the waves were made by relatively quick flicks of the rope, snakelike, by the enders, producing unsynchronised oscillations which run towards each other, causing real difficulty for the jumpers.

Girds and cleeks, and whips and peeries

Of many non-competitive pastimes, girds and cleeks was one of the most popular. A gird was a circle of steel wire of a gauge heavy enough to maintain its shape without distorting while in use, of various sizes from $1^1/_2$ to 3 feet in diameter. It was propelled along the street by a cleek made of the same metal. The cleek was a rod more than a foot long with a loop at one end to give a firm grip, and usually shaped into a hook at the other, which was angled and formed and held over the gird in the 4 o'clock position. Another form of cleek had a second closed loop instead of a hook and was attached loosely, but permanently, to the gird by a small separate loop. Girds were common but I never had one, neither can I remember any member of our group having one, which might account for a personal feeling of indifference towards them. Much practice was required for proper control, so as to get the most enjoyment from running round the streets with a gird, making it go where you wanted. There were opportunities to try it, but because of difficulties encountered, failing to understand that it needed plenty of practice to master it, gird running was looked on as a boring pastime.

Whips and peeries required only a minimum of skill and were cheap to buy, so virtually every child had them. A peerie was on average a 3" long by 2 to $2^1/_2$" in diameter wooden turning, one end of which was flat and smooth, the other having a rounded taper which ended in a dome headed nail driven in at the point. In shape somewhat like a short fat bullet. Full diameter was maintained for half the length before the taper began, and in the area near the flat end, along with other turned decorative lines, a wide shallow groove was formed for the cord of the whip to be wound in. The whip was just a length of cane usually, with a couple of feet of string tied on to the tip. The object was to start the peerie spinning, either by a flick of the fingers, which wasn't as easy for young fingers to accomplish as might be imagined, or by winding the string round in the groove by as many turns as there was string. Then, holding the peerie upright in a loose grip with the point on the ground, if the whip was pulled away quickly the turning motion imparted by the unwinding string set it spinning. It could then be kept in motion by lashing it with the whip, while taking care not to spoil the spin by hitting it accidentally with the cane instead of the cord.

Children who were deft could keep the peerie going almost on the same spot, while others tended to drive it in the direction of whipping. Still others, who thought that force was what was needed, would lash away at it so that the cord was unable to unwind quickly enough. If that happened the peerie could become a dangerous missile. Peerie spinning could be made more interesting by marking concentric circles on the flat top in different coloured chalks, and varying this with radial lines produced a kaleidoscope of colours that changed as you watched, and as the speed of rotation was altered with the whip.

Peever (or beds)

Peever and beds are two names for a game in which a circular piece of marble an inch thick and between 3" and 4" in diameter, with smooth faces and a rough edge, was used. Beds were drawn on road or pavement surfaces in chalked designs, two of which are recalled and described here. One was in the form of a large panel resembling a guitar in outline, beginning with a narrow three step ladder, at the foot of which was a semi-circular box in which the player stood at the beginning of each sequence of the game. At the head of the ladder were two large boxes side by side, compartments numbered 4 and 5. Next, 6 was a central single box, beyond which was another double box, 7 and 8. The final box, 9, was a large full width semi-circle, and the whole bed was about 10 feet in length by about five in width at the double boxes. It will be understood that these dimensions are average, for sizes depended on juvenile inclination and artistry and size variations were many within the basic outline.

Although I had a peever and played it with pals as described below, the game was mostly indulged in by girls. Taking turns and playing individually, the first move was, from the starting box, to slide the peever into box 1, where it had to land clean within the box, for if in this or any subsequent cast it landed outside the box aimed at, or on a line, it was a case of begin again at 1. With it successfully lodged in 1 the player, always missing the box in which the peever lay and avoiding treading a line, hopped on one leg into boxes 2 and 3, landed left foot in 4 and right one in 5 together, hopped to 6 then both together again in 7 and 8 and on into 9, which was treated as the starting box for the return stage. On the way back the player stooped on one leg and picked up the peever, then continued on to the foot of the ladder. The next cast was to box 2 and so on, the sliding throws becoming progressively more difficult as distance increased. On successful completion of the course, on reaching 9, the direction was reversed with the throws commencing from 9 in descending order, so that the hardest part was the long final throws into the smaller ladder boxes.

The best surface to play on was the smooth asphalt of the road (described in slightly greater detail in the following section) on which peevers glided smoothly. Pavements were also used but with their usually rougher surface, unless they were of the slate slab type, peever games were less successful. Unevenness of the concrete sometimes caused the peever, slid with the force needed to reach a distant box, to roll over on edge and travel clean out the bed altogether. Actually, the most common peever was an empty shoe, furniture, or linoleum polish tin, because it cost nothing other than the effort to search the middens if there wasn't one available at home. However, in recent years there has been talk of granite peevers used in the past, but I never saw any other than those of marble used in our district. This may cause people today to wonder where such as exotic material came from. In the course of renovat-

F

ing grocery and provision shops and cafes, the opportunity was taken to replace marble slab counters which had become scratched and chipped with use. Being of the correct thickness, I suspect these discarded slabs were the source of our marble peevers.

The other peever game is less clearly recalled, but details were supplied by an enthusiastic former beds player, and fellow (lady) member of the Govan Reminiscence Group, who has demonstrated it to children at Scotland Street School Museum. This beds game was laid out in the form of a broad ladder with each section divided into three lateral compartments, three roughly equal spaces. Both top and bottom of the bed had semi-circles, one of which was the starting box, no. 1. Numbers 2, and 3 and 4 were the central compartments of the ladder. Numbers 5, 6 and 7 were the boxes down one wing descending, and 8, 9 and 10 ascended the opposite wing, with 11 being the half circle mid-point-of-the-game just beyond. Operation of the peever differed here in that it was propelled, again hopping on one leg, by the outer edge of the foot being hopped on. On reaching it the process was reversed. The term 'beds' may derive from the fact that in drawing them out, as well as the ends, edges and compartment divisions of the last mentioned 'bed' were usually rendered with curved lines which conveyed the impression of quilting. Even less clearly remembered are yet another form of beds, what were called 'ba' beds', in which players hopped in turn round the course stoting a tennis type ball.

Roller skates

Most side streets in districts with older tenements had smooth surfaces laid with a material called asphalt. That knowledge is due to the occasion a road repair squad was relaying a patch in Skipness Drive at the corner of Holmfauldhead Drive. I happened to be one of a small group of boys watching with interest, as the new surface was being spread on the area that had been dug up. Three or four of us were sitting in a row on the pavement edge, studying the operation with unusual quiet fascination as the hot new tar-like material was spread out and levelled. The work completed, the two men involved sat down beside us and lit their pipes for a smoke before packing up, when one of our group said 'Whit dae ye ca' that' stuff, mister?' Probably as a reward for not being the usual annoying street urchins who would be liable to shout insults or interfere with the work or equipment, or generally get in the way, one of them, the older of the two who is remembered clearly because he had an 'interesting' face, turned and looked at us. He studied the row of young faces for a moment, then decided that we deserved a sensible answer rather than be told to '"Adjective" off!' as we half expected. He said, pointing first at the repair and then at the original material with his pipe stem, 'This is mastic, and that's asphalt powder — and raising his voice 'ah hope ye's'll remember tha'!' One more example of how a brief but interesting event of seemingly no importance from so long ago again remains in clear focus.

Roller skating was another of that erratic rotation of activities we took part in, and those smooth asphalt street surfaces were ideal for it. Today's roads have a surface designed for the rubber tyred wheel, pitted to help tyre treads get the best grip possible, during wet weather in particular. Present day plastic skate wheels appear to have a greater rolling resistance to that surface, which renders the sport less enjoyable. Roller skating seems much less popular with today's children than it might be, but if there was a convenient, suitable and safe surface to skate on, like the one described, without having to travel away to some distant place to get access to a rink, plus metal ballbearing skates, it would be more indulged in. It is impossible for children with skates today to use them on any road. None could be called quiet, and neither their surface, or pavement surfaces, are smooth enough and the latter are anyway for pedestrians. So this is a sport in which the fuller potential we attained is no longer possible. There are one or two examples of streets with asphalt surfaces still to be seen today. One, until recently anyway, was Elder Street, a derelict stretch lying near a recent housing development.

Not long after joining the Skipness Drive group and finding I was one of the few without skates, the next time they were in season I pestered my parents about getting a pair. I hear with memory's ear Mum saying to Dad: 'He's askin' fur skates noo — can we afford them?' Soon after, on a day of excited anticipation on my part, it would have been a Saturday afternoon because he worked in the morning, not as overtime but part of his normal working week, Dad took me 'up the town' to buy them. The date might have been September 1937 and they would therefore have been a birthday present. At that time certain Woolworth stores advertised and sold everything at two prices, 3d and 6d, and we went to the Union Street shop. Clearly recalled is the black (or navy blue?) coloured frontage, with gold coloured half-round moulded lettering portraying the company name and these two prices; during researches in the Strathclyde Regional Archives, a photograph was unearthed showing this same shop in the thirties. What puzzles me now is that my skates were bought there, and cost about 12/6 (twelve shillings and six pence — equivalent to $62^1/_2$p. That figure represented about one-fifth of Dad's weekly wage then, and the equivalent today would be close to £40. However, these skates turned out to be Rolls Royces of the skating scene.

To me, at first they were just skates, but when my friends saw them their eyes popped. The more knowledgeable of them said with awe — 'Ball-bearing skates', and looked at them with envy. Each axle had a solid rubber pad in its mounting which made them very comfortable and easy to use. Whether that purchase was by accident or design will never be known, but they really were the best in the street. One skate even survived a severe deliberate mutilation in being used to make a bogie. The last time they were seen was at Pollok, in a (then) recently unearthed box of long discarded playthings and due to be thrown out, when I may have been in my twenties. I distinctly remember feeling a pang of regret at their going and being convinced they were still usable. Back in Skipness Drive in 1937, some of the other boys were using skates of the cheaper kind that looked as if they had been handed down by more than one previous user. In one case the wheels were so worn down the owner was running on the wheel webs. Skating style is different now from what it was in the past, because our skates didn't have that important addition of today, the angled buffer under the front. Our technique in propelling ourselves was by leaning forward slightly, and angling each foot out alternately left and right in a pushing motion. The front buffer does away with this by allowing acceleration to be achieved with straight pushes.

Because they were so easy to use, my skates gave a false sense of my own competence. One day, a year or so after I got them, after using them a lot and feeling confident that the skill had been mastered, Mum and I were watching a boy speeding along in a very competent and smooth-flowing way. She said to me in a slightly querulous tone: 'Why can't you "go" your skates as good as that?'. To say I was speechless is an understatement. I looked at her and wondered if I had heard her correctly and said 'Surely I'm as good as that, if not better!' She soon brought me down to earth with the truth, describing my actions as being far too jerky (stumpy, I think, was the term used) and unco-ordinated. This completely deflated me and all I could think of in reply was: 'Well, I can go as fast as he can', which was probably true, but only helped mollify me a little.

It was a joyful recreation to indulge in on warm summer days, to be able to drift along effortlessly round the streets with a group of pals. From early on days of sunshine in high summer, with the sun's rays reflected from windows mornings and evenings making fragmented splashes of golden colour on the shaded side of the street, into late evenings of school holidays. Then it was up the stairs to get washed and go to bed dog tired, with a cup of milk and a slice of buttered plain bread and jam for supper and a comic, and be so tired that after reading only half a page I was asleep. Occasionally children felt hungry when playing in tenement areas. To save them from having to climb the stairs they called up to their maw for a piece, which mother duly spread if she was in the mood and not strained by pressure of housework. Then she put it in a paper bag and threw it down into the back court. Sometimes I was fortunate to benefit from this service although once or twice, when thrown from three storeys up, the 'poke' was unable to withstand the landing and burst.

Bogies

There were two types of bogies. The one most often encountered was made from a suitable plank of wood of roughly 6 ins x 1 in x 5 ft in length, a pair of axles with wheels, and a wooden box. Of these components wheels were the most difficult item to get hold of, and on the rare occasion when they did turn up the locality was scoured for other parts. For the other type, a roller skate could be used if no axles were available, but skate-bogies were uncommon, usually because in the course of fitting, the skate was knocked about and liable to be left unusable for skating. A primitive bogie could be made using simply the plank to which the axles were attached, maybe with a platform of some kind, but they were regarded as 'poor boys' bogies'. Addition of a box for a seat however, which had to be within suitable dimensions, raised it into the affluent class. If you were lucky enough to find a pair of axles complete with wheels, usually off a redundant pram chassis recovered from a midden, you were the most popular guy around with your pals.

One axle was fixed rigidly to the back end of this plank, with nails begged of 'borrowed' along with a hammer from someone's house. The difficult part now was securing the other axle at the front in such a way that it was able to pivot. The ideal distance to aim for between the two axles was if you could sit in the box seat, positioned over or just forward of the rear axle, with your feet comfortably resting on both ends of the front axle near the wheels. Holding on to a loop of rope fixed to the axle ends and, there being no convenient slopes in the district, with someone pushing, you were able to steer with both foot pressure and pulling on the rope. With one of its ends removed the box was nailed bottom down on the plank, near the end that would be the rear, with the open end towards the front, but leaving a small ledge at the back of the plank just sufficiently deep to allow a pusher to stand on in a crouch, so he could benefit from an intermittent hurl. During a bogie making season, there being such a run on them, suitable boxes might be impossible to find, so some bogie makers, late starters in the scramble to build one, had to settle for the primitive version and sit on the bare plank.

Because of constant use and rough treatment our bogies rarely lasted long. But sometimes it happened that a few of the four-wheel kind were in existence at the same time among different groups, and this would produce a rare sight, a sort of local Derby. It wasn't really a competitive event but it had its exciting moments. As each cart with crew of steerer and pusher (the latter would be the most physically able of their respective group who was prepared to co-operate) went careering along the street producing the fun we, the spectators, were hoping for — crashes and spills.

Skate bogies were designed differently. If the bolt locking the two halves of a skate together was removed, each half could be used in place of an axle and wheels set by nailing them rigidly in place at front and back. Once I saw instead of a single skate, a pair used one full skate at each end, but this was judged to be unsuccesful because the bogie was less easily steered. Bogies made with a single split skate were easiest to manoeuvre, which was done by banking-leaning over in the direction of turn desired. Also, cheaper rigid skates were much less steerable than those with rubber suspension. Making a skate-bogie the box, with both ends retained, was mounted standing on end at the front with the open top facing the rear. A strip of wood nailed across the top end to project a few inches on either side, acted as handlebars. That was my home made scooter, for that really was what it was. It was the only bogie I ever had, and immediately the superior quality of my skates showed when, on its first test, it was found to be able, without mechanical steering to U turn with ease well within the width of the street. Size of box was important too, and when a bogie making season started there was a run on the shops for those of most suitable size. If you were shopping late you ended up looking silly with a big one, like an orange box, or a small one over which you had to bend down in a crouch.

On one phase of this bogie building part of the play activity cycle, and it happened on the one in which I built mine, the game was cut short by the arrival of the 'polis'. The streets during school holidays were becoming rather crowded with them racing up and down, creating a hazard even with what little traffic there was, and with more under construction it could only get worse, when the bobbie arrived. Coming round the corner from Clachan Drive into Skipness Drive, he stopped the first bogie rider and produced his notebook. That was the signal for all other bogies to disappear up the closes. So ended my only venture into bogie making, and although it had been knocked out of shape a bit, the skate used was recovered and put back into service for its original purpose.

Vanished and mischievous games

One street game never encountered since this period was called 'French and English', a name which seems to date it from the days of Napoleon. It was a sort of semi-violent war game in which two teams set themselves up on opposite pavements. At a signal all the participants rushed towards each other with folded arms outstretched, to meet in the centre of the road in what was really a pushing match. The object was for one team to shove all members of the opposition back on to their own pavement, and the semi-violent label was apt because it could become quite boisterous. Another game was statues, the participants of which stood in a line as one of their number, beginning at one end, gripped each individual in turn by the hand and pulled him or her firmly behind and out of sight of the puller. Each one pulled moved on for a few steps and then froze in a position they considered striking or funny, but they had to hold their position while the puller was looking. If he detected someone moving that person was 'out', and the winner was the one with the best or most amusing pose and who remained frozen longest. Home made stilts were common, as was a version for younger children using a pair of cans. Two holes were punched in one end at the edge on opposite sides, and a knotted loop of string was put through. Length of loop was such that a child, standing on a pair of cans and holding on tightly to the loops, could clump about on the shoe extensions.

One of the least energetic games was Actors and Actresses, in which we sat around and took turns in suggesting a set of initials of our chosen film star for the others to guess their full names. WB was Wallace Beery, JC — no-not THAT one but James Cagney, or PO for Pat O'Brien, etc. MM was of course Mickey Mouse. Games like these needing no props were legion, and a primitive musical instrument could be made using a comb and a piece of tissue paper.

But it has to be the old style crinkly stuff which rustles when crumpled, which is seldom encountered today, not the modern soft variety. With a strip of tissue folded over the comb, if the comb is held gently to the almost closed lips and hummed through, it produces a pleasing fuzzy sound not greatly dissimilar to a Jews (or 'Jaws') harp.

Another game was Scotch Horses, where we paired off, each with someone who matched you in size and physical ability, for which standing side by side the pairs crossed arms behind. Linked together with left hand holding left and right holding right, we galloped off around the street or school playground, perfectly happy with our lot-until boredom set in. Until one pair, on one occasion, discovered that while still linked if each simultaneously performed an about-face, in opposite directions of course, they had instantly swopped sides.

A different kind of entertainment was available between autumn and spring in the church hall nearby. The Band Of Hope was a weekly gathering organised by churches to try to take local urchins off the streets during evenings and keep them out of trouble, by providing entertainment which was laced with religious messages. One or two of our group whose parents were that way inclined attended regularly, while others expressed an interest but were to reluctant to go. Another boy and I, kicking with the other foot and well aware of the implications of differences of faith, kept our distance. However, one warm evening our group happened to be playing near the door of the church hall when the entertainment was in full swing, and as the door lay ajar we were attracted to the sound of singing. Congregating round the entrance, we gradually worked our way in and found ourselves given a paper bag with a bun and a biscuit and, without quite realising how, seated on the stage just inside. A slide show by what was then known as a magic lantern began in the crowded hall, with the screen just over our heads, the content of which was the usual biblical story. But it was the novelty of my situation and the unusual projector medium that held my attention. Some of our group were members of the Boys Brigade, competition between various church groups of which was intense, locally 119 and 121 companies.

Some games were mischievous and designed to annoy the neighbours (always other people's neighbours unless you were thick) the simplest form of which was knocking on doors and running away. Its variation, which was to tie adjacent door handles together then knock both doors and make a bolt for it, was also indulged in. Fortunately we avoided real trouble because we seldom had access to anything other than easily broken string. One trick that could cause a householder a lot of annoyance, for which it was difficult for a new resident to find the cause, was called clockwork. It needed a long length of dark thread, a button or a washer, and a piece of sticky paper or insulating tape. It was usually only possible to practise this on low down houses with windows facing into the back court, although those one stair up weren't immune to adventurous youngsters brave enough to climb up a rone pipe.

The method was to tie on the button or washer about six inches from the end of the thread, then stealthily tape the extreme end on to the glass of a window pane high up in the frame. Leaving plenty of slack, the other end was then carried to a place of concealment, ideally lying flat on top of a dyke. By pulling on the thread it was possible to make the button tap the glass gently, which usually succeeded in making the householder appear at the window. But this was a ploy for which the evening gloom of the unlit backcourt was needed, so that it was almost impossible to spot the cause. When you thought they had settled down again you began tapping once more, and the man or woman came out into the backcourt to investigate, by which time they began to suspect that they were victims of the dreaded clockwork game they would have been well warned about. This was a once only thing for any house, and when you were preparing for it you had to hope the occupants hadn't experienced it before at the hands of other practitioners, for they might be ready to dash out and catch the perpetrators by following the thread.

During the season of dark evenings, in the course of our games we would sometimes pause to look with wonder at a bright glow in the sky to the east, which suddenly became visible from the street. We knew its cause from hearing adults referring to it as Dixon's

Blazes. The reddish glow was of course only seen after dark, and then only if other conditions were suitable. There had to be a low overcast of cloud with the atmosphere otherwise clear, and the phenomenon lasted only for a short time. I was intensely interested in it, and asked various people what could produce such a glow bright enough to light up the sky. Grandad Chambers, that source of so much other knowledge he was keen to share, said it was caused by a steel works over near Polmadie but was unable to elaborate further. Later, reading industrial history, it was learned that Dixon's Iron Works was an old established plant which produced pig iron until the early 1950s. It closed down then, and on the site today is Dixons' Blazes Industrial Estate, situated off Crown Street. The light we were seeing occurred when the lids were removed from the reduction vats and the molten metal poured into moulds. People who lived close to the plant said the fiery glow was accompanied by thick clouds of smoke, causing it to resemble what they imagined a small-scale volcanic eruption would look like.

CHAPTER 5

The Dykes, and School

A somewhat hazardous form of play we indulged in was climbing the dykes. This was something all parents worried about. But the dykes were there and the few who were less concerned about their offspring having an accident, those with an out-of-sight out-of-mind attitude, made it easy for other adventurous boys (and tomboy girls) with concerned parents to indulge. Who would go out into a back court in front of a group of children and in full view of every house in the block, and tell their offspring to 'Get down off there, it's too dangerous, you could fall off and land on the spikes', when they were one of a group who are obviously enjoying themselves, the others with the apparent approval of *their* parents? Thereby gaining a reputation of being a killjoy for themselves, and make their child appear a wimp in front of their friends. 'Dyke' was the term applied to the brick built washhouses and midden buildings in all back courts. In height, they were from 8 to 10ft. Most had a cast rough aggregate concentric roof with a slight slope, although some were of wood, pitched and slated. Each concrete roof section had a vent in the form of a quarter circle piece of six-inch tile piping projecting up on top at the centre, which also did duty as a seat for dyke climbers. These buildings were usually built in a row back to back, serving closes on opposite sides of the block in layouts that varied according to the ground plan of the block.

The block in which we lived in Skipness Drive was a broad oblong, which meant that individual back courts were long and narrow. Most of the washhouse/midden buildings, of eight closes — four on either side, were in a solid elongated block in the centre, while closes in each corner had smaller detached blocks. That arrangement is in contrast with the Drive Road/Hutton Drive and Hutton Drive/Kennedar Drive layouts which were long and narrow. Here, design of the block made individual back courts broad and shallow so that washhouse buildings stood in separate groups of four, two for closes each side of the block. While back courts were invariably separated by iron railings, spaces between washhouse island blocks here were filled in with a brick wall which divided one side from the other. For dyke climbers, this produced a continuous high level, and until you got used to it, stomach churning walk along the tops of the wall sections from one end of the block to the other. Those walls had a feature that was a major deterrent to would-be dyke walkers. They were topped by a hollow fired-clay capping, in section shaped like a broad spear-point, so that when walking on it you had to do so with very splayed feet, placing the arch carefully over the point, which required a lot of nerve to master with a drop of eight feet on either side.

The arrangement of dykes in blocks with a ground plan like ours in Skipness Drive, meant that in places there were gaps of different widths between these small buldings, which provided challenging leaps of varying degrees of difficulty. When the most difficult jumps of our own dykes were mastered, those that were within our current ability after much time was spent 'daring' and goading each other, we began to trek round neighbouring blocks looking for other gaps to jump to further test our nerve. As time passed we became more able and experienced, returning regularly to areas previously visited to try to conquer those we were too afraid to attempt last time. Considered now, the danger was appalling, not so much in falling off but what you might land on. In those days almost all railings had spikes, all of which were dangerous and some lethal, with railings separating back courts among the worst, having slim sharps spikes. Concern of parents was understandable, knowing their children were larking about and forgetting the danger, and their dilemma was great. In my own case I was warned off a couple of times in private, on being spotted from our window at the beginning of my climbing days, at the age of coming up for seven. The obvious way to climb out of sight of your parents was to go to another block, hoping that no-one living in the houses overlooking these dykes knew your parents and would 'tell' on you.

As time passed the contant interaction of our group, with occasional sessions of dyke climbing (and no serious accidents) meant that my parents, no doubt as others equally concerned had done before and since, slowly became used to it and apart from intermittent mild objections, eventually accepted it and in the end ignored it altogether. 'Fell aff a dyke' was a light-hearted expression used in those days which didn't consider the pain involved in a broken limb or fractured skull. In my experience accidents were few. The only one I was involved in was one of a small number of similar incidents where no injury was sustained, and happened when another boy and I tried to jump over the same gap from opposite sides at the same instant. We met in the middle and fell the eight feet, landing in a heap in such a way that we seemed break each others fall. Apart from some bruising we had nothing to show for it and were soon back up with the others as if nothing had happened. Over the years we heard of others outwith our area who suffered broken limbs in falls, and I remember being shown scars by somebody at school who fell on spiked railings, and seeing the marks where a spike had transfixed a thigh muscle. To get down off a dyke older ones could 'dreep it', that is lower their body off the edge and hang down by the finger-tips, well away from spikes, and let go. That introduced another element of competition — daring one-another to tackle progressively higher drops.

The wash-house and washday

Interiors of the buildings making up the dykes, and their functions, may be of interest to students of conditions of the period. The washhouse, the place where most tenants did their weekly wash, was provided with three facilities. In a back corner of a space roughly ten feet square, with walls of plain rough brick, stood a large copper boiler with a loose lid, with a capacity of between twenty to thirty gallons. It was set inside a squat round brick housing standing about four feet high, and was filled from a supply pipe with a tap above it. The top of the housing was slightly dome shaped, with the lid forming the cap of the dome. Under the boiler was a fireplace, with a flue in the corner leading up to a chimney-head on the roof immediately above, which had two chimneys, the other one from the wash-house through the rear wall. This heated the water but there was no outlet to draw it off. Boiling water had to be lifted out with a large tin half-hemispherical scoop with a round wooden handle, which held about a half gallon, and when this operation was under way scalding accidents were an occupational hazard. Against the outer wall, below the window stood two large deep white glazed pottery tubs each fed by a cold water tap, with a raised wooden batten between them as a mounting for a wringer. Above the sinks, the window was a large square 9 pane frame. Fixed permanently, a protective wire mesh cover over the outside of the window rendered it impossible to clean, so that it was quite opaque with dirt. Against the rear wall stood an unpainted wooden bench with a bleached working surface, for handling wet clothes.

Made by a local company in Bridgeton called Acme, the wringer, the predecessor of the spin drier, was a device for squeezing out most of the water from washed clothes before they were hung out to dry. It was fixed to the mounting between sinks by clamps set in its base at either end. It had two spring loaded hard rubber rollers mounted one above the other, geared together (at this period with unguarded coarse gears), and operated by a handle of a design similar to the starting handle of a contemporary motor vehicle. Wet clothes were lifted from the tub and put through between the rollers. Pressure on the rollers was adjustable by an open-wheel knob, which in a post-war design improvement became a decorative form of wing nut, on top of the wringer body. A big disadvantage was that it was severe on clothes, and buttons in particular tended to get broken. Fingers needed careful watching too for this job, particularly if two people were involved. Underneath the rollers a catchment tray with a spout either side was mounted on a rocking pivot, to catch water squeezed out which could be diverted to either tub. When the cauldron of water was boiling, enough was transferred to a tub with the scoop and cooled with cold from the tap to wash the coloureds, while white things were put into the water left in the boiler, with soap powder, to be boiled for a time. Lifting clothes out of the boiler was done with the stub of a brush pole, bleached with use and usually of the heavy-duty type as used for the scaffie's (street sweeper's) brush. The pole had to be kept horizontal so that no boiling water ran down and scalded fingers.

On washday, among items a housewife carried down to the washhouse in a large oval wickerwork basket with handles either end, were the clothes to be washed and all the other items required: a peg bag, clothes rope, bar of washing soap — Whitewindsor or Sunlight, packet of powder, Oxydol, Rinso, or Persil, or maybe the Co-op's Thistle, Soap Powder No.1 or No.2, scrubbing brush and wash board, and a final wise check was to see that the key of the washhouse door was in her apron pocket. The washboard was a flat wooden frame with legs, which stood about 2 feet high by 1 foot wide, with a ribbed glass, galvanised steel or aluminium plate set in it for scrubbing the clothes on. It was single-sided (although I once saw a double-sided example), and had a ledge near the top convenient for holding the bar of soap and scrubbing brush. Rubbing was done with the legs of the board standing on the bottom of the tub containing the washing, and the board top resting on the front of the sink. In this position it lay at a comfortable angle, and using an up-and-down push-and-pull motion over the ribs with as much force as could be exerted, the soapy clothes were alternatively dipped and massaged.

Some women used an additive called blue whitener, Dolly or Recketts, which was bought in small round cakes, like a section sliced off a piece of dowelling, tied up in blue fabric bags. It was easily crumbled between fingers into a blue powder, and put in with the wash as a sort of camouflage which was supposed to give a better 'white' finish to the white clothes. This kind of treatment is still in evidence with blue coloured washing powders available today. My mother never used it and seemed scornful of its supposed advantages, nor could I understand what the benefit was supposed to be, but this no doubt stems from our partial colour blindness.

The washhouse floor sloped in to the centre, and when the plugs were pulled in the tubs the contents poured out and ran down grooves to a drain there. The floor itself did get wet when boiling clothes were transferred to a sink, however, so to help prevent wet feet there was a duckboard to stand on. The plain weathered wooden door, it probably had seen paint at some stage of its existence, was kept locked by that eagerly sought implement, the washhouse key. It was always a source of concerned gossip along the lines of 'Who's got the washhouse key?', or 'D'ye know who's got it?' between neighbours, secure in the knowledge that the other knew perfectly well what 'it' was. It should be clear from the foregoing that before the arrival of the washing machine, washday work was laborious and time consuming, and apart from the labour involved there was the fact that housewives' hands were immersed in soapsuds for long periods, so that anyone with delicate skin, known today as allergy, had a difficult time. There is no recollection of seeing rubber gloves until long after this time.

There was a Corporation washhouse, a 'steamie', forerunner of the laundromatt which is really what the present day steamies are, fifteen minutes walk from Linthouse, in Harhill Street next to the baths. Virtually all our neighbours used the washhouse, and the question might be asked — why would anyone need to use the steamie when the washhouse seemed to be perfectly adequate? The short answer to that is that it wasn't. Because of the human factor trouble flared up now and again with disputes about allocation of turns. As in all other similar situations it could only be settled by discussion and mutual agreement, although as a last resort, before the police were summoned if violence broke out, and even that wasn't unknown, the factor could be asked to mediate. Two circumstances were the main causes of disputes. One was antagonism between individuals, and the other was a close with a greater than average number of large families needing a lot of washhouse time. Most closes in a three-storey tenement had twelve houses which, if they all needed a turn in the usual manner of one in the morning and one in the afternoon, it would take a whole week for everybody to get their washing done. However, a number, up to half in some cases, of people living alone, or couples, chose to do their washing in the kitchen sink, so this took pessure off the allocation of washhouse time, and there were the odd one or two who, for one reason or another, preferred the steamie.

To wash white clothes properly in those days it was considered necessary to boil them. In order to have the water boiling in good time the fire had to be lit at an early hour and attended to for stoking, so that it would be ready for, say, not later than nine a.m., sometimes much earlier. Once the housewife got to know how long it took to boil the amount of water sufficient for all her needs, she had to get the boiler filled and the fire lit so that it would be ready in time. A common routine was that if the husband was up for work early enough or rose earlier than usual, something like 6 a.m. would be about right, he carried the coal, paper and sticks down and lit the fire and filled the boiler. A cause of arguments here was that no matter how careful he had been the fire could go out after he left. If this happened and his wife was slow in arriving to check, it was pointless to relight it if there was insufficient time. At worst that would be her turn up in the air until another one became available later in the week. In freezing weather and if the water supply hadn't frozen up, a wife with an uncooperative or otherwise unavailable. husband had to be up in the middle of the night to do this chore. When the water was ready she had to slave away to get the work done, so as to be out of the way before the next person was due to get in. Sometimes the second turn of the day was lucky and found that the first one in hadn't used all her hot water, and so she saved time and expense. On rare occasions, with a high degree of co-operation three women could manage to get through their wash between dawn and dusk, and while there was no lighting candles were used in emergencies.

Descriptions in the previous paragraphs might give the impression of washday being a combination of having to rise early to see to the fire, and coping with the drudgery of the preparations. But the main object of it all still had to be accomplished — the actual washing of the clothes. There is no exaggeration in suggesting that labour involved on washday, for a woman with a large family who desired to be clean, would be equal to a good day's work in the yards for many men. Most women were fussy, and went to great lengths to ensure that when they hung out their washing it was sparkling clean. There always seemed to me to be an element of competition about it, with other people's washing being examined, and comments passed between friends on their appearance. 'Ah wish ah could get ma' white things as clean as that,' or, in the opposite vein, 'Look at the colour o' hur mans' combinations, ye'd think they'd never been in the tub!' It is a form of labour completely lost to present day housewives who have never had to do it, because of the convenience of washing machine, spinner and tumble-drier. If people who use modern appliances have never had to get through a big washing for a family, which included bedclothes, without a washing machine or access to a steamie or laundromatt, could they, I wonder, possibly imagine what it was like in the days before they arrived. Another point to take into consideration is this. Materials used for most clothes today are often modern inventions that are a good deal easier to clean than the natural fabrics of fifty years ago.

After that task was finished, the next operation with the clean clothes was relatively easy, if the weather was suitable that is, getting them dried. Again, most people today are independent of the only way of drying clothes then, by hanging them outdoors or on a pulley indoors. At the prsent time those with tumble driers, and others with no outdoor facilities for hanging them but who have other arrangements like an indoor drying space, certainly have an easy time. Before there were any of these facilities, in being dependent on getting the washed clothes dried outdoors it was a case of watching the weather, and that could be a heartbreak causing extra work. How many women working within the very limited horizon of the tenement block, and dependent on the appearance of that portion of sky visible from within it, were fooled into covering the backcourt with a big washing, when a wider view would have allowed them to see that rain would be arriving soon. Many are the times I heard my mother and other women say with heartfelt anguish, 'Ah had jist covered the back wi' mah washin' when the rain came oan, so ah hud tae rush an' take it aw in again, an' it's still rainin' so how a'hm a gonny get it dried noo?' To hang as much of it as possible on the kitchen or lobby pulley, and a clothes horse if one was available, and a few small items on the mantelshelf stretch was the only option. Of course in winter that problem was much worse, and it wasn't unknown, during long spells of cold damp weather, for some of the previous week's washing to be still taking up space on the pulley when the next lot needed to be hung up. It will be understood that a washing that had hung for a week in the kitchen would be redolent of the smells of the week's cooking.

The arrangement for hanging clothes outdoors depended on the shape of the back-court. In our block, back-court dividing railings incorporated high spaced out stanchions, while others had different arrangements, such as Hutton Drive with individually 'planted' clothes poles. The stanchions had hooks at the top onto which the clothes rope could be looped, and strung in a criss-cross pattern which covered the back-court. Although there were separate hooks for each side, friction between women from adjacent closes could develop because of someone thoughtlessly winding their rope round the hooks on both sides of a pole, in doing so trapping a rope hung previously on the other side. To provide as much rope space as possible, additional hooks were sometimes set in the walls of both the tenement itself and the washhouse, which gave additional stretches. Tension of the rope was important in that it shouldn't be too slack, or the weight of damp clothes would cause it to droop, maybe low enough to let them brush the ground. Or too tight, making it difficult to get the clothes pole to lift the clothes up to catch the breeze. Wooden clothes poles, bought from a hardware shop with contributions from all tenants and kept in the washhouse were lengths of 2-inch by $1\frac{1}{2}$-inch timber about eight feet long. A 'V' notch was cut in one end to hold the rope, and two cuts made at the opposite end, taking off the narrow edges, left a broad sharp point to dig into the ground to prevent it slipping. Our back-court surface was fully covered by a rough cinders-and-small-stones tarry mixture, while others such as those in Hutton Drive were part grass and part bare earth, with only a metalled path between close and washhouse.

When the clothes were dry the next stage was to iron the lighter things, and have the heavier items, mainly bed clothes, put through a mangle if one was available. Early smoothing irons were solid and heavy, and were heated by propping them up in front of the firebars, or sitting them on top of the draw-out plate above the fire. This must have caused difficulty in ensuring the ironing surface was clean before applying it to the fabric. These same irons might also be heated by gas on the stove, or on a purpose-made frame with jets connected to the mains by a flexible hose. As coal gas was also a sooty fuel, care must have had to be taken to clean the base and edges before using. Just how were women able to learn to judge temperature so that nothing was ruined? Touching it briefly with a fingertip moistened with a lick is a gesture recalled, but it seems now to be so haphazard that many mistakes must surely have been made. At that time use of starch was still standard practice on collars and cuffs of shirts, and on parts of certain women's garments, to stiffen up the limp natural materials then in use, for dressing up on special occasions. Shirts were made without collars, with the latter purchased in whatever quantities were judged to be needed. Six collas was the usual number, and they were fitted to shirt necks for wear using collar studs, one each front and back, which meant that with a fresh starched collar fitted each day a shirt could be worn for a week. I seem to remember that even my Dad's working shirts had this arrangement. *For work?* — although he habitually wore them without a collar.

A mangle was really a giant wringer of Victorian design standing over four feet high, with six-inch wooden rollers, and mounted on a blackened cast iron frame similar to, but heavier than the frame of a Singer sewing machine of the same era. It had the same kind of small iron wheels as a Singer, so care had to be taken when moving it inside the house, as its great weight bearing on their small surface area could cause it to cut through and break up linoleum, and floor boards weakened by rot. It was operated by turning an 18-inch diameter open cast iron wheel mounted at the side, having four spokes which curved from the rim in to a central boss. The handle for turning the wheel was fixed to the rim at right-angles, the operation driving the rollers through a gear train. On top of the mangle was a similar but much smaller wheel, for adjusting spring tension. Beneath the rollers was a broad wooden tray of what was once smooth timber, the grain of which now stood out in close set ridges with their tops highly polished by generations of use. The mangle I was familiar with, and on which this description is based, belonged to my mother's aunt-by-marriage, Auntie Mary Ann.

When she died around 1940 we inherited her mangle, and I dimly remember it being pushed carefully along the street on its tiny wheels from her house to ours, and carried by Dad, assisted by friends, with some difficulty up the three flights to our house. Of the people I knew who had a mangle they were nearly all older women, which may indicate that they were no longer being made, and those that were around had been in the possession of families for a long time, perhaps handed down through generations. Some women, Auntie Mary Ann was one such, could make a copper or two by taking in other people's washed clothes to put through their mangle, charging something like tuppence for an average wash and a ha'penny for a pair of linen sheets, linen being ideal material for this treatment. Laundries and small shops provided this service also.

Mary Ann's mangle travelled with us when we moved to Pollok in 1945, and was installed in the brick air-raid shelter in the back green of our terraced house there. It was in use for about a decade after this, then abandoned as washday requirements altered when, with the march of progress, Mum got her first washing machine. Eventually it was taken away by a scrap man for a shilling or two. In operation, it had to be treated with care and concentration especially if the work was being done by two people, more so than with a wringer for the larger diameter rollers of the mangle could more easily trap fingers. I became a victim on one occasion when working with Dad. In the gloom of the shelter, he was ca'ing the handle while I was feeding sheets into the rollers when, just at the point where the rollers begin their grip and I should have released mine, fingers of both hands were caught, and at that same instant he was distracted and looked away while continuing to turn. Although not bad enough to require hospital treatment or even a visit to the doctor, both thumbs and forefingers were badly crushed so that I lost thumb and index finger-nails in the weeks following as the injuries healed.

The midden

Next door to the washhouse was the midden and the less said about it the better, although some comment must be made. The interior was about six feet square, with an opening across which, in Skipness Drive anyway, a piece of slate which came to above knee height was permanently fixed. All rubbish was simply thrown in to pile up, and the cleansing department came round a couple of times a week and cleared it out. They operated a night shift for a time, wearing lights attached to their hats like miners, but this caused complaints because of noise disturbance and was discontinued. They had a horrible job, where one of their number had to climb inside and shovel the rubbish into large deep baskets for the men to carry out to the collection truck on their shoulders. This system was changed quite soon after. The piece of slate was removed and six square metal bins with side handles installed, making the job easier but no less distasteful, for they still had to carry the loaded baskets which, although lined, allowed a certain amount of ash to run through on to the carrier.

Vehicles used for rubbish collection, a large fleet of which was operated by the Cleansing Department, are worthy of describing in that their design, though appearing antiquated today, was then years ahead of its time, with two features not seen again for about twenty years. All road vehicles up to that time, other than trams, had petrol, diesel or steam engines up front, mounted over the front axle. The internal combustion engine was enclosed in a close-fitting housing or bonnet between the front mudguards, with cab behind. This placed the driving cab well back behind the front axle. But cleansing trucks were battery powered and had flat front ends. Because there was no engine as such it had a large cab mounted well forward, so that the position of the driver was well over the leading axle. The advantage of this arrangement became known to me in the early 1960s, when for a time I was the owner of a van of similar outline which was found to give excellent front end visibility.

A new school — St Constantine's Primary

Early in March 1937, within a few days of arriving home after five months spent in Mearnskirk hospital, I was marched along to St Constantine's Primary School in Uist Street by Mum. After an interview with the headmaster I was put on the roll and told to start there next day. St Constantine's had been built ten years before, so was relatively modern in design when compared with others in the area. Most of them, such as Greenfield, Elderpark, Fairfield, Harmony Row and Hills Trust, but not Drumoyne Primary in Shieldhall Road which dates from roughly the same period as St Constantine's, in common with most older schools in Glasgow, were built of sandstone as enclosed units. They had classrooms grouped around a central open assembly space within the building. Sir John Maxwell's in Pollokshaws and Shawlands Primary, are just two of many other examples of this design. In later decades these stone buildings were regarded as Victorian in a derogatory sense, considered antiquated, but after a further passage of time some of them are still in use, and now it is clearly seen that they were well built and substantial, and a few survivors are likely to outlast some schools put up since the war, even as late as the 1960s.

St Constantine's is a two-storey plus ground-floor building, partly constructed of red brick in the form of a broad flat U ground plan. Stairs, staff rooms and cloakrooms were in the wings of the U, and access to the classrooms by high-railed verandahs on the upper levels were within the U, with stairs and verandahs originally open to the elements. That arrangement went from one extreme of the Victorian enclosed design with its implication of a lack of fresh air, to the other, the open one with adequate fresh air, but subjected to weather penetration, deterioration and expensive to heat in winter. Considered now, the older buildings were definitely the better of the two types, because in the old, rooms had windows that could be easily opened to let in any amount of air, whereas the 'modern' design, with the open part facing west, could be adversely affected by wet and windy weather, particularly in winter. The stairs and verandahs of that building and Drumoyne school have since been enclosed.

On that first day I was put in a class below the level I should have been in according to my age. No doubt that was because a look at my record of attendance at St Anthony's would have shown how much had been missed. Classroom sequence commenced with room 1 low down at the south end of the building, and I was put in room 2. This lasted for only a few weeks, however. Then the school authorities must have decided that I hadn't missed as much as was thought or I had caught up somehow, and moved me on one, to the level for my age. Memories of this school are pleasant but hazy. The headmaster, Mr Docherty, was a pleasant individual with short grey/white hair with a bald patch, and a jutting forceful chin, who wore a bowler hat on his rounds. The assistant head teacher is the person who remains most clearly in my memory, because young as I was I recognised that he was skilful and efficient at his job. Most other teachers only managed to get through two or three subjects in any one day, but this man, Cameron I think was his name, always managed to take the class through all the important subjects *every day*. While others struggled to teach composition, for example, as a weekly subject, he made us do it daily. Somehow we managed it, most of us anyway, and thought nothing about it. He did not normally teach, but covered our class for a sick colleague for an extended period. I consider myself fortunate to have been taught by him, even for that brief period. He had that special requirement of all good teachers, the knack of making any lesson interesting.

Few names remain with me for the period of school attendance covered by these reminiscences (to 1939), other than about half those seen, and recorded, in the class photograph taken in 1938 in the north-east corner of the playground and reproduced in the plate section. It is regretted that our teacher did not choose to join the group, for if she had there might have been another name for the list. Other fleeting memories are of carrying a slice of toast in my school bag for a play piece, and the janitor ringing the school bell, a large handbell, at start and finish of school and at playtime. In those days the playground was divided in two; the half nearest Nimmo Drive belonged exclusively to the boys. That reference may appear pointless, but while most present day school playgrounds seem to have no rule of separation of the sexes, then it was a division strictly enforced by children themselves. There was no need for any supervisor to keep them apart, as no boy or girl would have been seen dead in the other playground, a strictly observed custom that remained throughout my schooldays. If they saw a ball game in progress one or other of the two priests from the adjacent church, Fathers John Battel and Bart Burns, eagerly hopped over the dividing railings and joined in. The latter was the most enthusiastic, but he frequently had to go looking for the janny to retrieve the ball, invariably a tennis ball, from the flat roof of the school building where it had landed after a demonstration of his high kicking ability.

Trench coat, blazer, a tie and skullcap was the uniform we were required to wear, and stockings reaching to just below the knees. In winter a helmet in the style worn by pilots of the open aeroplanes of the time was favoured. Short trousers were invariably worn by all boys all the time whatever the weather, until reaching the age of 14. Rather less than half the class were from families who could afford the full rigout, while the rest were somewhat haphazardly clad. Children then seemed to have no choice in what clothes were bought for them. Unlike today it was a case of, as with food, eat or wear what was provided whether you liked it or not. Food fads and wearer's choice didn't enter into it until you could afford to buy your own. The skullcap was the prize oddity; the very name confused me as to whether it referred to 'school' or 'head'. Made from triangular panels of thin grey felt, sometimes lined, and with a covered button on top at the point of convergence of the panels, with a small skip stiffened with card, they were ideal teasing material. In playground rough-and tumble they were easily snatched off and thrown from hand to hand by a group of mischievous boys, which sometimes left the owners in tears after a long and fruitless chase.

Pupils sat in pairs at double-width desks, which had a single lid over a large compartment for holding jotters and text books, but with individual lift-up seats, in plain heavy unpainted wood in a tubular iron frame. The same rigid division of the sexes applied here as in the playground, with an imaginary line down the centre of the classroom, and girls and boys keeping each other at arms length and barely on speaking terms. We boys were a curiously inhibited crowd who coloured up if it became necessary to speak to a girl. On top of each desk, at the front on the narrow transverse section forward of the lid, each pupil had two china inkwells, well separated and confined in recessed holes. One was for blue ink, and the other for red which was never used, except by teacher from her own supply, for correcting written work. There was also a rounded long groove in which writing implements were laid. Normal written work was done in pencil at first, then moved on to pen and ink for composition. At infrequent intervals some-one deemed sufficiently responsible was delegated by teacher to go round with a large bottle of ink and top up the wells.

Learning to write with ink created the serious difficulty of the need to *get it right first time!*, with no possibility of correcting mistakes by rubbing out. Nibbed pens and dipping ink were the normal means of formal writing then, until ball-point pens began to appear around 1950, except for those who could afford a fountain pen. The dipping pen was a development in metal of the quill (goose feather) pen of an earlier age, for which a sharp knife was required to cut a fresh point when the current one had worn down. Small knives, with blades which folded away so that they could be safely carried in a pocket, came to be specially made, and were called 'pen knives'. While today it would be risky to have such an implement on your person, in that less violent age earlier this century, like most boys and youths I carried one. Metal nibbed pens work on the same principle of capillary action as the quill, as does the ball point, but were liable to be extremely messy to use unless treated with special care. Pen nibs were made of brass and fitted into holders at the point of the handle, so were easily changed when the point wore down, but they could become distorted through misuse and would not hold the reservoir drop of ink in the narrow slot at the top of the split made to perform the function. In class, however, replacement was mostly made necessary by rough usage of the nib, seldom by normal wear. One prank when teacher's attention was elsewhere was to use them for dart practice.

Fountain pens were by no means a recent invention, but the cheapest kind were the most modern in writing technology available to us. Inside the pen body was a sac of rubber material. When the nib was held dipped in ink and the sac squeezed and released by means of a side lever or a plunger, ink was drawn up and filled the sac. This formed a reservoir to supply the nib, doing away with the need for frequent dipping. But buying a cheap fountain pen was a lottery because they had a tendency to leak. The cap had a clip to allow the pen to be carried attached to the inside or breast pocket of a jacket, so if a leak did develop it could be a disaster. I remember having one which was a treasured possession, with a gold tipped nib the softness of which made it a pleasure to use. But the main defect was that the rubber reservoir sac tended to perish rather quickly, and when that happened with a newly filled pen, ink could flood out, ruining clothes, although I was lucky and avoided any serious disasters with mine.

School china inkwells were made with a disc top which overlapped the edges, to give a supporting shoulder when placed in the hole in the desk top. The disc had a small hole in the centre just big enough to admit a pen. In use, an ordinary pen was replenished by being dipped frequently so as to carry a drop or two, but it needed controlled and careful handling or drips would run off onto clothes, hands, or work, and many were the pages spoiled by this. It had to be manipulated at the correct angle. If held too steeply it could spray ink over the page, for the point was liable to dig into the paper then spring free. If the angle was too shallow the reserve blob on the underside might touch the paper and flood out, causing that bane of everyone's school life, teachers and pupils, an ink blot. With one dipping a good nib could write maybe about a dozen words, so frequent replenishing was necessary. Ink writing did not dry quickly so that if the page was handled too soon it smeared. Drying was aided by the use of blotting paper, which was different from ordinary writing paper in being thick and absorbent. Folded into several layers it also served as a protective pad to lean on and help prevent sweat or dirt smudges on the pages. Pencil marks are easily rubbed out, but there was another writing implement for business use, the unerasable 'copying ink' pencil.

Teaching aids were primitive by today's standards. The main one was a tall narrow blackboard in a wooden frame mounted in a castored U frame, so that it could be easily moved around, with the pivot mountings at the tops of the U. Below the board a ledge held chalk, duster, and a pointer like a short billiards' cue. Teacher's desk was tall and narrow, again of unpainted wood, with horizontal wings on either side of the lidded compartment which projected out about six inches, one of which was a convenient parking place for the Lochgelly strap. Set in front was a tall shallow cupboard for storage of text books. The seat was a high spindly chair with a foot rest about six inches above floor level, giving teacher a good vantage point to oversee a class of over forty children.

Classroom conditions then were very different from today in that rigid discipline was enforced, to the extent sometimes of regimentation. We were often required to sit up straight and remain silent for lengthy periods, and keep perfectly still with arms folded or by our sides, then submit to inspection for dirty hands or fingernails. St Constantine's had an unusual feature incorporated in the classroom layout, which may have been present in other schools built during the 1920s. Divisions between adjacent rooms were in the form of moveable partitions of panelled varnished wood, with the upper portion in glass. The complete wall between each classroom could be folded aside concertina-like, opening up the whole of a flat or as many rooms as were required. There was one occasion when, as one of more than sixty children sitting the qualifying exam, when three classrooms were opened up to accommodate us, well spread out in one large class.

The strap!

What children of today will know of only as an exhibit in museums of education, the Lochgelly strap was a dreaded reality to us, girls included. To receive it you stood facing teacher with hand held out full stretch for a good whack on the palm. Certain seemingly sadistic teachers insisted on having both hands held one on top of the other. We used to wonder if they really thought it doubled the punishment. Some children, mainly girls, had great difficulty in maintaining the position when faced with the descending leather, and would draw their hand away just before impact. They would then be made to stand with their back to teacher and hold their hand out to the side. However, there were other children considered to be worse off than us, because some schools still used the cane. My parents said it was the norm in all schools during their time. I do not know for certain but it is possible that in the 1930s the cane may have been used private schools only, and had been banned from those of local authorities. As soon as they moved above infant class level any child was liable to have the belt used on them. To have it administered for serious misbehaviour was understandable. But for getting a sum wrong, for being unable to say the 7-times table, or for a reading or spelling error, or for a blot on our writing, one or two of the belt was an everyday fact of life, just part of the enforcement of learning as well as discipline in the system. Despite statements by people who agitate against the use of corporal punishment on children, I feel I benefited from it. However, I know it is wrong because it allows that tiny percentage of individuals who have a sadistic streak, and who lack intuitive ability to control a class of possibly difficult children, to be unprofessional. The common punishment today, writing out lines, was also used in some local schools but not in any of the three I attended.

If asked what would be the most abiding memory of school, I would say it was the rote learning of multiplication tables. The rhythmic chanting in unison by a whole class could be hypnotic, almost as if the ritual was designed to make it difficult to remember the information it contained. Sometimes it seemed to free your mind from the task of taking in the message carried by the recitation, until the next round-the-class test when you wished fervently you had paid attention.

Joys and hazards of schooldays

A particularly happy memory of schooldays does not belong to that school but to a woman who lived in the last close on the west side of Elderpark Street. She made toffee and sold it from her street level kitchen window to passers-by, mainly school children attending the two nearby schools. It was the best kind of toffee, candy as used for toffee apples, which she poured on a tray in a thin layer. When set it was broken up into small pieces and sold in small paper bags in 'guesstimated' quantities for a halfpenny a bag. I was seldom able to afford any, for my pocket money was generally doled out daily after school at the rate of a halfpenny a day, and spent immediately. It was only if some event intervened to prevent this, or an out-of-character oversight caused me to have something left, in the manner of 'finding' a halfpenny during school hours perhaps tucked into a corner of a pocket, enabling me to buy some of that delicious toffee. Very occasionally a gift of money, never more than 3d, was slipped to me by a benevolent aunt or uncle who had paid a visit the previous evening. If spotted by either of my parents, it was taken away 'for my bank' at the first opportunity after the visitor had gone. Once or twice I was lucky and the gift went unobserved, and next day, with a sum in my pocket equal to a week's normal pocket money, was able to buy some toffee.

Greenfield Primary School stood nearby and proximity of the two schools, Catholic and non-Catholic, might have been expected to have caused some friction, but like other unpleasantness, while there were a few stories circulated of serious battles between certain children, I never witnessed anything other than the infrequent shouting match. But an election campaign gave rise to a comical situation when a car cruised past along Nimmo Drive at 4pm one day, just as the schools were coming out. It must have been canvassing for the conservative candidate, for all the children lined up quite spontaneously at the edge of the pavement and booed loudly. Even although the home I came from caused me to be in sympathy with the sentiment, it seemed so very odd coming from a crowd of youngsters. Apart from technological advances, the main difference I see in the schools of my grandson's day is in the numbers attending. Playtime today has less than half the number of children present in playgrounds of the thirties.

Today, school hours seem flexible in that pupils can be seen sauntering in up to 15 or more minutes late, quite unconcerned, showing no sign of the apprehension we would have felt in that situation. Mothers too accompanying latecomers, are equally unfazed. In times past we would have dashed along breathlessly with worried expressions, for starting times were rigidly adhered to, and if you arrived after the last of the line-up of classes had trooped in, you had to queue up with other latecomers for the strap. The main difference from today's hours of attendance was a later finish then. Infant classes finished at 3pm and primary and secondary at 4pm, so that in December and January, on dull gloomy days we walked morning and evening almost in pitch darkness. However, summer holidays were longer. Because of the habit then of taking the odd day's holiday for saints' days over the rest of the year, Catholic schools had eight weeks while others had nine.

Except for pockets like the Nethan, Shaw and Wanlock Streets area, West Govan (west of the Cross that is) seemed to be a reasonably prosperous district. There was a certain number of children who, from their ragged unkempt appearance (and smell), could be regarded as neglected. One boy in my class never had dinner. He passed the time walking all members of the class home in rotation. What stays in my mind is that the first time he came home with me, he was pathetically pleased to find that I lived farther away from the school than any of the others he had gone with up to then. The sad aspect of the occasion escaped me at the time, for I thought he was doing it by choice while, it is quite obvious now, it was more than likely that there was probably no-one at home or anything to eat there. Of course I quizzed him about his seeming lack of need for a mid-day meal, but accepted without question the statement that there was 'Naeb'dy in' at home. The expression for this heard with remarkable frequency, when asked 'Whit did ye get fur dinner the day?', the answer, perhaps in jest but quite likely to have been true, was 'A run roon the table and a kick at the cat!'

Apart from the life-threatening illnesses, less serious infectious diseases seldom encountered today were rife, such as scabies and impetigo, and head lice too, weren't uncommon. Are there any children today who have to subject themselves to a degrading head-search? Then, if any vermin are found have their hair shaved off, which made them stand out like a beacon and a target for ridicule by others. It nearly happened to me on one occasion when a member of a group I had associated with was found to be infected. The drill was, using a special fine-toothed comb and lying over a chair with my head over a sheet of newspaper or a basin of water, my mother ran the comb over my scalp. It was dug in with not a little force and had to scrupulously cover every square inch, so that any crawlers present would be dislodged and easily spotted. Fortunately none were found. Cases of scabies occurred at intervals, and when I developed a rash with a crust, a visit to the doctor, to querulous accusations of mother that 'You've picked it up from somebody', was vital. Impetigo, only marginally less repulsive, was diagnosed, for which I spend a week in purdah with large areas of skin covered with gentian violet.

Other pests encountered frequently then which are not often seen today, except in circumstances usually involving birds or animals, are fleas. The first time I remember having picked one up was complaining to mum of having had a disturbed night in bed because of an itch. I was promptly hauled up, then and on subsequent occasions, and stripped and examined closely. Sometimes the telltale signs were found. Red spots over an area of skin identified the culprit, and immediately Mother, after inspecting my pyjamas closely without finding anything, would rush to the bed and slowly peel back the covers, all the while studying intently the newly bared surface. 'There it is' she would cry, making a grab for something invisible. Fleas are so tiny that squeezing one hard between finger and thumb did not always dispose of it. Once, she made a great show of catching one, chasing it over the surface of the bed until, with a cry of triumph, she appeared to catch it (it was invisible to me). She then came to me aiming to display her 'catch', saying the best way to kill it was to get it between thumb nails and press hard. I have to admit to being somewhat sceptical, because I had seen nothing, and still think I saw nothing, except a tiny black dot in the centre of a spot of blood on her thumb nail. The nearest bug to compare them with for size are midges.

In 1938 or 1939 a show was organised by the school authorities and staged by pupils in South Govan Town Hall, for which individual classes were encouraged to, as it was termed then, 'put on a turn'. Led by teachers of course who had the job of organising the entertainment. We were expected to put on a playlet, sing as a choir, or perform a mini pageant etc. A couple of teachers were fortunate in having in their class a child with a good singing voice, or who could recite a poem, and something could then be organised round them to bring in the rest of the class. As there was no talent in our class, we were coached to sing a song (or nursery rhyme, it was 'pat-a-cake baker's man') and perform actions in unison signified by the words, for which we were dressed in white blouses and short trousers. Material of the garments is recalled as being silk-smooth and shiny. The main hall, small but well fitted out at that time with an elevated properly lit stage, was packed to capacity by parents and friends, and we did our stuff with only a few hilarious moments. However, I was uncomfortable and had a feeling of impending disaster, and could hardly wait to get off the stage when our turn ended with no mishap having occurred. My parents' first words to me later were 'What was wrong with you; why did you fidget so much?, you looked as if you had St Vitus's Dance!' Well, perhaps I was more round-shouldered than the others for I was the only one so troubled, but my braces, of white silk like the rest of the attire (if silk it was? although it is more likely to have been a cheap substitute), were slipping off my shoulders so that I was terrified my shorts would end up round my ankles. (St Vitus's Dance, an uncontrollable twitch, is now known as Huntingdon's Chorea.)

On a frosty day of wintry sunshine the whole school was in a ferment in anticipation of a planned visit by the Lord Provost, Paddy Dollan. From the Golden Jubilee booklet of St Gerard's Senior Secondary School, it is known he conducted the official opening of that school on the 20th of December 1937, and the Scottish Film Archive has in its collection a very brief film of the LP, described as scenes of him visiting three schools in Govan at that time. Also, a still photograph of him with pupils in St Anthony's has been seen, so it seems likely that St Constantine's was the third school of the tour, significantly all of his own religious persuasion. His arrival was supposed to have been around mid-morning, and while we were full of enthusiasm and were looking forward to the event, it wasn't really due to any appreciation of his position. Through the grapevine, probably a teacher let it slip, we heard that at the end of the visit we would be sent home for the day, so, as far as we were concerned, the quicker he arrived the sooner he would leave and we would be off home. But time passed and there was no sign of him.

Thinking about it now makes me curious about whether there was communication between schools, and I wonder if they were connected by telephone, so that the visitor's location might be known and his arrival anticipated. Perhaps school authorities of the time were reluctant to make use of such information, considering it 'unfair' to take advantage of what was a by no means new medium, that they should simply hold themselves in readiness by habit. However, lunchtime release time passed with still no sign of the LP. We were then told to go home and not return. As the crowd of excited children went surging down Uist Street in the slanting sunshine of the day before the winter solstice, revelling in our release and free for the day and with the Christmas holidays due to start soon, the official car appeared from the Langlands Road direction. Going on past us it drew up at the school entrance. Having been released first we younger ones were in the lead, and most of us dutifully made to turn back as we fondly imagined would be expected of us, only to be carried on by the dense throng of older children rushing along behind who had no such intentions. Except for a fleeting glimpse through a window as the car passed, of Paddy's quite distinguished looking head, with gaunt features, deep set eyes and flowing white mane, that was the only time I saw him. Although he was a socialist, his reputation with the far left at that time had been tarnished and his name was mud with the ILP. In particular, my father was very scathing about him, although in this case I suspect Dad's religious intolerance might have had much to do with it. John McGovern was another political figure regarded in the same light.

Building the Vogue cinema

During 1937, at the corner of Langlands Road and Crossloan Road work commenced on building the Vogue cinema, which was to open in the summer of 1938. Behind the site and situated in the northern section of Uist Street was McLean's boatyard. The Vogue was to be a first class hall, on a par with the Lyceum, the last of the four extant cinemas in Govan to be built, and may even have been the last designed in art deco style in the country. Walking to and from school I passed it most days, observing the progress of work from site preparation, through the foundations being laid and the building going up, until it was completed. The activity was observed in a sort of half interested way without realising what it was to become. Without knowing that for a decade it would be a palace of enchantment and the last word in entertainment, which I and countless others would enjoy attending many times.

Scotch derrick cranes were once very common. As well as on building sites, they were used for lifting and moving about heavy loads in places like building contractors' storage yards, timber yards, steel stockholders etc. It was one of the first items installed on the Vogue site, for use in preparing the ground and unloading construction materials. As the name might suggest they were a local invention, cable operated usually by geared hand crank, with larger ones steam or internal combustion engine driven. However, they were static, depending on a long jib to give reach. Constructed of timber beams, individuals of the type had a vertical post set in the ground, and two others in inverted sloping V formation as bracing, with the point of the V fixed to the top of the vertical, and the legs spread well out and anchored in the ground. Jib winding, luffing and lewing machinery was located at the base of the vertical post, on the opposite side from it.

Construction work was fascinating to watch, and once or twice I was late for school or returning home, when some operation of particular interest was under way and held my attention. Such as a squad of men with shovels mixing a batch of cement in that pre-mechanised age. When working a large batch, the mixing was tackled by a group of half-a-dozen or so surrounding the heap of ingredients. Each man circled round it, following the man ahead of him, shovelling the mixture non-stop from start to finish, with water being added to the well, or void, in the middle. Bricks were carried up a series of ramps incorporated in the wooden scaffolding of the time, to the places where the bricklayers were working, by men using a curious device called a 'hod'. It was employed on all building sites using bricks, until mechanisation brought in first man hauled and then motor driven lifts. Made of solid hardwood, the hod was a right-angled V platform, with one end of the channel blocked off, mounted point down and braced with stays on the end of a stout pole. Length of pole was such that with its end on the ground the channel came to just below shoulder height. With it carefully balanced, the labourer loaded it up with about a dozen or so bricks. He was then able to place his shoulder under the V and lift and carry it. A load of bricks would weigh something like a hundredweight, but it was easily controlled on the shoulder by the pole, with the channel lying at an angle, blocked off end down and slightly over the back to retain the load. Other routes to school were used, via the park and Drumoyne Drive and Nimmo Drive, and we, my schoolfriends and I who lived in the Linthouse area, changed from one to another with permutations, as the mood took us.

When the Vogue opened at the beginning of July 1938 the owners (the Singletons?) held a gala and fair day in Pirrie Park off Langlands Road. Pirrie Park was Harland & Wolf's employees sports ground, which had been set up on land that was part of West Drumoyne farm, and named after that company's managing director, Lord Pirrie. One of the Vogue management team, a well built young fellow who I think was a member of the owner's family, was involved in what should have been a spectacular display. In a marquee, entry to which a nominal charge of something like a halfpenny or a penny was charged, and dressed only in shorts, he had a circular cage of shiny metal rodding lowered over him. It was connected to a d.c. generator, so that with the power on and probably set at a low voltage, he held a metal rod which he was supposed to run up and down the bars, the current passing through him to earth. With him standing barefoot, this should have produced showers of sparks while delivering only a mild kick. Unfortunately for him the voltage regulator must have developed a fault for he, with sweat pouring off him, was receiving plenty of kick but there were no sparks. We got refund.

South of Pirrie Park but separate from it, the land must have belonged to the Education Department. An interesting building lay on an area laid out as sports pitches, access to which from Ardshiel Road was by a hedge lined path between the gardens of houses there. It was a long low wooden structure with a pitched roof and covered verandah, and a stepped frontage similar to the British Legion pavilion in Holmfauld Road. An outlyer from Govan High School, it was used as a sports pavilion and was known as 'The Ranch'. The name probably derived from its resemblance to buildings of that type seen in the Western films so popular at the time.

McLean's Boatyard in Uist Street closed around this time, but there is a vivid memory of walking on one occasion in Langlands Road near Drumoyne Road a year or two before with Grandad Chambers, when a traction engine hauling a large trailer carrying a boat approached. It must have been early in the year of 1936. We stood at the pavement edge to take in every detail of the spectacle, of this seemingly enormous white boat with ropes dangling in even loops round the outside from the gunwales. Grandad took his pipe from his mouth and pointed with it. 'That's a lifeboat, and it's going to Clydebank to be put on the new Cunarder', later named the *Queen Mary*. This story raises two questions. First, it must have been a Sunday, otherwise he would have been at work at John Brown's. Second, why was it travelling west in Langlands Road?, for the picture I retain is of a bulk appearing to fill the road as it passed Govan High School which might have been a bit too big for the ferries. From Uist Street it should have been heading for the town centre to cross the river by KGV Bridge. Perhaps it was being taken to KGV Dock to be put in the water there, for onward movement by river.

Parks of the district

We were fortunate in having locally three safe recreational and play areas in the form of parks, of which Elder Park was the largest. All had high boundary railings, those of Elder Park substantial. Smallest of them was in the form of a right-angled triangle, at the junction of Moss Road and Langlands Road with Langlands Drive on the third side. It really was too small for ball games needing a lot of space, but it had a grassy central area surrounded by a made-up path and, like the other parks, a border of bushes and trees which made it ideal for hiding games. At its southern tip there was (and still is) an electricity sub-station, surrounded on three sides by bushes which I remember sneaking round in the course of a game.

Between Greenloan and Greengairs Avenues is the rather larger roughly oval park, also bordered all the way round by dense shrubbery. It was of better size and shape for ball games, and the central, oval grassy area had an unusual border of trees spaced out all the way round the edge. At that time the trees were an ideal distance apart, so that it was possible to pick two opposing pairs to use as goals. This gave a choice of either setting up a pitch for a small game with a few players by playing across the narrow centre, or along the long axis for a big game with a lot of players. Three occurrences in this park come to mind.

The first was when, approaching the age of nine, I had been pestering Dad to teach me to ride his bike. He agreed eventually, no doubt with reluctance born of the knowledge that once proficient he would have to put up with interminable requests to go cycling. His original bike was an older model of Raleigh make with a fairly heavy frame, having the straight-across type handlebars he favoured, midway between the older upright kind and the latest 'droop' sports style. After a couple of years he acquired the sports model referred to before in the story of the pulleys, a Daytona Elite with droop handlebars. Both these bikes had Sturmey-Archer 3-speed gears. Why he chose this location for my first attempt isn't known. Perhaps he felt that if I was going to be a failure it would be better to find out away from the sight of folk who knew us. Anyway, we went round there and he put me on by myself. I had gone with him before for runs riding on the crossbar, known then as a 'baurie', but they were brief and governed by how long it could be tolerated before my backside and thighs became too painful. Even with the bar padded, Renfrew and back was about the farthest.

We started out in Greengairs Avenue with him walking alongside holding me up by the rear of the saddle, assisting with the steering and giving instructions. After going what seemed like a few yards I got the hang of the steering, and he disappeared out of sight behind but I sensed that his steadying hand was still holding the rear of the saddle. Then, becoming more confident I asked how I was doing, and getting no answer after a pause asked again, this time turning my head partly round. Still there was no reply. In addition I could not see him, and diverting my attention was making me wobble rather a lot. Making an effort to regain control I snatched a quick look behind, only to see him walking about twenty feet away. Realisation that I was on my own gave me a start for an instant, but then, with a surge of elation realised I was actually 'going' a full size two wheeler. Soon we were venturing on even longer journeys to Barrhead, Erskine Ferry, Campsie Glen, Stewarton, etc.

Unlike today's mainly mute bikes, virtually all cycles then were equipped with an audible warning. Most had a bell of the type currently seen, and heard, on film from the Far East, particularly China, clamped to the handlebars. From the smallest child's trike to full-size uprights and sports machines, almost all had them, their musical trill a more tolerable warning than strident contemporary honking motor horns. The bell was mounted convenient to hand grips, and the sound generated by rotating weights on a return spring, which was triggered by a thumb lever projecting from the side, striking a small metal dome which screwed on over the mechanism. The de luxe model which I longed for but never acquired, was two-toned, producing a very musical trill from double top-and-bottom or sometimes side mounted domes. However, some usually older people had small air operated horns worked by squeezing a rubber bulb. Cycles of an older vintage than this had what was called a 'back step'. Because of adult usage the term persisted, and often youthful cyclists on up-to-date machines, were asked by their bikeless pals for a ride using the phrase, 'Can I get a hurl on your back step?', even although there was nowhere for passengers to place their feet.

The second event was walking to that park with a group of pals to play football, and finding a team of older boys already there, playing with a near full-size ball. There were mutual acquaintances between the groups so they agreed we could join in. But my first kick brought disaster, for the bladder proved much too heavy, and in attempting a kick with it coming towards me fast I sprained my foot and had to limp off home in agony.

The final event happened during the war when, like many things, fruit was so scarce, except for poorer quality home produce, as to be virtually unobtainable. While playing there with pals on a warm early summer evening, a certain weed was much in evidence in full bloom. After a while some of us lay down on the grass to rest, and I had plucked one of them and was absent-mindedly rubbing the seed pod between my fingers, when I caught a whiff of the scent it gave off. The smell was of apples, not ordinary apples, but the distinctive sweet smell of MacIntosh Reds that we hadn't seen for a couple of years. We lay on the grass in the warm evening sunshine enjoying a smell none of us had experienced for a good part of our lives, while trying to recall what apples from Canada tasted like.

Elder Park

Elder Park was nearest and by far the largest of our parks. It had a putting green, swing park and a pond for sailing model boats and catching 'baggie' minnows. There was bowling and tennis we could watch if we felt like it, and large grassy ares, extensive flower beds and a hot-house. The swing park, then situated in the north west corner which made it very convenient for us in Linthouse, was the biggest attraction, having ideal facilities for children. It was closed off from the rest of the park by chest high railings, with a single entrance gate. At that time a deep border of bushes and mature trees ran all round the boundary, cut through only by entrance paths, which was particularly dense at the swing park corner, especially in full leaf of summer. In the swing park section children were shielded from the noise of traffic on Govan Road, and the residents opposite, there and in Drive Road, were screened to some extent from the noise created by crowds of youngsters enjoying themselves. During the late 1960s, road improvements connected with the Clyde tunnel cut away this corner, taking with it the swing park, and a poor substitute in swings and other amusements was provided near the tennis courts, in a part of one of the most extensive grassy areas.

The main attraction was a pair of large frames of tubing, each containing four swings with wooden seats suspended by two chains with an inverted 'Y' section at the bottom. One frame stood on each side and to the rear of the centrally placed attendants' building, a small substantially built pavilion of red brick, with a pitched tiled roof topped with red coxcomb ridge tiles. It contained a central room for the attendant with a toilet either side for boys and girls. There was also a maypole, a roundabout (then called the joywheel), a circular paddling pond bordered by a ring of sandpits, divided into four sections by access paths, and an area of grass with a scattering of benches for mothers accompanying the younger children. Strangely, there was no shute.

In front of the pavilion was an original Parks Department cast iron drinking well standing between three and four feet high, with a thick heavy shell having vertical ribbing. A domed overhanging top, also ribbed, was surmounted by a knob shaped like a large seed emerging from its pod. Another knob, with ridges polished smooth from twisting by more than one generation of little hands, projecting horizontally on the right-hand quarter, turned on the water, which came from a spigot moulded in the shape of a lion's head set under the edge of the cap at the front. There was a cup, also of cast iron, very thick and heavy to withstand constant rough handling, which imparted a metallic taste when you put it to your lips. It had a rounded base with a loop moulded on, to which a chain was attached, with the other end securely fixed to the well cap and left to dangle. At the base of the shell, near ground level beneath the spigot, a semi-circular catchment moulded as part of the body was kept permanently filled by spillages — for animals to drink from.

That area was closely supervised by an attendant, a deeply tanned old soldier with a good supply of stories of army life in distant lands. He used to hold us in awe with tales of his experiences in India. It might have been noticed earlier in these reminiscences, that an interest in discovering what the rest of the world was like was developing. I liked to get around and was always keen to go with anyone, family or friend, who went walking or on a journey by tram, and holidays and other events which took me farther afield were looked forward to with growing awareness and anticipation. This interest in new places was manifesting itself in a liking for, and an outstanding ability at, school geography lessons. Too bad it was the only subject I was outstanding at. At secondary school, when a particular set of end-of-term results was announced I had scored 95 per cent for geography, which carried the average one point over the 50 per cent minimum needed to be moved up a class, otherwise that year might have had to be repeated.

The maypole held an enigma for me. I could go on it only for a short period because it made me feel squeamish. But it wasn't motion that caused it — it was the smell of the rope of the harness. The pole was like the old-type tall thick heavy steel lamp-post, with a cap under which rotated a ring with a number of metal loops. To these were fixed lengths of chain long enough to reach to about head height of an adolescent. The lower end of the chain had a loop of heavy rope attached, into which the upper torso was placed. It was this rope, which had a distinctive and peculiar odour similar to but not quite the same as creosote. Obviously it was the smell of the preservative. The puzzle was I seem to have been the only one affected in this way, having to be off to recover after a couple of minutes, and thereafter keep away from it. Once or twice after standing near it for a time watching others having fun, and seemingly out of reach of the smell, the same twinges of nausea were felt. Which now makes it seem that as well as having a physical effect it also had a psychological one. After a time even the continual ringing noise produced by the chains striking the pole, which occurred with normal boisterous use, threatened to bring on the same symptoms when heard from as far away as the far end of Skipness Drive. It might have been caused by an allergy in my system to some chemical element in the preservative.

A great innovation not observed in any other south side swing park was the paddling pond. It was shallow with smooth concrete lining and easy sloping stepless sides, which allowed the youngest children to paddle with a minimum of supervision. In good weather it was well used, but had to be emptied daily for cleaning. A major difficulty was caused by the nearness of the sandpits, because sand was continually being walked into the pond on children's feet, and thrown in too when the attendants' back was turned. Throwing balls of damp sand to splash someone standing in the water was a favourite pastime, but anyone caught doing it was banned. If sand was allowed to accumulate it blocked the drain and allowed the pond to overfill in wet weather, and it then became a hazard. After the summer season was over and it was taken out of use, its sloping sides made an ideal scooter or fairy cycle track, a 'fairy' cycle being the smallest kind of bicycle. Design of the joywheel was different from modern examples, in that the current ones are built for riding on by standing on board a low platform close to ground level, and holding on to radially set rails. The older design was of flat topped open tubular construction, built up to flare outwards from the centre with the faceted or segmented outer rail at about waist/chest height. This open frame allowed a number of children to position themselves within the frame and run, pushing on the bar ahead, permitting a somewhat dangerous speed to be worked up, another activity the attendant had to look out for and put a stop to because of the risk of injury to younger ones.

Except where they were original, furnishings and fittings were of the same standard design in all parks and green areas, however small, throughout the city, with the possible exception of major items like boundary railings and bandstands. If, like those in our park, they dated from the days of the independent burghs, before they were taken over by Glasgow and came under the control of the Corporation Parks Department, they were usually of different design. Other features were low shin high single-bar railings, having broad uprights with a sleeved hole at the top through which the heavy square section rail passed, installed around grassy areas from which people were excluded, of which there were plenty in the parks of old. Higher (waist high) fuller railings, nicely designed in thin rodding, the tops of which were a pair of harmless double concentric semi-circles, were all of a common design, which was repeated in railings fronting all council housing built during the 1920s to mid 30s. Recently, I was amazed to see some sections of these same railings still doing duty in Househillwood at certain corners near the library. Also, there were the numerous signs requesting you to 'PLEASE KEEP OFF THE GRASS', with lettering in relief on low broad cast-iron plates spread around on the forbidden areas.

Perhaps most distinctive of all park furniture were the numerous bench seats spaced out along path edges, except in the flower bed area which had unique seats of its own. The more common benches were of rustic design, with a pair of supports near the ends, uprights in cast iron which formed two legs having an extension at the rear which angled up as a support for the bench back. These were intended to resemble tree branches of irregular but identical shape, with a simulated rough bark surface which innumerable coats of paint had rendered smooth. Photographs showing scenes in parks dating from before this period show simple single-plank seat and backrest benches. But those recalled were each about eight feet long, with a single-plank backrest, and double-plank seat with an unfortunate spacing that could trap fingers. Modern park seats are of similar design but are made from pressed sheet metal. Flower bed seats were of the slatted kind, with narrow slats fixed horizontally close together in continuous rounded flowing curves. These were supported at the extreme ends by intricate cast iron supports containing a moulding of a coat of arms, which, come to think of it, would in all probability have been those of Govan Burgh.

The bandstand was used regularly in summer, with concerts at weekends and occasionally on weekday evenings, weather permitting. On days when a concert had been arranged, a union jack flag was flown from the tall flagpole which stood between the bandstand and tennis courts to the west. Simple individual folding seats were laid out on the broad surrounding path before the concert started unobserved, appearing and then disappearing mysteriously. The bandstand itself was located roughly at the park centre where the six paths seen today converge. It was an ornate octagonal cast iron structure, with a pagoda type roof supported on eight round columns. Its platform, about four feet above the level of the path, had a waist high cast iron screen round the edge, with steps up to an opening in one of the facets. In the 30s that screen was fretted, but the fretting isn't visible in the none too clear picture on which, as a memory aid, I've based much of this description.

If viewed from a position away from the platform entrance, the screen gave musicians a slightly comical appearance, with only the top half of their bodies visible. The narrow area between the bottom of the screen and the surrounding path was banked up with earth and laid out as flower beds, and the whole encircled by a high spiked railing with facets and a gated entrance matching those of the bandstand. A number of bands and concert parties gave performances in it, but the only ones recalled now are the Salvation Army Govan Citadel, SCWS and Govan Burgh brass bands. The bandstand itself came to an ignominious end during the war when, probably during the operation of scouring the country for any metal not doing an essential job, although it might just have been necessary because it had become unsafe, it was pulled down. A rope was tied round a pillar and the other end attached to the back end of a lorry. One pull from the lorry and the structure collapsed. We heard about it later from someone who had seen the event, and it was one I felt cheated at missing. It may be thought that in collapsing the whole district would have been alarmed by the noise. But it was wartime, and anyway surrounding industry most likely made enough racket to cause it to pass unnoticed.

The boating pond, oval in shape and, when compared with other park ponds, of medium size, was a magnet for us in summer and no doubt still is today for youngsters of the district. More for fishing than sailing model boats, because the models we possessed, home made because nobody had parents who could afford anything better, tended to have a short life. After a couple of years' service my yacht, the present from Dundee, had reached the end of its sailing life. Its mast was broken, so the hull was only fit for use as a pull-along model. With a length of string tied to a point on the deck edge called the 'quarter', it was towed round, staying out from and keeping parallel to the bank. A ledge, running all the way round the edge just above water level, provided a good platform for pondside activity, and on days when there were few fishers I could walk round towing the hull until boredom set in. At that time the pond sides below the ledge sloped down to the bottom at a convenient 45 degrees. The broad stone piers at each end of the pond had low well worn square stone pillars at the outer corners, making ideal vantage points for spotting minnows. These pillars were hotly contested for by fishers, because of the 270 degree sweep of water area accessible from them.

At the height of the minnow season there would be scores of children parading around on the ledge carrying their nets on canes, intently eyeing the water on the lookout for a likely prospect. Some days there were so many it seemed remarkable the pond wasn't fished out within a couple of hours. Fishing for minnows, baggy minnows we called them (shortened to baggies, no explanation is known for that term) could be very competitive among us to see who could catch the most and biggest. In those days jam was bought in 1lb and 2lb glass jars of standard shape. Every jam manufacturer used only those sizes, and an empty jar of the larger size was ideal for keeping minnows. With a piece of string tied round the neck, incorporating a carrying loop, it provided the usual method of transporting home the catch at the end of a couple of hours' fishing. Second choice was a milk bottle of the wide necked design of the period. Fishers would hold their bottle or jar up for inspection, for the usual comparative arguments to rage as to who had the best catch.

Usually, winners in this competition with no prizes, except ego boosting it is obvious now, were those with the most patience. Initially I was scornful of one method of fishing. The odd one or two to be seen moving their nets slowly and cautiously towards a likely catch were using stealth, when it seemed to me that speed was essential. However, they were the ones who invariably had the best catches, because their stealthy movements did not alert the fish, while allowing the net to retain its shape in not causing the wire stiffening loop to be bent back by a too forceful thrust. Moved slowly, the net retained its widest mouth setting and greatest catchment area, and I, slow in the uptake, never came to realise this until it was far too late to benefit from the knowledge. We rushers pushed our nets through the water violently in the natural urge to be quicker than the minnows, but were usually more successful in scooping up weeds, mud and debris from the bottom than fish. I used to look longingly out into the middle of the pond sure that, with no paddle boats therefore no access for junior fishermen, there would be plenty of fish out there. Big ones which never came near the edge and so survived longest. Then someone was observed using a device which opened up the possibility of getting access to what was fondly imagined to be a vast shoal of fish, possibly big enough to eat even, which must be swimming about out of reach — a lure.

The lure was in the form of a bobbin of thread on the end of which a scrap of red cloth and a white shirt button were tied, and a nail to weigh it down, which was thrown out a few feet and pulled in slowly with a slightly jerky motion. Although he had only a short length of thread, the boy using it seemed to make it work well enough, in that a few minnows followed the piece of cloth and button to within netting distance. But the technique he employed with the net was less successful than it ought to have been, partly because he was working the lure and trying to use the net simultaneously. After studying it for a while it appeared to me that the operation could be improved on. For example, by having a long enough length of thread to get as far out as possible; trying other materials and different colours; tying the weight on some inches away from the lure, because it caused a disturbance in being drawn along the bottom by stirring up sediment, which tended to obscure the lure and probably scared off the bigger fish; and setting up in partnership with someone else to share the two tasks. But surely best of all, why not set the net up in advance laid flat on the bottom and camouflaged with bottom debris, and then pull the lure over it so that the fish following would pass over it and be easily netted with a quick lift. This last idea seemed to be the clincher, the one that would make me famous as the boy who could fill jam jars with fish in a very short time.

Like most juvenile schemes, the reality was a bit different. After scrounging a bobbin with a long length of thread from Mum, and getting her to produce a suitable scrap of red cloth, a button and a nail for weight, the lure was made up. Then agreement was reached with a pal about operating the scheme, and we set off for the pond full of optimism, carrying a couple of jam jars in which we were confident there would be insufficient room to hold our catch. On trying the first cast, as far out to the middle as I could manage, it was found that the catch was unlikely to be anything other than weed, clumps of which caught on the weight and deterred minnows from following the lure. Of course that was where it had the chance to grow undisturbed by the many thrashing nets of the mobs of fishers. Soon, by trial and error, we found the best distance for the lure was to throw it not too far out, a little beyond the four or five feet or so of the boy with the original lure was about right, and we got to know places where it could be thrown farther without snagging anything. We succeeded in losing lures which had caught on obstructions the thread was too weak to dislodge them from, or through tying components on unwittingly with a 'granny' knot which came loose. But the biggest disappointment was that the minnows lured in were the same as anywhere else in the pond. Camouflaging the net, too, proved to be something of a dead loss, because fish were more difficult to see against it when it was covered with debris of the same colour as that surrounding it, except when it was sunny. Nevertheless, we had some successes.

Experience taught us that minnows were unaware of, or indifferent to, a net of white fabric lying on the bottom, for there were enough other similar items like sweetie papers and cigarette packets scattered around for them not to show any awareness of a net. The result of this scheme was that sometimes we did well and others we didn't, and soon others were using the same technique with a variety of lures and varying success, so we abandoned our grandiose plan as a waste of time. At the height of its efficiency the lure would be drawn in with a string of fish following, so that we waited for the biggest to pass over before making the 'lift'. But the excitement generated among the inevitable spectators very often meant that an inadvertent premature movement of the net spoiled the operation by frightening the fish off.

Later that season a partnership was set up with an older boy, Ivor McCallum of Clachan Drive, a better catcher of baggies than I. Weather conditions must have been ideal for their growth, for the minnows were bigger than usual during the summer of 1938. We were, or he was, catching some exceptionally big ones, the largest of which we had trouble fitting into even the larger size jar. One monster, it must have been between four and five inches long, when put in the large jar seemed to occupy so much room that we tipped out the rest of the catch to accommodate it. It was a prize specimen, but because of a problem at home (his mother had threatened to put it down the lavy pan) Ivy decided that I should be entrusted with looking after it. I proudly showed it off to my mother and after negotiating with her about where it might be kept, it was agreed that it could sit outside on the (three stairs up) kitchen window ledge.

Next morning, on going to check on my charge I was dismayed to find the jar empty. What had happened to it, we wondered. Mum also, for she too was mystified. Had a seagull snatched it, or had some envious youngsters climbed up the rone pipe, up the three flights, to steal it? If so, why leave the jar? Did he put it in his pocket? After more wild speculation we began to think sensibly about where it had gone. At that point I recalled hearing stories of people who kept goldfish being careful not to fill the bowl up too near the top, or they would jump out. There was no trace of the fish on the window ledge, but on going down to the backcourt sure enough there it was — dead. Obviously, after lying there probably for most of the night. My main concern was that Ivy would say about this. But in the event, after a bit of leg pulling along the lines of 'no bein' fit even tae look efter a fush,' we went back to the pond to try again.

Because of numbers and size of the minnows, and continuing good weather, the pond was crowded each day, with dozens of children milling around and getting in each other's way. Ivy suggested we try an expedition to Victoria Park pond, which is a little bigger than Elder Park's and might be less crowded. So off we went on what was for me a daring journey of adventure, across the river on the ferry to a place visited in the past only when accompanied by an adult, usually Granda. However, we found that conditions there were the same as in our own park and that we were among non-too-friendly strangers, so that expedient was abandoned and we returned to our own park to fish among familiar and friendly acquaintances. My one and only visit to the Fossil Grove took place around this time.

The only opportunity of seeing bigger boats on the pond was when club members sailed their yachts at weekends during summer. They were kept in the clubhouse, which again was built of the same pleasing red brick as most other buildings constructed by the parks department, and which is still standing at the north west corner of the pond area. Regattas were held at intervals, when club members' boats made a spectacular showing on days of suitable weather conditions. To my mind it wasn't fair that grown-ups had the privilege of sailing models that should have been the preserve of children, so why were there so few youngsters to be seen with them? Certainly there were some dads, grandads and uncles with children, but they were never permitted to use the pole, with its rubber ferrule, to turn the boat away from the pond edge on the opposite track — something I longed to get to do.

Another attraction of the pond, a permanent resident which was almost an institution, was a one legged swan called Jock. Permanent because its disability meant that it could not leave. To begin with I was rather afraid of it because it had a fierce reputation and hissed menacingly at anyone approaching too close. Then one day I saw a dog having a go at it, growling and snarling in a frightening manner. It looked to me as if Jock could not possibly survive this, but I was reassured by Grandad who said that the swan was quite capable of looking after itself, and that its wings were powerful enough to injure the dog if it came too close. Visitors took scraps of food along to feed it, so that although it was unable to feed naturally by being restricted to a comparatively small area, it seemed fairly well off. In summer I used to feel sorry for Jock because visiting swans, with their cocked up wings, sometimes numbering up to half-a-dozen, arrived to occupy the pond for a time, and they always chased 'our' swan off so that it spent much of the time on one of the nearby grassy areas.

In winter, if there was a long enough spell of frost and the ice became bearing, the pond was turned into a fantastic playground, but Jock was always looked after and a patch kept clear of ice for him to dip into. There used to be hundreds of children and young adults thronging the surface, skating and sliding, producing a phrase I remember being used by grown-ups to describe the scene set in the white landscape of winter — 'the pond was black with people'. Ice forming during a long hard frost with calm conditions gave a good sliding surface so that we could slide on any part of it, but if it became bearing after a period when the temperature fluctuated, with partial thaws, particularly if there had been sleet or snow, the surface could be too rough for comfortable sliding. On those occasions, and they seemed to predominate, children formed groups which concentrated on a particular section, and smoothed out a strip by sliding repeatedly over the same narrow area which was gradually extended. A serious hazard could be introduced, in that after ice began to form and in the interval before it became thick enough to walk on, the edges were continually being broken up and pieces thrown all over the surface. When the temperature rose above freezing and dipped again those pieces froze and stuck, leaving obstacles dotted about on an already tricky surface. Minor injuries were caused by people sliding, tripping on one piece and falling, and their momentum causing them to slide on, then being caught by another.

Two events are recalled which happened during prolonged frosts. The first of these was two periods of hard frost with a thaw between. The first freeze made the ice bear for a few days. Then a thaw set in for a few more days causing it to be broken up round the edges by children, the melting leaving a gap of about five feet of clear water between the bank and the main body of ice. Frost then returned for an extended period, producing a situation to test the nerve of any adventurous boy or girl, with the ice left from the original freeze lying five feet out surely bearing by this time (or was it?), with edges not quite thick enough to get us out there. I remember seeing brave or foolhardy youngsters, the lightest in weight who could be 'persuaded' to try it, moving out sideways slowly and cautiously, while holding on desperately to a pal standing on the pond ledge, each clasping tightly the outstretched hand of the other, and the brave one ready to fall towards the edge should the surface give way. The action of trying to leap or scramble or make any sudden move would surely cause the ice to break, but fortunately, if it was dangerously thin it usually gave out warning cracking noises before giving way. Anyone finding themselves in this situation had a hard decision to make, for any attempt at a sudden move to safety would increase the chance of a breakthrough and give them an icy dip. The best method of overcoming the hazard was to take a run at it to pass over the thin ice quickly, and this was what happened eventually, providing that it was perfectly safe in the centre and that there were some brave youngsters around. Soon the area of thick ice was full of the young and not-so-young, but it was quite hilarious watching the more timid who were desperate to get out to the safe ice, trying to pluck up courage to run over the thin stuff.

When the long cold spell ended there was a period of unseasonally mild weather and a repeat of the weak edge-ice phenomenon, which caused the winter sports to come to an exciting conclusion. It was apparent that the edge was more and more risky but there were still plenty of people prepared to chance rushing over it, and even with the sun shining and the air mild nobody gave it a thought that the centre might be becoming risky also. With quite surprising abruptness ominous cracking noises were heard, causing looks of horror and panic to appear on the faces of the large numbers still enjoying themselves. The surface began to clear as if by magic as everyone made a dash for the safety of the bank, but over the whole area it had rapidly become unstable and one youth on skates went through. However, he managed to keep upright and found himself standing on the pond bottom up to his thighs in the freezing water.

Soon, many people from the surrounding district had heard about the break-up and the excitement it was generating, so that as well as those who had got clear and were lining the pond, many others arrived to enjoy the spectacle. The crowd was humorous, offering advice to the unfortunate 'paddler', telling him to swim for it or fly out, or look for so-and-so's boat which had sunk the previous summer. After trying to climb up on to the edge of the ice a few times, causing it to break again, eventually he was successful and found a temporarily safe region on which to decide his next move. A quick inspection by onlookers — it had to be quick for he had to keep on the move because of continual cracking noises, suggested he try a particular place. Taking a long run to gather as much speed as possible, he flew across the thin section and on to the low step. But his momentum carried him on to the high step, over the broad path bordering the pond, over the low railings and on to the forbidden grass where he had his leg pulled further about trespassing — 'Can ye no' read?'.

The other event, occurring during another winter, was a period of hard frost that lasted for an unusually long time. The ice on the pond was of unprecedented thickness, seven or eight inches if memory serves me right, with freezing conditions lasting well into March. After a couple of weeks of spring-like mild weather, which seemed to have little or no effect other than make the surface slick, it became very warm for mid-April with the temperature climbing to around 60 degrees. The effect of this was that there we were playing on the ice clothed for summer. Soon after, to allow the yacht club boating season to begin, it was reported that park employees had used chains to break it up to make it melt more quickly.

A curious sight encountered in the flower beds which lay between the putting green and the old park superintendent's house, is what appeared to us to be a short flight of stone stairs and entrance to a mansion. But there was no house. The story at the time was that it was all that remained of the original Lint House, abode of the local landowner, which naturally we assumed had stood there. However, recent reading indicates that it is the Italianate portico from John Elder's house, Fairfield Mansion, which stood near where the fitting-out basin was constructed. Contemporary maps show house and, to the west, the basin in existence at the same time, but the mansion and its associated outbuildings were probably cleared away to allow expansion of the works in the 1890s. The portico, if it is the original it must by now be well over 200 years old, was considered to be of such architectural merit as to be worth preserving, so it was carefully dismantled and rebuilt in the park.

In the thirties the path leading to the swings from Drive Road continued beyond the swing-park entrance, to run parallel with and close to Govan Road and on to the pond at the boathouse. Lying between pond and swing-park was a group of low buildings, in one of which the park superintendent lived. Between the house and that path lay a courtyard enclosed on the north side by a high brick wall. A gate in the perimeter railings here was used by the public, but also by park staff and vehicles to gain entry to the courtyard through solid double doors in the wall. Around the courtyard a group of buildings, which were used by employees to store machinery, and by gardeners for their equipment, had the appearance of having strayed there from the countryside. On the east side of the yard were two hot-houses, while on the south side was the rear of the super's house which, from this aspect looked like an old farmhouse. From the study of old maps it is now believed to be, for one or two of the original group of buildings are still there today, the original steading of Fairfield Farm. Also, as far as can be judged, the same maps indicate that Holmfauldhead House was situated near and a little to the west of the junction of Clachan Drive and Skipness Drive.

A third-of-a-mile or so to the north west, Linthouse Mansion stood inside Stephen's shipyard. I was certain of having seen it on the left inside the main gate when passing by in Holmfauld Road, because the first time a photograph of the house was encountered it seemed familiar. But reading one of the many books on local industrial history by Messrs Moss and Hume indicates that it was demolished during the early 1900s. The office building next to the gate looked comparatively modern in the thirties, so the mansion was probably originally used as offices until it was found to be too small, then demolished to make way for the new building. Linthouse Mansion had been built by the man responsible for the lint producing industry established there in the seventeenth century, hence the origin of the name.

An alarming event occurred during a summer storm of thunder and lightning. A friend and I were playing in the street together when the sky turned as black as night and it began to rain. We moved into the close of Number 12 for shelter as the downpour became tropical and the flashes and crashes came nearer. Considering ourselves grown-up and feeling brave, at first we enjoyed standing at the closemouth waiting for the flash, then dashing inwards to escape the subsequent peals of thunder. The kind of terror the phenomenon used to generate when I was younger, when Grandma and Mum tried to calm me with 'Ach, it's jist the boats gettin' coal!', were firmly behind me. But during that cloudburst, with the sky at its blackest, we were awaiting the next flash, by this time not a little scared by the inky blackness and violence of the phenomenon. There came a flash and crash together, the brightness of which momentarily blinded us; so loud was the sound we were deafened, which caused us to fly into the innermost recess of the close, where we remained, petrified, until the sky began to lighten.

After the storm passed there came a report of a lightning strike in the park. The avenue from the bandstand to the north-east entrance was lined with beautiful mature trees, one of which grew at an unusually steep angle, and this was the one affected. Local people flocked to inspect the damage, a deep scar in the bark exposing white wood on the underside of the leaning trunk, running from high up to ground level. The scar remained visible for decades, but looking for it recently I could not find it. The puzzle then was why the lightning bolt took that path, but it is clear now that in the downpour rain would run down the branches and merge, forming a stream of water pouring down the underside of the trunk which would have been a perfect path for the electrical charge. Examples of this have been observed elsewhere, on trees similarly affected.

Standing in the other flower bed area in the Langlands Road/Arklet Road corner, Mrs Isabella Elder's statue is a well-known landmark to West Govanites, and many families, like ours, probably have family group photographs taken there. Inside the north-east park entrance is a curious monument in granite with the inscription: 'To the memory of the civilian and naval personnel who lost their lives in the Gareloch in the K13 disaster in 1919', which stirred a desire to find out what happened. Part of the history of shipbuilding on the Clyde, it is a tragic and harrowing story, but it is unnecessary to re-tell it here, for the details are accessible through library or local history group.

Like other large parks, Elder Park was constantly patrolled by uniformed rangers or park keepers. We called them 'parkies'. Compared with the very few who do the job today, who skulk around in vans and are provided with two-way radios, in the thirties they walked about all day in all weather in a smart uniform with skipped cap, equipped with a whistle which they had no hesitation in using. The uniform, of ubiquitous Corporation dark green, gave them a kind of military bearing and made them look 'official'. Large areas of the bigger parks were strictly forbidden to all, like the outer boundary of shrubs and trees and some scattered clumps, the flower beds, and carefully manicured areas of grass which were fenced in with low iron railings. Anyone daring to put so much as a foot there was whistled on as soon as they were spotted, and told sternly to 'keep off'. A vivid picture of one experience is of finding myself between the distant figure of a parkie on one hand, and a trespasser on the other, with the former blowing his whistle at the transgressor and shouting at him to 'keep to the path — or else!', the youth in question meekly doing what he was told with a sheepish look. All parkies seemed to have an authoritative presence and an ability to confront a wrongdoer and command him to stand to attention to receive a dressing-down, then send him on his way cowed.

In summer the shrubberies round the perimeter were dense and high with a good scattering of trees, where the gardeners turned over the ground regularly to keep down weeds, which made it a place to keep away from in wet weather. During a dry spell, however, it was particularly suitable for hiding games, but it was a no-go area of which the parkies were exceptionally vigilant on their patrols. The border varied in depth, being quite deep along the Langlands Road section of boundary. Occasionally, it happened that on expeditions through the park we found ourselves in that area, so the braver elements sometimes ventured into the depths to play. Initially they kept a lookout for the parkie, but pressure of the game could soon divert attention. It took more courage than I possessed at first to do this, and I always pleaded another engagement like my maw needed messages or it was time for me to go up. Until one occasion.

On being joined by others unknown to me who were acquaintances of my pals, I found myself caught up in the enthusiasm of a game of 'cowboys'. In the excitement caused by being part of so large a crowd, the threat of the parkie was forgotten. We played happily for a time, running through the bushes without a care — until suddenly I realised I was on my own. Abruptly a parkie appeared out of the dense summer growth and grabbed me — *me*, out of upwards of a dozen or more who had been milling about seemingly but an instant ago. This ranger obviously had plenty of practice in scaring the daylight out of wee boys. He went on in a harsh voice about how he had reported me to my mum and dad and they were going to give me a leathering, and the polis had been told about me, and so on. After a while he let me go and I made my way home on rubbery legs in trepidation. My knees felt weak as I went up the stairs and, cares of the moment having made me forget to whistle to have the door opened, knocked and stood on the doormat expecting the worst. When the door opened and nothing happened my panic subsided, and realisation came that I had been conned. Nevertheless it was a long time before I ventured into the bushes again — as no doubt was the intention.

Closing and locking the park was carried out strictly to time in the past. All were completely enclosed by railings with lockable gates. Hours of opening at this time were dawn to dusk in winter and 7 a.m. to 10 p.m. in summer, these times being displayed on large ornamental boards at each entrance, which also carried the extensive list of by-laws, rules and regulations like No Cycling, No Gambling, No Consuming of Intoxicating Liquor, etc, etc, etc, all of them rigidly enforced. Two small removable panels on the board displayed the hours current at the time, and somehow a memory remains that the idea of being locked in accidentally was a cause for major concern, even among grown-ups, despite it being a fairly simple matter to climb out over the railings. Unless of course you happened to be elderly, infirm, or a woman, for no women wore slacks. Despite the spikes, why this impression should remain with me isn't clear. As closing time approached the parkies (in summer there was more than one on duty at any one time) walked about blowing long blasts on their whistles to warn people to get out or risk being locked in. All equipment in the swing-park was immobilised. The swings and maypole were chained and padlocked, and the joywheel was locked by a rod set in the ground.

The main entrance, at the north-east corner in Govan Road near Elderpark Street, in terms of size and mini-grandeur in respect of the surrounding district, is in keeping with the Victorian age which produced it. Standing inset from the back line of the pavement, in a recess with curved inner corners, it has substantial stone pillars which once carried heavy cast-iron double gates flanked by smaller pedestrian gates. Inside, the short length of broad drive for the few yards to the K13 monument was, like the main road, laid with cobblestones. Many features visible in photographs taken a hundred years ago on the occasion of the park's opening ceremony, and later, are still to be seen there today. Only a few alterations have been made to the layout of paths and ornamental cultivated areas during that time. One photograph taken shortly after the opening in 1887, is a view looking west towards Linthouse. Taken from high up in the tenement in Elderpark Street (or Thompson Street as it would then have been), it shows a sector of the park from a point overlooking the main entrance and gates described above. Beyond the park Merryflatts buildings and clock tower, then comparatively new, can be seen, in a view unimpeded by the tenements soon to be erected in Drive Road and beyond. Behind the trees in the centre of that picture, and obscured by them, and roughly in line with the superintendent's house in the centre background, should be the first tenement after Linthouse Buildings to be constructed in Linthouse, at the north end of Drive Road.

The long tenement in Drive Road between Skipness Drive (then George Drive) and St Kenneth Drive, must have been in the course of building, because my great grandfather, Alexander McFarlane, is recorded in the 1891 census living at 13 Royal Terrace, as it was called before being changed to Drive Road. Visiting that area today produces a feeling of 'belonging', and it is strange yet somehow comforting to consider that the scenes in the pictures of Elder park in the late 1880s and 90s, must have been familiar to my paternal grand and great-grandparents. My father's mother was one of a family of nine. Her father, the Alexander McFarlane referred to above, had five or six addresses in the area between Helen Street and Drive Road between 1871 and 1901. Dad was one of at least eleven children and his father, the barber with a 'saloon' at 56 Queen Street, lived at five addresses over a rather wider area.

Another institution from a decade or two later is Elderpark Library building. In the late 1930s it was under 40 years old, a remarkable building with character, something worth pausing to admire. Today, after a further 50 years, it is showing its age and the exterior is being patched up. I first came to use its facilities at the end of the decade being written about, and here opened up a world of previously unimagined interest. After school on cold winter afternoons I used to wallow in its warm comfortable atmosphere, where talking above a whisper just wasn't allowed. It was redolent of the smells of fine timber, highly polished like the brass fittings to be seen around the interior, and, I suppose, the leather-bound books in the reference section. For me books became the essence of enjoyment, although I have no recollection of any from the childrens section. It was in the adult non-fiction department, where there were a great many on foreign countries and their people, which interested me most. Among the specialist travel books were accounts by adventurers who indulged in that then fledgeling sport, mountaineering. I read about Irving and Mallory on Everest with awe, and wondered if it would be conquered in my lifetime, resolving that if the opportunity occurred I would take it up. This even although I tended to suffer from vertigo. Heights have always made my toes curl.

CHAPTER 6

General Events and Random Observations

An unlikely supplier of information, with an article on what was described as the ultimate source of energy, was a children's religious magazine produced in monthly editions by the Irish Catholic church and sold from church bookstalls, called *Our Boys*. My aunt bought it for me for a year or so. All the stories and most of the articles it contained were slanted towards its mainly Irish readership, with children in country adventures 'running down the boreen' and such-like Irish idioms, with some of it in Gaelic. At a time of change from picture books and comics to written material, I found it interesting but irritating, in that most of the story settings in Ireland were strange, because they contained elements of the supernatural mixed up with religion, as might be expected because of its origin. However, one feature was a column of brief news items in which there was a reference to the atom, and some kind of matter (or material) which had been discovered, from which power (or energy) could be extracted, giving mankind the prospect of unlimited development sometime in the future. That was how I learned for the very first time of atomic power.

One aspect of life completely revolutionised is in the realm of food. While most dishes served up fifty years ago would be quite recognisable today, at that time any of foreign origin were unknown in working-class homes. The most exotic meal recalled is French toast. Bread and potatoes were the main providers of bulk, while rice, served up occasionally in our house, was always in the form of a sweet pudding. Stews and mince served at dinner time were generally of the cheaper cuts, and sausage figured frequently. Something which made an occasional appearance on our table was skirting, a name unknown in this context to most younger people, because though tasty, it tends to be rather tough even when well cooked. Today its use is restricted to older people (with good teeth) who relish it, and the rest used, well minced, as filling for pies, bridies and sausage rolls. There being no fridges or freezers, leftovers were to be avoided, and usually anything perishable not consumed by the following day had to be thrown out. Many foods now available the year round were only on sale in season. Salads were a summer only dish because lettuce and tomatoes could be bought only between April and September. Our main meal on a Friday was always fish, and, a fussy eater as a child, it was one of many items I had to be made to eat. Economy reasons meant that every scrap of what was set down in front of me had to be consumed, but the one item I really loathed was pudding in any form. At this time tins of Heinz baked beans contained tiny pieces of pork, which made them a favourite. That novelty disappeared during the war and only recently reappeared under the guise of 'beans with ham'.

The 'black hole' toilet and pleasures of a pipe smoker

Joe Chambers, my grandfather, smoked a pipe. He used thick black tobacco, the reek of which sometimes caused me to have a spasm of coughing. When that happened he immediately laid it aside. My grandparents' house had no electricity to the end of their tenancy, and in common with most other gaslit houses of similar design, had no provision for a light in the toilet, or even in the lobby off which it opened. The toilet was tiny, a square, virtually windowless cubicle which gave me problems when I needed to use it, for I had a child's normal fear of the dark. The only illumination to penetrate into it came from the landing through a tiny slit of a window set high up in a wall. Even on the brightest days only dim daylight got through, and at night the stairhead gaslight was weak and set too low down to be of any benefit. After dark you had to do the business in pitch darkness. It was a case of finding your bearings with the doors to kitchen and toilet open, to illuminate the interior, then closing the latter and hoping for the best.

It could on occasion be a dreadful dark smelly and frightening (though not unclean) hole to enter, but the biggest drawback for me was after granda had spent time in it enjoying a smoke while on a natural function (known as a 'number 2'!). If during this time I was seized with the urgent need to go and had to wait until he was finished, there were occasions when on dashing in desperate for relief I found myself in a much worse state, for the tiny compartment was full of smoke, a predicament I continued to experience in later life. For economy reasons there was no such luxury as tissue toilet paper. What happened was that newspaper was torn up into handy sized squares, then, with a hole pierced in a corner of each sheet, a length of string was put through it and tied into a loop. The loop with its bunch of sheets was then hung from a nail convenient to hand. I do not recommend anyone on an economy drive to try it because, speaking from experience, it really is a dead loss.

Pipe tobacco in one-ounce packets prepared ready for smoking was available, but many pipe-smoking older men bought theirs by the stick, or cut from a roll or coil. The leaf was compressed to resemble rope of size and consistency similar to, but denser than pepperoni sausage, and was cut from the coil and sold unwrapped. As well as Thick Black there were other brands, one of which was Bogie Roll, smokers of which were generally considered to have an above average constitution to withstand it, for it was powerful stuff. When bought by the ounce the coil was lifted from the drawer beneath the counter, and the 'rope' end uncoiled and laid out to have the requested amount cut off, an estimated half-ounce or an ounce or more, with a knife, the blade of which was stained and encrusted with tar, and weighed on scales.

Preparing for a smoke was ritualistic, beginning with production of the items needed. A plug of tobacco, a penknife with a blade much reduced by honing, the grindstone (which was in frequent use), his tobacco pouch, made of soft leather and considerably worn through years of use, and a small, much scored flat piece of hardwood. And of course a pipe, chosen from among a selection of half-a-dozen suspended on a pipe rack hanging on the wall at the fireside by his chair, with its cap with spring-loaded retaining clips which fitted over the bowl, and a taper or box of matches. Other pipes in his collection had lids fixed permanently, opening on a hinge. First, a few slices were cut from the plug, then laying them on the wood he cut them up carefully into smaller and smaller pieces, turning them this way and that as he did so. What fascinated me was how he managed to do this without cutting himself, for his fingers were constantly in close proximity to the blade. Then the crumbs were rubbed in small amounts between his palms until they reached the desired texture, which may explain why, in some old adverts for cut tobacco, certain brands were described as Ready Cut and Ready Rubbed.

The pipe was then held with the bowl resting at the outer end of the crease in the palm of his hand, at the chopping edge, and the rubbings guided carefully into it and tamped down with a fine judgement of pressure. Not too firm or it wouldn't draw, or too light or the tobacco would burn up quickly. Usually the whole plug was treated in this way and the rubbings stored in the pouch for future use. Then, with the pipe gripped firmly between his teeth, a taper was lit from the fire, gas stove, or mantle, and he would sit back and puff away with a contented expression on his face. He had a spitoon which he used, constantly sitting on the floor at the side of his chair — a flat white enamelled-metal dish with inward flaring sides, the loose lid of which had a shallow full-width depression with ribs running down to a hole in the centre. Memories of these scenes are the source of another emotional conflict, for although the smoke might induce spasms of coughing and unpleasant feelings in my bronchial tubes, the smell of it has ever since generated, and continues to do so in certain circumstances, a sensation of pure longing for a return of the happy times I spent with him.

Of brands of tobacco and cigarettes then available, one or two had exotic names. One was made by a Paisley company called Dobbie and their brand name was 'Four Square', the meaning of which was a square deal for your money. Their product was sold in round flat silvery tins of two-ounce capacity. Another brand was called 'Balkan Sobranie', and recently reading a work by Solzhenitsyn, Sobranie (sobranyie), described as a Slavic word, was defined as meaning 'pick of the crop'. John Player sold a ready rubbed tobacco, and cigarettes, called Prize Crop, and W D & H O Wills had another known as Gold Flake. Two other brands of cigarettes come to mind — Craven A with the advertisement inviting you to 'For Your Throat's Sake Smoke Craven A'(!), and De Riske Minors and Majors. With more smoking then, spitting was more common, and pubs had sawdust scattered and spitoons strategically placed on floors. Worst offenders were older men who *chewed* tobacco, and public transport used to have notices prominently displayed at the front of lower decks reading 'No Smoking', and on the upper deck where smokers were confined, 'No spitting — Penalty 40 Shillings'. Having to keep away from tobacco smoke, I sometimes wonder are 'Willy Woodbines' still available?

Despite having ultra-sensitive bronchial tubes smoking fascinated me. I fondly imagined it was the thing to do and that all men did it, and couldn't wait to grow up to indulge in it. There was an occasion when I found myself with three-halfpence, and through listening to talk among pals knew that two Woodbine could be bought, extracted by the shopkeeper from the then popular unsealed paper pack of five, with that sum. Confiding in the boy who was then my closest buddy I went into Dick's and bought two Woodbine. The old man in the shop gave me an odd look but handed them over for the cash, and having made sure to acquire matches well in advance, we retired to a place of concealment. We lit one each and puffed away for a while, assuring each other how much we were enjoying the experience, although it seemed his look mirrored the way I felt — rather queasy. Months later the opportunity occurred to repeat the experience, but on going into Dick's with the request, he regarded me rather severely and said 'If you don't stop this I'm going to tell your father!' Dad called there daily for his *Evening Citizen* so, quite apart from not really enjoying the experience, that put the hems on smoking experiments for a while. From then on I looked on Mr Dick as an ogre who had deprived me of the opportunity to experiment with adult things. He was a rather sad figure with a deformed leg and walked with a painful limp, and is recognised now, rather late in the day, as someone to be congratulated for trying to keep me on the straight and narrow.

It was around this time I heard talk somewhere that tea could be used in a pipe instead of tobacco. One day, in a friend's house when his parents were out, I mentioned this, so he produced a clay pipe

H

and the tea caddy and we tried it. Be assured it works, producing a peculiarly pungent aroma. When his mother arrived home, she went around the house sniffing and looking at us in a way which indicated that she was sure we had been up to something. Quite rightly, she suspected me, and I was never again invited into that house. Then we found an alternative — cinnamon stick. I noticed them on sale for a ha'penny a stick in Annie Bennie's sweet shop but never had the opportunity to sample them, until one of our group announced that he had heard they could be smoked like cigarettes. This revelation electrified us. With much secrecy, which probably meant that half the street knew what we were up to, we tried it out and found that it too worked. So for a while my ha'penny a day pocket money was spent on cinnamon sticks for smoking (never inhaling I should emphasise), the 'in' thing until our mothers started asking awkward questions about the peculiar smell clinging to us when we came home. At that point we decided it was better to find something else to occupy our time. Anyway, by then we had tired of the smoking caper and were longing for the usual fare of soor plumes, swizzles, sherbet fountains, liquorice sticks, and the figures in cheap chocolate, which could be bought with our ha'pennies.

Treating an injury

In a previous chapter, there was reference (in the section on the coal fire) to how the kitchen fireplace was protected at floor level by a fender, and a description given of the one we had which had a pair of padded boxes, that could be used as seats. As a further refinement this fender set had a thin plate of the same metal for a base, which lay flat, completely covering the area within the fender, the stone or cement hearth. Its function really was decorative, for when polished it was a considerable improvement on the original surface, although being thin it tended to distort. It had sharp edges, but the weight of the fender held it down firmly enough while covering them over. That plate was the cause of a quite serious accident that left me with a scar which has remained throughout my life, and was included in a list of identifying features used in my description by the army authorities on being called up for national service. The accident happened on a day when Dad was helping with the household chores and was using the cylinder vacuum cleaner, our first suction cleaner which had only recently been acquired. My mother preferred this type to an upright model and never during her lifetime would she have a Hoover. In the course of using it the fender was always pushed back from the front edge of the platform, the side pieces being able to slide so far into the boxes, to allow cinder and ash that invariably gathered there to be drawn up. When the vacuum cleaner operator moved on to save them stopping, anyone else available in the kitchen would be requested to replace the fender in its correct position.

On this occasion I had been asked, but because of dilatoriness Dad had progressed round the kitchen to a point opposite before I moved to comply. Getting down on my knees facing the fender I gripped it to draw it out, in doing so lifting it up so that the plate beneath also lifted about an inch above floor level at the front edge. At that instant Dad, in the course of making a sweep from the other side of the apartment and moving backwards so that we were back-to-back, took a backwards step and his heel struck my foot. With only my light weight on it the force of the push thrust my left leg forward, so that the knee came in contact with the edge of the plate with such force that a wide deep gash was cut across the kneecap. The would was so deep that the bone itself will probably still show the effect after all those years. Apart from the pain, on seeing the injury I went into shock and do not remember much of what happened for a while. There was one brief glimpse of Dad, holding my leg while I lay on my back on a chair, with a basin of water and disinfectant below it, and him lifting a soaking cloth or sponge and letting the fluid run into the wound, filling it until it overflowed.

Even through the haze affecting my mind I was aware of the exchange of recriminations which went on between my parents, with Dad saying to me 'What were you doing down there anyway?' and Mum reminding him rather forcefully that I was just doing what he had asked of me. A result of this, something I enjoyed but could have done without, was being kept off school. Proper treatment of an injury like this for folk unused to it is often a matter of guesswork, for while there was a hospital casualty department there was no easily available taxi transport to get you there. Telephones were few and far between and there was a fear born of ignorance of how to use them, and the proportion of people having a telephone then could be compared to those owning a video camera today. Virtually no working class home had one, and anyway the doctor had to be paid for.

In those days, dressing an open wound like this was a case of dipping a piece of lint in boiling water to sterilise it, letting it cool and laying it over the injury, then binding it firmly with a bandage. With hindsight it is easy to see that this was wrong, for blood seeped through and soaked the lint, and at the start the bandage as well, before hardening into a crust or scab which forms a protective cover and allows the healing process to go on underneath. But when the dressing had to be changed, three times a day was judged to be about right, and the lint lifted off, it takes the scab with it leaving the process to start again almost from the beginning. In my case this went on for most of the following week, and as it eventually appeared to be healing there was talk along the line of 'Back to school soon.' Then I became aware of a stiffness in the leg and although I had been walking a little, carefully, it became painful again but in a different way. It felt as if the leg was becoming rigid, while showing a tendency to turn outwards at the knee. Without anyone really looking to see how it was progressing I was accused, in a half pretending/wholly in earnest way, of faking to avoid going back to school. I suppose Mum might be to blame for this, because she would have had the task of attending to changing the dressings. But it has to be borne in mind that with her colourblindness, and mine, we would not have been alerted by the red aspect of the wound, and leg in general, caused by the inflammation, and here I speak from personal experience of similiar situations in later life. By the next day the leg had begun to swell and develop a really angry red appearance.

The doctor was summoned urgently and diagnosed a septic wound, for by then it was leaking pus, and gave my parents fits for not calling him sooner. Today, antibiotics would take care of sepsis and banish it in a few days, but the treatment then was unpleasant and long drawn out. A piece of material called skin, similar to the thicker plastic used today for bags of the kind which used to be available at certain supermarket self-service fruit and vegetable counters, a little larger than the lint, was laid over the wet lint, then bandaged up. This drew the poison from the wound by sweating it out, but it meant much more frequent changes of dressing, two-hourly if I recall correctly. The healing process was considerably lengthened because the wound could not begin to knit until all the poison had been drawn out. I think I was off school about a month in all, and it brought on the only visit from the school board officer. He was the truant chaser, one of the officials then employed by the education authorities to go round the homes of absentees to check that their absence was legitimate, that they were not doing so without their parents' knowledge.

Some toys of the times

My earliest remembered toy was a tin putt-putt boat, so called because of the noise it made when working. It was about four inches long with a bath shaped blue painted hull made in two halves, top and bottom, which had been pressed together. Inside, along the pressed groove simulating a keel, lay a thin tube which was heated by a pellet of flammable material. Just how the propulsion system operated escapes me now, but sitting in a couple of inches of water in the big tin bath, the tiny boat could be made to move slowly along making the gentle putt-putt sound. Of course the naked flame requirement meant that this amusement was available to me only as a spectator and under adult supervision. Another item never seen today, but played with among the toys in Mearnskirk Hospital was a pop gun, a wooden tube, probably cane, with a plunger like a cycle tyre inflater. A cork, attached to the barrel by a length of cord, was rammed in the open end, and when the plunger was pushed in vigorously it was fired out with an explosive 'POP'.

In the 30s Malcolm Campbell was attempting to be the fastest man in the world with his Bluebird car. Models of Bluebird were on sale and I had a beauty about a foot long. Although of tinplate it was very realistic, with its low-slung body of futuristic design complete with disc wheels and vertical fin at the rear. It gave a lot of fun although I have no recollection of whether it was powered or not, but it may have had a clockwork motor.

Among many toys and playthings of the period there was a torch with coloured filters operated by thumb levers, and a kaleidoscope. Details of the colours cannot be given for obvious reasons, but the torch was a favourite plaything which there is a vague recollection of having while in hospital. Colour changes were effected by pieces of coloured celluloid which pivoted over the beam, although just how this was done cannot now be recalled, but what is remembered is that affording the short life batteries of the time was a problem.

My kaleidoscope was a sealed tube with a slight taper about a foot long, made of mirror glass with the mirror side inside, one end of which, the viewing end, was plain glass. A section through the tube was, in shape, like an arrowhead, in that one side, held uppermost when viewing, was half as wide as the other two. The opposite, larger end from the peep-hole was angled at 45 degrees. A plain glass opening opposite the angled section, at the end of the narrow side, allowed light to be reflected along the tube to the eyepiece. Inside were tiny pieces of brightly coloured and sparkly card of a variety of shapes which, when the tube was shaken and the pieces allowed to settle, looking in the eyepiece with the light shining in the opening at the other end, the viewer saw a pleasing multi-coloured regular repeated circular design which altered with each shake.

Tiddley-winks was another common competitive sedentary pastime played, for preference, on a card table, it having the most suitable surface. Each player had a coloured disc of stiff plastic type material that may have been horn or celluloid, about the size of a 2p coin, and six others of the same colour of smaller 5p size, all having rounded edges. Taking turns and using the large disc it was possible, by pressing down on the edge of a smaller one, to make it jump up and forward, the object being trying to be first to flick all your small discs into a cup.

Another present received at this time was the picture-gun mentioned earlier. It was a quite realistic looking pistol in cast mazak type metal which split into two halves through the centre, with hinges along the top of the barrel. Inside were guides in which ran a loop of film containing about twenty frames. The sides of the film were slotted, into which a tag, part of the trigger mechanism, engaged so that when the trigger was pulled the film moved forward one frame at a time, in much the same way as modern film is moved in camera and projector. Looking just like a silencer, a lens, contained in a short polished metal tube which fitted into the muzzle, could be moved in or out to focus the projected picture, and two pen-cell batteries were held in the handle. As a hand gun its appearance was extremely effective, and when the war began and batteries were in short supply it was used very effectively in games as such. It arrived in a presentation box containing a number of films in cartoon style, of highly condensed versions of, for example, Davy Crockett, with real actors depicted, Lew Ayres being one. Another was noticed in 'Hollywood', a history of the film industry programme on TV a few years ago — Ella Raines.

Train sets

For my first Christmas after coming home from Mearnskirk hospital in 1937, I was given as a present an 'O' gauge passenger train set. It was a good quality outfit by the German company Marklin, but wasn't what I really wanted. Having earlier seen in the house of a neighbour of the Chambers a quite elaborate Hornby set, which I was permitted to watch briefly as the children of the house played with it, my heart was set on one like it. 'O' gauge was then virtually the only commonly available scale, and catalogues had been obtained which showed the large range of sets and accessories manufactured by Hornby. Rails and sleepers of these sets were thin tinplate pressings, made in straight sections about a foot long and performed curves, each being of one-eighth of a circle. What gave them a most unrealistic appearance, though, was that each section had only three wide spaced sleepers. In the smaller less expensive sets which included rails, there was usually just the eight curves making up a circle. The next stage was sets with two straight sections, making an oval. But my set had four straights so that it made a larger than usual oval. With the exception of the clockwork motor, everything was tin-plate. Each part of the set was of the high quality for which the Germans were and are renowned, and it continued to work well for the next decade despite the usual rough treatment by a juvenile to which it was subjected. My memory of the model was of an 0-4-0 tender locomotive with outside cylinders, and three four-wheel coaches of vaguely British outline.

Included with the set was a 'tunnel' and an early form of remote control, a sliding lever which fitted to the track. The cab of the engine had two two-position knobbed rods projecting through from the motor, for direct setting of the controls. One rod was for stop/go and the other forward/reverse. Connected to them through other levers, were metal flaps which projected below the motor at rail level, and set across direction of travel. These could be triggered according to setting, by a moveable tooth in the three position device which clipped into the track. Position one was free of any control, set at two made the engine stop, and in the third position it reversed direction. Though fascinating for a youngster to play with, that device was the opposite of realistic, for it made these changes while the engine ran at the only speed possible — maximum. Carriages were of the type common in toy sets, but unusually there were three of them with the peculiar Marklin type coupling, the only part which gave trouble. This was of course caused by rough treatment, for their design intended that they would be unable to uncouple accidentally. If the train was lifted when coupled, held by the outer ends it bowed, this caused the couplings to distort and lock, making it impossible to separate them. For many years the three coaches remained coupled up, which rather irritated me because it was impossible to put them away tidily in the box, a situation which lasted until I grew stronger and able to use pliers to free them.

While catalogues had been acquired showing the large variety of accessories available in the Hornby and Meccano rangers, I had not seen any comparable Marklin catalogue so did not know whether this company had a similar range. Long after, I found they had, but the items were not as freely available in this country as those of Hornby. Apart from the Marklin set, and a Meccano No.

OO construction set which came later and which generated additional desires, these catalogues sustained me for a decade or so. It may have been that had much of what I saw, and craved, in the illustrations in these booklets been made available to me, they might have caused disappointment. However, many an hour was spent pouring over the pages looking at the fascinating variety of train-sets, models of engines, rolling stock, track and points, stations, level crossings, tunnels, signals and so on in the former, and all the vast variety of parts in the Meccano list, that only a scarcity of funds, for what my parents regarded as a somewhat frivolous desire, denied me.

Mechanical devices fascinated me, especially trains, road vehicles, ships, aircraft or models of these forms of transport. It was an obsession not assuaged until middle-age was reached and satisfaction came at a significant point in my life. As a long time member of a model railway club and having constructed a number of unusual models (scratchbuilding is the term), mainly of diesel locomotives of which there were then no commercial models, I was approached by a group of fellow members for advice on some point or other. Lacking confidence to advise on the matter in question I suggested they ask other older members who were surely better qualified, telling them to consult 'the experts', when one of them said 'But what are you if you aren't an expert?'. Realisation dawned that I had reached the point of seeming competence at which, as a new recruit at the start of my membership, I had regarded those who were then the older members. I am indebted to Arthur C. Clarke for providing the following quotation which he thinks may be by Freud — Happiness is a childhood dream achieved in adult life!

Other playthings, games, books and comics

Would any young person today know what 'blow-football' is, and is it still around? It was a sheet of stiff paper about 4' x 2' marked out as a football pitch, which folded up like a map to large envelope size. There were collapsible card goalposts with their bases glued in position, which self-erected when the sheet was unfolded, and a dense marble-size ball of cotton wool was attached to the centre spot by a length of ordinary cotton thread, long enough to reach beyond the goals. Being naturally short of breath I was not much good, but still derived a lot of fun with it, in which the added refinement of using a straw to concentrate 'puff' helped. Folded up it was easily carried around from house to house, and was extremely popular with children — and adults, as a good if less energetic substitute for the real thing on wet days or the dark nights of winter. My father was a keen footballer in his younger days who at one stage, which must have been before I became aware of it, travelled more than once to Wembley for international matches. The tartan tammy complete with a toorie he wore, which seemed to have been, along with a scarf, the gear worn by supporters of the time, lay around our house for many years. What struck me most about that tammy was that it appeared to have been made from extremely coarse wool. I found it too prickly to wear for more than a few minutes. He and I sometimes played blow-football when he would often let me win.

In my grandparents' home there was a very unusual domino set going up to double nine. A normal set to double six has 28 dominoes, but a nine-high set has 55, and although it may not be as uncommon as is imagined, a set like it has never been encountered anywhere else. These dominoes were made of two layers, the topmost of which was bone or ivory discoloured by age, to what seemed to my partly colourblind eye to be a dark russet yellow, on which were the recessed black dots. The backing was of ebony and the two were held together with a flush brass pin. On some of them, however, the halves had become separated allowing them to pivot independently on the pin.

Collecting cigarette cards was a popular pastime with us. Of roughly business card size, sets were produced portraying in a range of pictures various scenes on a particular theme, such as different models of motor cars, motorcycles, aeroplanes, types of trees, flowers, ships etc. Each card was numbered, and the reverse side gave a description of the picture. They were found singly inside most brands of cigarettes. The object was to collect them into sets of up to 50 cards, but having no close adult relative or friend who smoked who might have saved them for me, I was at a disadvantage. Nevertheless, by swopping and trading around it was possible to make a collection, but to my lasting regret I never managed to gather a complete set for these were highly prized. My favourite was the W.D. & H.O. Wills set entitled 'Railway Locomotives of the World'. Most men had no interest in the cards and tossed them away when opening a fresh pack. During the usual randomly occurring season in which collecting was in vogue, we boys would scour the pavements outside newsagents in the hope of picking up discards. Following on from this, hanging around tobacconists in Linthouse with a pal is recalled, waylaying men coming out after buying a packet and pestering them to part with the card, with the plea 'Any cigarette cards mister?'

As a keen reader I had a collection of children's books received as presents over the years, which were read and re-read many times. One or two appealed quite powerfully and certain details of stories and illustrations in them have remained with me through all these years. Just recalling them can bring on that lovely feeling of nostalgia. It was around this time Walt Disney began with Mickey Mouse, but one book among the collection was entitled *Walt Disney's Silly Symphony* which may have been published before MM arrived. Among children's comics *Mickey Mouse Weekly* was for a time the most popular common reading material and just then, as well as the *Dandy* and *Beano*, later progressing to the more meaty stuff, the 'stories without pictures' in the *Hotspur, Rover, Wizard*, and *Adventures*. These names were always recited by us in the order of our personal preference.

A domestic chore delegated to me, was the pleasant job of going each Saturday morning to McGregor's newsagents in Harmony Row to collect the weekly papers, such as the *People's Friend* for Mum, the *Radio Times* and other magazines, and in doing so was allowed to choose one for myself. Although the choice was limited to one comic at a price of, I think, $1^1/_2$d. That apparently odd situation of travelling so far for magazines which could be bought in Dick's paper shop across the street, was because of trader loyalty which had lasted for twenty-five years. McGregor's shop was near the close in Harmony Row in which my grandparents had lived for more than a decade, from where they had moved in 1912. The proprietor of the shop and his family had lived nearby also and had become friendly, and the loyalty had endured all that time and was to continue for a while yet.

Referring to a preference for a particular comic sets up a conflict in my memory, for there are fond recollections of good stories in all of them. However, much detail contained in one particular serial in the *Hotspur* has always stayed with me, and at the time its powerful effect was sustained by a half-held belief that it was a true story. It was called 'The Truth About Wilson', the author of which was anonymous, for comic-book stories were never attributed. Only drawings, by the original artist, Dudley D. Watkins, were signed. In that story I had my first encounter with fantasy fiction (after nursery and fairy tales). It was a sports story set initially in the north of England in the (then) present day, about a mysterious man who appeared to be young, who had phenomenal physical abilities, who won by a wide margin every athletic event he entered, who was, it was gradually revealed as the story unfolded, about two hundred years old. It ran through a number of series ('The Further Truth About Wilson etc.') over the period during which I was a reader, and told the story of his life from when, in his youth, he went to Tibet to live with a mystic and learned all kinds of body control devices which gave him the incredible longevity and ability of a super-athlete.

It will be understood that at that time stories of this genre enthralled me, which of course is why it is possible to recall those details after the passage of more than half a century. Trying to interest my Dad in it I encountered, for the first time, the slightly scornful rejection I was to experience soon after with astronomy and science fiction. However, Dad wasn't a reader. He occasionally toiled over a book on the subject which interested him most — politics, dipping into it occasionally, sitting with it on his knees in a crouch and holding his head in his hands, and repeating the words slowly sotto-voce, but I cannot recall that he ever finished one.

Other comics were *Radio Fun* and *Film Fun*, in which personalities from those mediums in the form of actors and comedians, such as Laurel and Hardy, Arthur Askey, George Robey, George Formby, as well as detectives, magicians, cowboys etc, from many film series and radio programmes, were portrayed as comic strip characters. Also, there was *Tiger Tim* for the very young, and one of the best, the *Knock-Out*, had a great selection of comic strips and stories. *Magnet*, the Billy Bunter comic, was never very popular with us, no doubt due to its mainly upper-class slant and the Bunter stories set in an English public school. All these magazines were ideal trading material among children and were swapped around with enthusiasm, so that if you were keen enough and sufficiently motivated you could get to read every issue of each comic. I seem to have been unfortunate with this because frequently, when following up a serial story, often I failed to locate anyone with the issue needed who was prepared to part with it for what I had to offer. Daily papers all had their strip cartoons, and of these my favourite was 'Miffy' in the *Evening Times*. The *Daily Record* had 'Lauder, Willis and Gordon' based on living Scotch comedians, Harry Lauder, Dave Willis and Harry Gordon, all of whom I saw in pantomime.

The *Sunday Post* had 'The Broons' and 'Oor Wullie' which was first brought to my notice in the house of my grandparents' neighbours, the Patersons. I was captivated by them, along with 'Nosey Parker' and 'Nero and Zero, the Rollicking Romans', and the half page of jokes, crossword and other puzzles, as well as rhymes, dot-to-dot pictures to draw, and other trivial pursuits for children. The Broon Twins would be ages with me at that first encounter, and now 55 years later, they are still around seven years of age and here am I past sixty. Mum was pestered to buy the *Sunday Post* but there were socialist principles involved, for the editorial policy of that paper was, and still is, anti-union and my left-wing socialist father would not allow it in the house, describing it and others with similar policies as 'rags', so for a long time I had to depend on the Patersons keeping it for me. Somehow, the fact that the *People's Friend* was published by the same company was overlooked. Many years and the hostility of Dad were to pass before Mum eventually began to buy the paper, but by then I had outgrown the 'funnies'. Today, the puzzle is the kind of reading material juveniles prefer, for my grandson, Paul, shows no interest in what I found absorbing until approaching my twenties. Is it really too tame for him and his generation? No doubt TV, computers, electronic games and other attractions have taken over.

Among other books beloved of boys were two, booklets really, devoted to stories about detectives, 'Sexton Blake' and 'Dixon Hawk'. I may be wrong but I think one was a police officer while the other was a private eye. Anyway, one had an assistant called Tinker. They were written in an exciting 'Richard Hannay' style of what was then the popular type of small-format pulp magazines, and came out as periodicals, usually with one story per issue and we found them irresistible. None of us could stretch our pocket money to buying them, having to depend on picking them up from various sources, one of which might be the midden. They were treated like gold and had a high value in any swop transaction.

Straying for a moment once again beyond the (beginning-of-the-war) date limit of these reminiscences, a present for Christmas 1939 was a curiosity which baffled everyone — not just me. Even the person giving it, now forgotten, did not know its purpose. Wartime scarcities were just beginning to make their presence felt, and items suitable for children's Christmas gifts were hard to find, so that practically anything was being snapped up — even objects with obscure functions. Much time passed before its extremely simple action was discovered. It consisted of half-a-dozen pieces of unpainted quarter-inch plywood about four inches by three, the edges of which were smoothly rounded, with one of them having an extension for a bat-type handle from a broad edge. They were linked by three narrow strips of coloured ribbon in the following way. When the 'plates' were laid out flat in a line with the one with the handle at one end, and with all the shorter edges not quite touching, one length of ribbon was secured by a drawing pin or staple at the outer edge of the outermost plate. It was then laid along the middle of all the rest of the pieces, in the manner of over the first under the second over the third and so on, and secured at the outer edge of the piece at the opposite end. The other two ribbons were laid in the same way, but in the opposite sequence and near the outer edges. I cannot remember exactly how, but the ribbons must have been loosely stapled to each plate or secured in some way, or the plates would have tended to fall out, but that did not happen.

That puzzle arrived as a neat pile of smooth plates and ribbon, but nobody could figure out what it was meant to do. The best we could manage was to hold it by the handle with the pieces stacked up on top and heave it up in quick successive lifts, although all this did was to allow the plates to separate momentarily, accordion fashion, like a simple bat-and-ball game with a captive ball, then settle down again with a rattle. Then one day, held by the handle the plates were accidentally allowed to fall over and hang down like a long flag or pennant — not for the first time I must say. But this time I happened to turn the handle over through 180 degrees in the vertical plane so that, retained by the ribbons, the flat surface of the piece with the handle met that of the one below it. What happened then was that the second piece toppled down, within the ribbons, through 180 degrees to meet the next one in line, which then flopped down on the third, and so on to the final plate. This meant that each plate had performed an about face within the line. Such were the simple amusements available to us in those days, and they were as highly thought of as the latest electronic game might be today.

Once again, is there anyone today among the younger generation who knows what a bagatelle game is? I had one, and so did my sons, but I haven't seen or heard anything of bagatelles since that time, and I suppose the electronic toys revolution is to blame. While bearing a passing resemblance to pinball encountered in amusement arcades, bagatelle was a tabletop game played on a board on which were confined a number of marble-sized ballbearings. The board was of distinctive shape, with one end rounded, and they were available in different sizes. The object was to score points by propelling bools into various compartments, having different scoring values, spread over the surface. My board as 3ft x $1^1/_2$ ft with a solid plywood base and all round thin ply edging an inch high, the game being played from the straight end. Along the foot was a narrow compartment with a sliding lid, stretching almost the full width of the board, in which the bools, ten in number, were stored. Next to it, along the right-hand side, was an open slot confining the bool being played, which stretched up to near the start of the curve at the top. The curved end was raised, creating a slight slope, by peg feet inserted in the base, by an amount that could be varied according to their position in a selection of holes in which they could be placed. Scattered over the playing surface of the board were compartments which were mainly circular, but with one or two V-shaped, made up of spaced out partly punched in nails with a springy bounce. These were laid out in the form of compartments, with a restricted opening at their high point for rolling bools to enter.

The first compartment, a large circle near the top of the board, was divided down the centre with the easier to enter left hand compartment having the lower scoring value. A second divided circle of similar size in the centre of the board, had inside it a smaller concentric circle making three compartments, each again numbered according to ease of entry. There were other circles and V shaped catchments formed with nails, also small depressions in the board surface backed by a single nail placed to halt and trap rolling bools. All had different values in the scoring line-up, with the highest value points allocated to the most difficult targets. Method of play was to place a bool in the slot and, using a wooden rod shaped like a drumstick, propel each bool with carefully judged force up the slope for it to pass quickly anti-clockwise round the curve at the top. On reaching the 9 o'clock position the bool struck a nail, placed strategically close in at the side, which caused it to deflect out to the centre and, according to the amount of force applied, hopefully roll into one of the catchments and score points. Much excitement was generated by the ball bouncing, as in pinball, from nail to nail down the length of the board in an erratic and extended path until it came to rest. Other bagatelle boards had a spring loaded plunger installed for firing the bools instead of using a pushing stick. Initially, the steepest angle the board could be laid at was chosen, but eventually it became obvious that a shallow angle was best, with a bool's slow progress seeming to give better results. It was really a game of chance because the only opportunity for the application of skill was in pushing, and the level required was much too finely balanced for anyone other than a fanatic.

A very-early-age favourite was a humming top. These tops are still available today, but because plastic is an unsuitable material to make them from they are less common than they once were, for they are best made from tinplate. My top was so large that adults had to operate it for me until I reached school age, and of course it didn't last long after that for the corkscrew push-rod for operating it rapidly wore out and finally bent over, finishing it for good. What strikes me now about it is that it was bigger than most others I ever saw, and the noise it produced when pumped up to speed was quite organ-like, a very satisfying deep harmonious hum. Another plaything that gave a lot of pleasure, and amusement, was a mechanical mouse, simply a clockwork motor with a permanently fixed winding key inside the made-up body of a mouse, which ran on three tin disc wheels. It was the correct size and extremely realistic, and many were the unsuspecting visitors, women mainly, who received a bit of a shock when it scuttled across the floor when released from a suitable hiding place. But that type of mechanism would not work on today's carpeted floors. Another item, longer-lasting than most others was a John Bull printing outfit. It consisted of an ink pad and a small wooden stamping block with slots, into which oblong pieces of rubber with a letter formed on the end were placed. It wouldn't have stood up to today's demanding standards of quality, for the oblongs tended to be of slightly different lengths. This meant that it required more weight than I could at first bring to bear, when trying to make a proper clear impression after pressing on the ink pad. However, the set lasted a long time so that eventually, having gained the required weight and strength, effective prints could be made.

A different kind of amusement, and one still available today, is 'transfers', something not indulged in much, because getting satisfactory results with them eluded me. They could be bought from most newsagents' and sweetie shops, where they were sold in sheets of ten or a dozen, like stamps, at a cost of a ha'penny a sheet. About an inch square, each transfer depicted comic scenes popular at the time in the same way 'He-man', 'Transformers', 'Thundercats', and 'Turtles' were favourites in more recent times. Produced on a kind of blotting-paper-like backing paper they were placed face down on wrist, arm or back of the hand and *licked* until the paper was saturated, after which the backing was supposed to peel off, leaving the picture stuck to the skin. During a season when they were popular some children went round showing off arms covered with them, with each one successfully transferred as if painted on individually. Then there were others like me who found it impossible to make a success of it, and I wonder now if certain skins, or maybe saliva, contain an element that made it easy, which others lacked. I even remember taking a course of instruction from another boy who was always successful with them, doing everything in step with him, but while his transfers were perfect mine were the usual dead loss.

Joe Chambers and Sandy Paterson were quite friendly but they tended to argue rather a lot about politics. One day Granda and I were going for a walk when Sandy was somehow invited to go along. During a stroll out Renfrew Road to Shieldhall they went at it hammer and tongs, and one word, used mainly by Sandy, kept cropping up. It was totalitarianism, which had absolutely no meaning for me and made me heartily wish he hadn't bothered to come. I would have much preferred to have had my favourite all to my self, for him to describe the interesting things and places we were passing and go on relating his fascinating stories.

A rare sight — foreigners

Coloured people, or foreigners of any nationality, other than Italian, were almost unknown. There were no Pakistani, Indian, West Indian, Chinese, Greek or Turkish shops or restaurants at that time. All small shops which today are owned by Pakistanis were then run by local people, but proportionate to the population there were many more of them. The only time we encountered foreigners other than café- and chip-shop-owning Italians, were coolis off cargo boats docked at Shieldhall and Princes Docks who, from Shieldhall, occasionally passed through Linthouse to visit shops in Govan and beyond, for things to take back home to the Indian subcontinent. Invariably, they were dressed in ill-fitting crumpled suits and peculiar hats made of a kind of blue dungaree material, which were probably shipping company issue, sometimes barefoot in summer, or wearing shoes without socks even in the coldest weather, walking in a manner that made it obvious they were quite unused to them.

The following story was recalled by a recent newspaper article on some of the difficulties encountered by Italian immigrants in the early decades of the century, when in trying to run a business they had to put up with a certain amount of insolence and interference from local worthies. My father sometimes told the story of how, with a group of pals, they would go into the local Tally's, who provided entertainment in the form of playing records on a large ornate gramophone, and order a plate of hot peas, apparently a favourite dish in those days. When the proprietor's back was turned they would entertain themselves by tossing peas into the gramophone. When he discovered this the man berated them with 'You no' spit-a-da peas doon'i' gramophone'. HIlarious at the time, it is something to be regretted now.

Radio Moscow

Around 1930 my mother had corresponded with a remote and unusual organisation. Radio Moscow was broadcasting programmes in English of general interest at the time, with sections devoted to the home, women, recipes, etc. and had invited people to write to them on any subject in which they were interested. Mum had done so three times and received a reply on each occasion, but whatever the subject was is long forgotten. The letters, with their Soviet stamps, lay about our houses, from Howat Street to Pollok, for decades. They were the kind of keepsake taken out, like our collection of photographs, and looked at with interest every so often. Here was a tangible souvenir from an isolated and mysterious part of the world to dwell on with wonder. Soviet Russia was regarded with an odd mixture of wariness, fear and benevolent curiosity by people in our level of society, but with implacable hostility by the establishment. Through time the letters became mutilated and defaced by being used for scribbling and drawing, and of course the stamps were cut off, the intention no doubt being that they would one day be the foundation of a stamp collection. Eventually they all, letters, envelopes and stamps disappeared from sight, probably into the fire. The broadcasts were probably a propaganda exercise by the Russians.

A brief glance at Victoriana

Perils of the rocker

Mary Chambers and her sister-in-law, my Auntie Mary Ann each had rocking chairs dating probably from Victorian times. They were much favoured by older folk and children found them irresistible, but although no-one seemed aware of it at the time, the rockers of these chairs were a trap just waiting to cause serious injury to some unsuspecting toddler. The rocking surfaces were two gently curved strips of wood on each side running the full depth. Each strip was about two inches wide and rested on flat slightly wider bearing surfaces, part of the heavy open plinth base. Chair and base were held together by a single powerful coilspring fitted on the inside, in the centre of the rocking sector. Amazingly, that mounting was completely unguarded. Anything soft or breakable getting between rocker and the surface it rested on, like fingers or toes, would be severely crushed, depending on the weight of the person sitting in the chair. Even empty the force exerted by its weight, and the strength of the spring, would have caused severe crushing to tiny digits. Somehow, despite early memories of playing on and around that chair, I managed to avoid the danger and while there is no recollection of hearing of anyone actually being caught in it, it was the kind of hazard that today would not be permitted to exist unguarded.

Mary Ann Himsley had an organ which operated by air pressure generated by pumping foot pedals. It was of quite large size, not as big as an upright piano, but still an impressive instrument to sit at.

She used to let me try it, but I didn't then possess the co-ordination necessary to allow me to do more than one thing at a time without a lot of practice, so never progressed beyond the one-finger messing-about stage. The main problem was that my junior height did not permit sitting comfortably on the stool, and working the pedals while trying to play. An abiding memory of the instrument is the pleasant musty smell of Victoriana that came from it, probably from the aged wood and many decades of dust. The stool fascinated me as much as the organ. It had three lions' feet which flared out at the base from a thick hollow cast iron column, and a round padded seat on a giant screw which could be turned inside the column to alter its height, like a mini joy wheel. We used to wonder what happened to that organ and the painting of Bonnie Prince 'Chairlie', as the family called it, that hung above the bed in her bed recess when she died and her house was cleared out in the early 1940s. The only thing I recall my parents gaining was her clothes mangle. It was in her house that I first tasted Cremola Foam and another delectable bottled drink called Boston Cream, which I think later became American Cream Soda.

Styles of the 1930s

Older women invariably wore clothes which informed the world they were old. Ankle-length black or dark hued dresses and coats, hats of similar dark colours, thick stockings of dark grey, and low-heeled shoes, shaped to accommodate their bunions, were common apparel. Bunions are seldom encountered today for they were caused by wearing poorly-fitting shoes. Poverty was the main cause of this and progress made on shoe design and fitting, plus the ability of even the poorest of the young and old to buy cheap shoes which fit properly, has all but eliminated the condition. Another affliction affecting feet and hands never heard of today (except in reminiscences like these), is chilblains. They showed in the form of painful red welts on feet and hands, mainly fingers and toes, and were attributed to excessive exposure of these members to cold. It sounds now very much like frostbite.

Another item of women's apparel never seen now is the 'stole', which was worn draped round the neck and resembled a bulky furry scarf. Mum had two — one for normal dress wear and another of better quality for more important occasions. Stoles were usually made from the full skin, including paws, complete with claws, of a single fox, although others, made with the skins of more exotic animals, such as mink and silver fox, were also owned by the affluent. The skins were complete with head and tail, treated of course for elegant wear, and worn draped over one shoulder and fixed under an arm with a length of dark silk cord having a tassel, or simply looped round the neck like a scarf. Mother's stole had a wooden spring clip in place of the animal's lower jaw which, with it draped round a shoulder, clamped on to a section at the base of the tail on the opposite side just above waist height. Another fashion she followed was wearing a hat with a veil when dressed in her best togs, generally of the large mesh draped type sometimes shaped to fit under the chin. Indoors, day wear for most housewives was a sleeveless housecoat of cotton print, which crossed over a the front and fastened at the back with tapes, and a dust cap made of similar material. Mother generally wore one of these until in later years the 'pini', the apron which older women still wear today, came into use. A change in nomenclature is evident in that what she used to call a 'frock' is now a 'dress'.

Photographs of street scenes from last century and early years of the present taken in slum areas of Glasgow will show 'shawlies', women with babies who needed their hands free for carrying. They were usually the very poorest who could not afford a pram or go-chair, and had been unable to acquire someone else's discard. The difficulty was overcome by wrapping a large shawl tightly round the body in such overcome by wrapping a large shawl tightly round the body in such a way, under one arm and over the other shoulder, that the infant could be carried somehow suspended inside. They were still to be seen in my time, giving the impression that the wearer had plumbed the depths of degradation. While some could appear respectable, clean and tidily dressed, with a nice white crocheted shawl, it was mainly the sight of those in the worst slums in Govan that remains in my memory. In Nethan Street and McKechnie

Street/Wanlock Street areas they could be seen dressed in little more than rags, using a check or tartan blanket, the colours and pattern of which were obscured by dirt, in place of a shawl, often with an edge draped over their head and held under the chin. When not carrying an infant, the excess material of the blanket was gathered up and wrapped round folded arms in front like a muff. The local term for that was, I think, a 'mutch', which may have been the origin of the saying 'Yer granny's mutch' when ridiculing someone. Mother used to knit a lot and she also crocheted shawls for many people, which the recipients prized. There is no doubt that as a baby I would have been carried around in this way if she had found it necessary. I certainly remember seeing her carry my sister, born 1941, in a shawl, but this may have been due to scarcity caused by wartime conditions, which made it difficult initially to find a pram at the time she was born, just six weeks before the Clydeside blitz.

Another curiosity from the past which disappeared around this time was gaiters. Just thinking about having to wear them in winter conjures up memories of an interminable and excruciating ordeal. Made from thin stiff leather or rexine, they were worn wrapped round the calves so that the shaped bottom came down over the tops of boots in an extremely tight fit, the tension making them difficult to fasten. The method of securing them was peculiar. The fastening was a row of tiny bead-like buttons set close together along the full length of one edge of the gaiter, which were levered with some difficulty through tiny button holes along the other edge, for which a device known as a button hook was used. My mother had one — a rigid wire hook, the other end of which was bent back on itself in a loop to form a handle, which was put through the hole to catch the button and pull it through. Some women's footwear also had this type of fastening, particularly calf-length boots. The buttons had a piece of wire passing through them, which ended in the tiny loop by which they were sewn in position. My gaiter-wearing days dated back to pre-school times, and what I remember about them was that they were an ordeal to put on and very tight and uncomfortable to wear. However, they would have been ideal in providing support for the elderly and anyone suffering from varicose veins. Another contemporary item of children's wear was pants for outdoor winter wear with straps which looped under the shoe instep. Then called pantaloons, they were similar to the present-day garment called 'leggings', but were made from a stiff rexine type waterproof material.

Pantomime

Faint but fond memories remain of going to the pantomime at Christmas, with two visits in particular coming to mind which date from when we lived in Howat Street. The first was when I, as one of a small group of acquaintances from the locality, travelled with our mothers by subway from Govan Cross to Kelvinbridge. We went to the Empress Theatre near St George's Cross. The highlight for me was the two trips on the underground railway, which is all I really remember of the occasion. The other visit was to see the then famous show at the Alhambra in Wellington Street, where Harry Gordon and Will Fyffe did their stuff, keeping the audience, the bulk of whom were children, in stitches. One episode, reminiscent of clowns at the circus, greatly amused everyone except me. For some reason I was terrified when, after a large black box with external quilted padding was brought on to the stage, one of the comedians sat on it. Suddenly, from a door in the side behind the sitter, a figure appeared at a bewildering speed, so fast he was just a flicker, and whacked the sitter on the head with a balloon — then disappeared below. The sitter, in mock puzzlement, then moved round and sat with his legs over the trap-door from which the balloon wielder came. Of course the apparition with the balloon, who was suitably made up to frighten, appeared again from behind, in an ongoing sequence that had the audience in stitches. All except me. For there was something menacing and frightening about that scene in the way the man from below was attired and the manner in which he moved, that I hid under the seat, much to the mystification of the others.

More street scenes

Before the telephone was invented, the post office operated a system of transmitting urgent messages by wire, using the dot-dash code, called telegraph. This is why young folk might hear older people refer to poles carrying telephone wires as telegraph poles, although that term dates from a time before the oldest person now alive. The telephone service, then part of the GPO (General Post Office) as a branch known as GPO Telephones, continued to expand in the 1930s, but installations were confined to businesses and upmarket dwellings. My first opportunity to use a telephone, dating from 1941, left me awestruck by the encounter with technology. Instruments were generally still few and far between, and anyone with an urgent message for a distant destination could send a telegram. It required a call in person to a post office, and during hours of closure I think there was an office in Glasgow which gave a 24-hour service. Probably by the 1930s messages were transmitted verbally by phone between offices. A supply of telegraph forms was kept in a special small rack in every office convenient for lifting, and after filling in the message and presenting it at the counter, the charge was calculated on the number of words. The receiving office then despatched their 'telegram boy', who was dressed in a uniform resembling that of the Boys' Brigade in having a waist and sash belt with a pouch for carrying the messages, and a Foreign Legion pillbox type hat, to the forwarding address on his distinctive red and white upright bicycle. They were seen occasionally in all districts, passing by or going up closes to deliver messages, but they were regarded with apprehension as liable to be harbingers of bad news.

Maintenance of roads with cobbled surfaces was an ongoing feature complicated by tram lines. The Tramways Department was obliged to maintain the area within a foot on either side of the tracks, for which they had a squad to attend to that as well as maintain the track itself, while the Highways Department looked after the rest. Any photographs of tramlines on cobbled roads in Glasgow will show these boundaries. The Highways Department had numerous squads, because it covered a much greater area, and the labour intensive work was slow and laborious. Cobbled roads did not suffer from surface break-up and the potholes which are encountered today. What happened was that areas became depressed and liable to flooding, so repair work involved lifting the cobbles over a section of road, building up, smoothing out and levelling the bottoming, then re-laying them. A regular squad worked out along a main road towards the suburbs and, because of the nature of the task, all manual with no mechanisation, it proceeded at little better than a snail's pace. At a guess, to cover one side only of Govan Road at Elder Park between Elderpark Street and Drive Road might take two weeks. Everything was done by hand, with each individual stone having to be broken away from its neighbours and levered out using a pinch — a long heavy steel lever with a chisel edge — and lifted clear and stacked in random heaps away from the area being worked on. The sound made by cobbles being bumped together is still recalled today, in the almost identical deep 'glunk' produced by curling stones, or bowling green bools striking. What used to intrigue was 'how did they get the first stone out from the continuous dense layer?'

Once re-laid, the task of tarring the cobbles in was undertaken. The tar boiler was a large black tank with an estimated capacity of about 500 gallons, which ran on four spoked iron wheels with flat treads with a towing bracket attached to one pivoting axle mounted under the firebox end. In shape it was something like a bath with flat ends and a lid, and a large tap somewhere low down for drawing off the molten tar. It had a firebox which was fed from one end, in which coal was burned to melt the tar, and a tall thin chimney emerged low down from the opposite end. When fired up, as well as smoke from the chimney, the tank gave off clouds of white acrid fumes that always took the breath from me, although it was reputed to be good for 'clearing the (bronchial) tubes'. Tar arrived at the site in rough large block form, which had to be broken up into smaller pieces, which were dropped into the tank, the top edge of which stood at about head height. This was hazardous because of the risk of being splashed with the hot stuff as the lumps went in. The material did not set in the way modern mastic would, melting and hardening being solely affected by temperature. Hot weather caused it to melt and run and shoes sometimes became contaminated, causing it to be unwittingly walked into houses and deposited on carpets. The molten tar was drawn off into large metal buckets with long spouts and a carrying handle which could be hung on the tap when filling. It was poured in to fill up the gaps between the stones when they had been relaid. The squad had one of the most unpleasant and backbreaking jobs around, what with having to work in a stooped position all day, keeping the fire going, and manipulating the tar bucket.

Although they weren't used to level relaid cobbled roads or the local asphalted roads, steamrollers (or steam road rollers) were sometimes seen in operation. Traction engines too were employed to take heavy engineering loads to the docks. Both of these were a source of excitement to children because they travelled at not much more than walking pace, and could be followed for as long as we cared to tag along. Their attraction for me came somewhere between railway engines and ships, the big advantage being that small boys could get much closer to them than any of the other forms of traction, to feel the heat as well as see the smoke and steam. With steam and smoke puffing out from the tall chimney, they really did give the impression of being a living entity, the controls being somewhat imprecise, with the same fidgety behaviour as a horse. But the broad steel large-diameter wheels and roller of the road roller must have given a ride that was marginally more uncomfortable on cobbled surfaces than the narrower solid rubber-ised ones of the traction engine.

At this time all main streets were hosed down once a year in summer by a squad of men who worked their way round the city. They operated during the night and as I grew old enough, in the next decade, to be out late in the evening, perhaps journeying home from the cinema, they were seen with their barrow which carried the reel containing sections of heavy hosepipe of fire-brigade dimensions, heading towards the scene of their night's work. They connected into the fire-fighting water supply, one of the small number of groups permitted to do so. Street washers probably covered about a couple of miles a night, going over the full width of the street from the back edge of the pavement on either side, so that in the morning the washed section was sparkling clean. Although aware of them trundling through the streets and setting up the hosepipe, I never actually saw them in action until I came to drive the buses in the 1960s. Bus crews all took their turn on night service, and the street washers were one of the dead-of-the-night hazards to watch out for. They worked only from late spring to autumn, to avoid the risk of icing up the streets. The operation ceased soon after that time, probably with the last of the horses, for they were the main reason why it was needed in the first place, to flush dung from roads at a time when there were so many that a spell of wet weather did not do the job properly.

A different kind of stitches

My mother spent much of her spare time knitting. She was able to keep family and friends going with jerseys, sweaters, pullovers, cardigans, socks, scarves and gloves. Her production of shawls using best quality white Cashmere wool was much appreciated, and she had many commissions through the years, to the extent that there may even be some in different parts of the world that are now handed down as antique heirlooms. All wool was then bought in 4 oz hanks, loops about two feet across, that for convenience of the knitter had to be unwound and rolled into a ball. This was done with the aid of a helper who held the loop out loosely between hands spread wide, for Mum to uncoil and roll up into a firm ball, a job I regularly performed from when I was old enough until after I married. She could do it on her own but always complained that it took her twice as long.

A ball of light coloured wool had to be kept in a bag during knitting, but any of darker colours lay on the floor at her feet, and tended to roll gently around as it was used up. Sometimes this tendency to wander could be a problem if her attention concentrated on the work, allowing the ball to roll un-noticed into a danger zone. If one of us walked past her chair without due care and tripped over the strand, although not strong enough to trip anyone other than a child, serious disruption could result to the knitting. When that happened you had to keep out of the radius of the swing of her arm or risk getting a clout. I like cats and always wanted one at home, but my pleadings were ignored and it is obvious now that it would have been impossible. For a cat would have ruined the knitting operation by chasing the ball all over the floor, as is well illustrated in a recent TV advert. As a youngster I used to watch fascinated as the strand of wool unwound off the ball, climbed up to the flashing needles and metamorphosed into an item to wear at a quite brisk rate. Although her products were never of professional standard, for if they had been she might have been able to earn something from her work, her garments were quite serviceable and must have saved the family quite a bit over the years on what would have otherwise had to be bought.

The betting school

In the nineteen thirties betting was against the law, not being legalised until 1961. Prior to then, there being no betting shops, The bookie had to conduct business surreptitiously, with him and his customers slinking up closes and hiding in back courts or, for preference, on any vacant ground hidden from public gaze. Bookies had assistants called 'runners', and the ones I knew of were invariably either wiry young unemployed adults or still spry older retired men, for all had to be fleet of foot. Their job was to go round regular customers collecting bets and, much less often, delivering winnings, as well as keeping a lookout for the 'polis'. No member of my family or any acquaintance indulged in it that I knew of, and it was regarded in our house with the same abhorrence as alcohol. So, except for fleeting glimpses of the activity, I didn't find out what it was all about until well into my teens. Police played a game of cat-and-mouse which I am sure they enjoyed, with much spying and frequent raids on known haunts.

Most of what I relate here about betting is hearsay, for it only intruded at the edge of my awareness, and local haunts were unknown until one occasion when, with a group of pals, we were exploring an area somewhere around the top of Helen Street, close to the railway in the area where the bus garage was later built. We passed through a screen of bushes on to a large patch of bare earth which was probably used as a football park. Immediately we saw a group of men of all ages, from their appearance obviously unemployed, standing in a circle with their attention fixed on a small knot of people in the centre. Instinctively we froze, sensing that something outwith our experience — well mine anyway — was going on. We turned round and crept off as quietly as we could, hurrying away until we were at a safe distance. The more worldly of our group knew well enough that it was a betting school and suggested we had been lucky, for it we had been spotted we might have been taken for spies, and dear knows what might have happened. My feeling now is that no harm would have come to us. The worst we could have expected was simply to have been chased off, for the times were less evil than are those of the present.

It is intended that the next instalment of these reminiscences will be mostly concerned with the period from September 1939 to 1945, the war and how it affected the community of West Govan.

A final reference to the decade dealt with in the present volume, is the memory of receiving as a present a cellophane wrapped length of fruit rock type candy, in the shape (and colour) of Prime Minister Chamberlain's umbrella. It was probably intended as a light hearted omen that his efforts in Munich might succeed.

Selected Bibliography

Barr, William, *Glaswegiana*, Richard Drew, 1981

Blake, George, *The Gourock*, The Gourock Ropework Co. Ltd., 1963

Blair, Anna, *Tea At Miss Cranstons*, Shepheard Walwyn, 1985, & *More Tea*, 1991

Brotchie, T. C., *The History of Govan*, Cossar, 1905

Dow, James L, *Greenock (history of)*, Greenock Corporation, 1975

Feachem, Richard, *Guide to Prehistoric Scotland*, Batsford, 1980

Fenton, Alexander, *Country Life In Scotland*, John Donald, 1987

Hume, John R. & Moss, Michael S., *Workshop of the British Empire*, Heinemann, 1977

Hume, John R., *Industrial Archaeology of Glasgow*, Blackie, 1974

Hume, John R., *The Industrial Archaeology of Scotland–1, The Lowlands & Borders*, Batsford Ltd., 1976

Kinchin, P. & J., *Glasgow's Great Exhibitions*, White Cockade, undated (C. 1987)

McArthur, William F, *History of Port Glasgow*, Jackson Wylie & Co., 1932

McDonald, Dan, *The Clyde Puffer*, David & Charles, 1977

McKean, Charles, *The Scottish Thirties*, Scottish Academic Press, 1987

McKie, Euan W., *Scotland: An Archaeology Guide*, Faber & Faber Ltd., 1975

McNair, James, *James Maxton — The Beloved Rebel*, Allen & Unwin Ltd., 1955

Morton, Henry, *Old Glasgow*, Richard Drew, 1987

Oakley, Charles, *The Second City*, Black & Son, 1990 ed.

Nock, O. S., *The Caledonian Railway*, Ian Allan Ltd., 1973

Paget-Tomlinson, Edward, *The Railway Carriers*, (Wordie & Co.) Terence Dalton Ltd., 1990

Riddell, John F., *Clyde Navigation*, John Donald Ltd., 1979, & *The Clyde*, Fairlie Press, 1998

Roberts, David, *For To Do The Country Good*, Strathkelvin District Council, 1987

Sinclair, Maureen, *Murder, Murder Polis!*, The Ramsay Head Press, Edinburgh, 1986

Stewart, Ian, *The Glasgow Tramcar*, Scottish Tramway & Transport Society, 1983, and various other members thereoff with other publications too numerous to mention but well worthwhile seeking out.

Smith, Sydney, *West of Scotland Rambles*, Molendinar Press, 1978 (now out of print)

Smout, T. C. & Wood, Sidney, *Scottish Voices 1745–1960*, Collins, 1990

Thomson, David L. & Sinclair, David E., *The Glasgow Subway*, STMS, 1964

Various Contributors:, *The Victoria Infirmary of Glasgow 1890–1990*, Victoria Infirmary Centenary Committee, 1990

Walker, Fred M., *Song of the Clyde*, Patrick Stephens Ltd, 1984

Wordsall, Frank, *The Tenement — A Way Of Life*, W. & R. Chambers Ltd., 1979